In the Common Cause

American Response to the Coercive Acts of 1774

IN THE
COMMON CAUSE

*American Response to
the Coercive Acts of 1774*

David Ammerman

Florida State University

University Press of Virginia

Charlottesville

THE UNIVERSITY PRESS OF VIRGINIA
Copyright © 1974 by the Rector and Visitors
of the University of Virginia

First published 1974

Ammerman, David, 1938–
    In the common cause: American response to the Coercive acts of 1774.
    1. United States—History—Revolution, 1775–1783—Causes. I. Title.
E210.A45   973.3′116   74-2417
ISBN 0-8139-0525-7

Printed in the United States of America

To the memory of
Calvin Eugene Patterson

Why did he choose to plunge into nothingness, into the void of faceless faces, of soundless voices, lying outside history? . . . Where were the historians today? And how would they put it down?

. . . What did they ever think of us transitory ones? . . . who were too obscure for learned classification, too silent for the most sensitive recorders of sound; of natures too ambiguous for the most ambiguous words, and too distant from the centers of historical decision to sign or even to applaud the signers of historical documents? We who write no novels, histories or other books. What about us, . . .

Ralph Ellison, *Invisible Man*

Contents

Preface

ALTHOUGH scholars have long debated the causes of the American Revolution, they have seldom distinguished between the general conditions that led to unrest in the British colonies and the immediate events that precipitated the war. It now seems obvious, considering the instability of all colonial relationships, that the Americans eventually would have assumed an equal station among the nations of the earth regardless of the means by which they pursued that objective. What is not so clear is that the pursuit of equality need have included violence or that the equality sought necessitated independence. Consequently historians may find it more profitable to ask why the American Revolution occurred when it did and why it assumed a particular form than to search endlessly for clues about which particular aspect of the imperial structure was most objectionable to this or that group of colonists. Great Britain forced the colonists into the status of second-class citizens politically, economically, and socially, and that in itself is sufficient to account for general dissatisfaction. It does not, however, account for the outbreak of war.

In attempting to explain the advent of armed conflict in British America, the months between May 1774, when news of the Coercive Acts first arrived in the colonies, and April 1775, when the British troops clashed with provincials at Lexington and Concord, are of crucial importance. Prior to passage of the first of the Coercive Acts a variety of courses lay open to both the British and the colonists; after the engagement at Concord there was almost no possibility of avoiding full-scale civil war. In that brief period of time, both sides defined their respective positions, asserted an unyielding determination to maintain those positions, and provided troops to demonstrate the seriousness of their intents. Men who would have shuddered at the suggestion of war in March 1774 were encamped on the battlefield by April 1775. Why? What had happened during those twelve months to explain the remarkable unanimity with which the colonists greeted the final event? That question provides the main focus of this study.

It seems arrogant to speak with any confidence of the motives of men long dead when we are often unable to understand the forces that direct our own lives. Indeed, each colonist's decision to join or to oppose the American Revolution depended as much on his individual temperament as on any other factor. For some, the pace of events seemed always too slow. Sam Adams, whether in Boston or Philadelphia, worked methodically and indefatigably to reduce and then to eliminate the ties with Great Britain under which he had chafed for so many years. Others were bewildered by the rapidity of change and found themselves struggling to remain abreast of the tide. John Dickinson had greatly advanced anti-British sentiment in America with his famous pamphlet, "Letters from a Pennsylvania Farmer" (1768), and yet from 1774 to 1776 he labored as hard as any man in the colonies to slow the drift toward independence. Dickinson in the end cast his lot firmly with the new nation, but he did so only after long and agonizing efforts to find a suitable alternative. Still others, like Robert Beverley of Essex County, Virginia, were unable to join in rending the imperial tie. What pains Beverley suffered, what secret feelings he hid from even his closest friends we can never know. It is certain only that he attempted to divert his neighbors from a path he feared and then retired in dismay and grief from excesses he believed could culminate only in disruption and mob rule.

Recent historians have paid little attention to the months preceding the Battle of Lexington, perhaps because they have found the period unsuitable to their interpretative bent. Whereas nineteenth-century historians, most notably George Bancroft, portrayed the American Revolution as the penultimate battle in man's struggle for freedom, twentieth-century scholars have tended to search for evidence of economic and social divisions underlying the facade of colonial unity. Because the initial phases of the Revolution constituted the high-water mark of American consensus, the period has been generally ignored in recent years. One exception is Arthur M. Schlesinger, Sr. Writing in 1918, he dealt at length with the Coercive Acts and the First Continental Congress but focused so narrowly on the merchants in the colonies that he produced a one-sided account. Because his study, *The Colonial Merchants and the American Revolution, 1763–1776*, has gone generally unchallenged and because it is, despite the author's bias, an excellent work, it has had great influence. Modern writers have relied heavily on the volume and have consequently continued to exaggerate factional divisions during a period which was more notable for the temporary muting of discord.

It is not my intention to swell the ranks of the so-called consensus historians. Large numbers of Americans were unrepresented at the meetings of the First Continental Congress, and little is known about their attitudes. At the same time it seems fairly certain that many colonists looked toward the Congress for direction in the troubled fall of 1774, and equally certain that the men who attended those meetings were surprisingly united on objectives and methods. Divisions existed in the several colonies but did not surface to any considerable extent in the Congress itself. The American Revolution was successful precisely because the sympathy of so large a percentage of the colonists was wedded to the cause of resistance in the initial phases. That unanimity, in turn, was possible because the only group that could claim to speak for all the colonists did so in a clear and undivided voice.

It is hardly remarkable that as resistance hardened into revolution, a significant number of Americans withdrew their support or that the divisions which later weakened colonial unity reflected economic, political, or social differences in the society at large. Many who opposed British policy did not fully support the boycott of trade; many who supported the boycott refused to take up arms; and many who took up arms could not justify the move to independence. Still, the greater the number who participate in the initial phases of such a movement, the greater the number who will see it through to a conclusion. It is therefore notable that the Coercive Acts of 1774 brought almost every man in America into some degree of sympathy with the opposition to Great Britain.

The British seem to have done almost everything wrong. They enacted a program which alienated an overwhelming majority of the colonists and thus provided the broadest possible base on which an opposition could be erected. Having established a past record of retreat, the mother country encouraged, perhaps even enticed, the Americans to commit themselves to a position from which there was no retreat. The ministry then precipitated a military engagement from which the colonists emerged not only victorious but convinced that the onus of aggression lay with their oppressors. The men in Whitehall had created a broadly based opposition, backed it into a corner, and then allowed it to win the first battle. Such a policy could only fan the nascent, localized spirit of resistance into a full-blown national movement.

The Americans of 1774, like colonial peoples in other places and other times, looked forward to an ever-increasing degree of autonomy. Complaints to the contrary notwithstanding, most Americans seem to have believed that their colonial status had gradually improved, and they expected, until passage of the Coercive Acts, that it would continue to do so. Great Britain, fearing that the colonists were drifting toward independence (as I suspect they were), decided to reverse that trend. The colonists objected, and since the mother country did not have a governmental or military apparatus adequate for exercising direct control over America, objection easily turned into resistance and culminated in revolution. The American Revolution shows once again that when men perceive themselves to be deprived —economically, politically, or socially—they are likely to resist and, given a plausible chance of success, to resort to violence if their demands are not met.

It would be impossible to name all those persons who have contributed to this study. I am especially grateful to Curtis P. Nettels, Professor Emeritus at Cornell University, who suggested the topic, and to Anne C. Loveland, who succeeded, despite innumerable obstacles, in keeping me at it. Stephen G. Kurtz, until recently Director of the Institute of Early American History and Culture, and Edward M. Riley of the Colonial Williamsburg Foundation provided encouragement and excellent working conditions during my stay in Williamsburg. At various times I have been given advice, inspiration, and technical assistance from a number of others: John and Alice Zeugner, Pete and Martha Ripley, Joy and Arthur Barnes, James M. Smith, Thad Tate, John Selby, David Brion Davis, Elizabeth Fox, Richard M. Brown, Jane Carson, Michael Kammen, Sung Bok Kim, Ann Withorn, Jim Hutson, Harold Gill, Paul Smith, Wayne Harris, and Maxine Stern.

In nearly every depository where I worked there were individuals who went beyond the call of duty to be of assistance. Especially helpful were the staffs of the Historical Society of Pennsylvania, Olin Library at Cornell University, the New-York Historical Society, the New York Public Library, the Connecticut Historical Society, and the Research Library at Colonial Williamsburg, where Marylee McGregor and Patricia Gibbs supplied an answer to my every question.

Financial assistance for the project came from the Colonial Williamsburg Foundation and from a Faculty Development Grant provided by Florida State University in Tallahassee.

In the Common Cause

American Response to the Coercive Acts of 1774

CHAPTER I

The Die Is Cast

THURSDAY, December 16, 1773, dawned over Boston damp and sunless. A steady rain, beginning early, drummed on the rooftops of the little town, collected in puddles along the unpaved streets, and swept down over the harbor. It was a dull, uninviting day; a day for staying indoors beside a warm fire and taking care of tasks that did not require venturing into the elements. Surprisingly, the Bostonians seemed unaware of the inclement weather. Throughout the morning, from all parts of town as well as from the surrounding countryside, hundreds of people appeared in the streets, hurrying through the rain toward a common destination.

The cause of this unusual activity lay along Boston's deserted waterfront, beneath the rain-splattered decks of three ordinary vessels. There, protected from the hazards of the weather, stood chest after chest of dutied tea sent to Massachusetts Bay by the East India Company—tea that had for three weeks been the subject of a bitter dispute between the town and Thomas Hutchinson, acting governor of the province. The town insisted on returning the cargo to Great Britain with the taxes unpaid. The governor refused. It was this controversy that had driven the Bostonians from their warm homes to the draughty spaces of the Old South Meeting House.[1]

Puritan Boston had no illusions about either Thomas Hutchinson or human nature, and the town feared that the determination of the former and the weakness of the latter might combine to defeat years of colonial resistance to parliamentary taxation. Each of the five thousand persons who attended the meeting that December morning knew that British law allowed the governor to confiscate goods standing in port for twenty-one days without payment of duties. They also knew that the period of grace would elapse within a few hours, and feared that the governor would then use force to land the tea and deliver it to the merchants for whom it had been intended. Once the fragrant herb lined the shelves of Boston shops at the reduced prices made possible by the newly adopted East India Company Regulating Act, who could doubt that New Englanders—being but human— would succumb to temptation and purchase the duticd article. What

---

[1] For a detailed study of these events, see Benjamin Woods Labaree, *The Boston Tea Party* (New York, 1964).

arguments could then be mustered against new taxes or further exercises of parliamentary authority? Surely Boston must protect herself, not only from the machinations of the government but from the weaknesses of the flesh.

The meeting voted to send Captain Francis Rotch, master of one of the tea ships, to visit Hutchinson in a final effort to secure the governor's permission for the vessels to leave port. Since Hutchinson was then at Milton, several miles from Boston, the meeting recessed pending return of his answer. During the afternoon, while Captain Rotch pursued his errand, Old South buzzed with arguments, predictions, and discussions of past confrontations between the colonies and Great Britain.

Sam Adams, unquestionably the most important and persistent leader of the opposition to British authority and to the governor, must have felt considerable satisfaction as he observed the temper of the crowd. Not only had the town turned out in force, the tone of the meeting evidenced a determination to resist landing of the tea. One speaker had reminded his listeners that Britain had campaigned relentlessly for nearly a decade to force colonial recognition of Parliament's right to tax. Had anyone forgotten Boston's determined stand against the Stamp Act in 1765? Could anyone doubt that New England was eager to defend her constitutional rights now as she had been a decade before? Would any man in Massachusetts, excepting possibly those indebted to the Crown for their exalted stations in life, speak in behalf of parliamentary taxation? The hall was silent.

Other speakers may have reminded the meeting that in 1767, only one year after repeal of the Stamp Act, Charles Townshend had attempted to force American acceptance of taxes on glass, paper, lead, painters' colors, and tea. How foolish Townshend had been to play on a supposed distinction between internal and external taxes when the colonists had all along objected not to the form of taxation but to the fact. Once again America had resisted, and in 1770 Lord North repealed all of the Townshend duties except the tax on tea. Unfortunately, the colonists had allowed themselves to be bought off too easily. America should have continued the boycott of British trade until Parliament had repealed all of the duties. Surely it was now obvious that the weakness shown by the colonists had only encouraged the British to yet another effort at fixing a precedent for taxing America.

As Adams reflected on these several points—points that he had helped instill in the minds of the Bostonians if not all Americans—he may have speculated on the probable outcome of this latest conflict between the colonies and the mother country. He was pleased by the apparent American determination to resist parliamentary taxation but also aware that the mother country seemed equally determined to effect its authority. Even the repeal of the Stamp Act had been less than a complete victory for the colonies. The British legislature had indeed withdrawn the measure, but at the same time it asserted absolute sovereignty over America, claiming in the Declaratory Act a right to legislate for the colonies "in all cases whatsoever." During the decade following repeal of the Stamp Act, Adams had found no shred of evidence to suggest that the government had altered this all-encompassing and insulting position. The North ministry in repealing the Townshend duties had insisted on retaining the tea tax, apparently for the same reason that had dictated adoption of the Declaratory Act—the desire to assert Britain's unlimited authority over the colonies. Historians cannot dispute the fiery Bostonian's judgment. George III's private correspondence reveals that the king did indeed defend the tax on tea as a symbol of Britain's determination to "keep up the right."[2]

Sam Adams was a determined, effective, and indefatigable leader. He was also a consummate politician. Even as he noted with satisfaction the apparent unanimity of the meeting in Old South, he recognized here and there the face of a political enemy. Adams knew that a number of merchants, supported by others with property or status to protect, feared that economic or political disruption would upset the balance of society and threaten the established order. These men shifted uneasily in their seats as they thought of the riots that had accompanied demonstrations against the Stamp Act, and they instinctively felt that Sam Adams and his ilk were not to be trusted.

Propertied Bostonians were, in fact, caught on the horns of a dilemma. On the one hand they viewed the authority of the mother country as a bulwark supporting the existing social order; on the other, they had found that same authority infuriatingly insensitive to their own needs. Long before Parliament initiated efforts to raise a revenue in America, the merchants and other economically privileged classes had raised their voices, if not their arms, to complain against laws affecting trade, western expansion, domestic manufacturing, currency emission, and the judicial system. If the taxation dispute extended back over a decade, the roots of other disagreements reached into another century. Wealthy Bostonians, like their counterparts in other colonies, had chafed under restrictions imposed by the Navigation Acts of the 1660s as well as the Woolens, Hat, and Iron Acts, all passed in the first half of the eighteenth century. Significantly, it was to be the more conservative members of the First Con-

---

[2]Hon. Sir John Fortescue, ed., *The Correspondence of King George the Third from 1760 to December 1783*, III (London, 1928), 131.

tinental Congress who would put up the strongest fight for including acts affecting trade and manufacturing among the cardinal grievances of America.[3]

Nor was taxation the only issue involved in the dispute at hand. While Sam Adams hammered away at the East India Company Regulating Act as yet another parliamentary effort to fix a precedent for taxation, many a wealthy merchant thought instead about provisions of that act allowing the East India Company to monopolize the sale of tea. If Parliament could permit one company to decide who had the privilege of selling tea in the colonies, might she not also establish monopolies in other areas?

Adding to the general discontent over British policy, especially among the mercantile interests, was the abominable ignorance of American conditions repeatedly evidenced in the policies of Whitehall and Westminster. Efforts to tighten the Acts of Trade and Navigation, for example, had given birth to a complicated system of rules and regulations which made it impossible for even the best of subjects to treat the law with respect. Not only were the requirements foolish, but the great distances separating local officials from the center of authority had encouraged arbitrary enforcement and so further strained imperial ties. What was a loyal American merchant to do? How could one choose between Adams and anarchy on the one hand and submission to British economic interests and ignorance on the other? If only Hutchinson would compromise his stand and permit the ships to leave port, no doubt the crisis would pass. The Boston merchants could then return to their business and forget not only the mob but, though one dared not say it aloud, the laws of Parliament as well.

Thomas Hutchinson, unfortunately for the peace of the empire, was made of sterner stuff. As he listened to Captain Rotch deliver the town's ultimatum, the governor was angered by this evidence of a growing tendency toward mob rule in Massachusetts Bay. Hutchinson sympathized with Boston (or at least its "better" elements) on many points, but he firmly believed that laws must be obeyed. In 1765 he had acted on this belief, working to defeat passage of the Stamp Act in Parliament but, once it was adopted, doing his best to see it enforced. He had been rewarded first by a Boston mob that gutted his home and then by a British ministry that repealed the act after the damage had been done. These ministers had repeatedly ignored his warnings; and he may have wished that they could experience the impotence and frustration of a royal governor who attempted without arms or patronage to force unpopular laws upon an aroused

---

[3]The delegates from Pennsylvania and South Carolina seem to have been especially concerned about these acts. See chapter 4.

population. But Hutchinson certainly would not agree to the terms proposed by the town. Convinced that leniency in the past had only fanned the flame of rebellion, he informed Rotch that he had no authority to permit vessels to leave port without payment of duties.

By the time Captain Rotch returned to Old South Meeting House candles had been lighted to dispel the gathering dusk of the waning winter afternoon. As he explained the failure of his mission, tension mounted in the hall, and then, according to tradition, Sam Adams took the podium to announce that "this meeting" could do nothing more to preserve the liberties of America. That announcement, with an emphasis on the demonstrative pronoun, may well have been a signal, for Adams was answered by war whoops in the street, and a band of "Mohawks" straightway descended on the waterfront. In a few hours the contested cargo floated on the tide. The "Indians" and the cold salt waters of the Atlantic had settled the dispute, destroying in the process private property valued at thousands of pounds sterling.

Later, as night settled over the town, there was little to suggest that this had been other than an ordinary day. The streets were quiet and dark, except perhaps for an occasional uncovered window reflected in the puddles still standing before the houses. For the most part, the citizens of Boston gathered behind drawn curtains and talked quietly. Some may have rubbed a bit of warpaint from their foreheads as they sat down to dinner; others no doubt brewed a defiant pot of tea and cursed the unruly mob; all speculated about the results of what they may already have termed the Tea Party. But three thousand miles of ocean separated old from New England, and it would be spring before anyone in the colonies would know the nature of Britain's response.

That response, when it arrived in early May 1774, was so harsh as to surprise even those who had condemned the destruction of the tea. The Boston Port Act, first of the so-called Coercive Acts adopted by Parliament in answer to the Tea Party, arrived along with the newly appointed governor of Massachusetts Bay, General Thomas Gage. The act closed the city's harbor with a blockade to go into effect on June 1 and forbade the export of goods to any foreign port "or any province or place whatever."[4] Boston could ship no products out of the harbor and could import only provisions for the king's troops and such fuel and victuals necessary to sustain the inhabitants as might be carried by vessels trading along the coast. Parliament had decreed that the harbor should remain closed until the king decided that the colony was prepared to obey the law and that British trade could once again enter the port safely. However, not even the

[4]The text of the Port Act is in Peter Force, ed., *American Archives . . .*, 4th ser. (Washington, D.C., 1837–46), I, 61–66.

king could relieve the city until full satisfaction had been made "by or on behalf of the inhabitants" of Boston to the East India Company for the destroyed tea. Clearly the ministry intended to punish Boston by depriving the city of its main industry and to bring home to the citizens of all America the potential power of the empire. One advantage of the act, from Parliament's point of view, was that enforcement lay primarily in the hands of the British navy, a factor obviating the possibility of effective colonial resistance.

The colonists raised a number of objections against the Boston Port Act. Men asked why Parliament had given the Massachusetts capital no opportunity to testify in its own defense. The British legislature had heard the case, passed judgment on the city, and enacted a severe punishment without making any effort to solicit information from the Bostonians themselves. Then too, the act forced the innocent to suffer along with the guilty. Even so confirmed a supporter of the Coercive Acts as Norfolk's James Parker admitted that he was "very sorry for the Innocent people in Boston. Doubtless there are many such who are punished for being in bad Company."[5]

By a stroke of the parliamentary pen Boston had become a besieged city. Never before, not even during the French wars, had an American city faced a blockade, and now the mother country proposed to effect what no belligerent power had even attempted. Landon Carter of Virginia, upon hearing of the Port Act, charged that Parliament had "declared war against the town of Boston and rather worse, for they have attacked and blocked up their harbor."[6]

Perhaps most important, at least outside Massachusetts Bay, was the widespread belief that Great Britain had intended the act as a warning to the rest of the continent. Thomas Wharton, Sr., a moderate Quaker merchant of Philadelphia who later turned tory, concluded that "all this Extensive Continent Considers the port Bill of Boston as striking Essentially at the Liberties of all North America."[7] From Norwich, Connecticut, Ebenezer Baldwin wrote that the inhabitants felt a "deeper Concern...than in the time of the Stamp Act. The present Measures tis thot [sic] forbode something more dreadful to the Colonies than that detested Act so pregnant with Mischief."[8]

[5] Parker to Charles Steuart, June 7, 1774, Charles Steuart Papers, National Library of Scotland, Edinburgh (microfilm, Colonial Williamsburg Foundation, Williamsburg, Va.).

[6] Jack P. Greene, ed., *The Diary of Colonel Landon Carter of Sabine Hall, 1752–78*, II (Charlottesville, Va., 1965), 817.

[7] Wharton to Thomas Walpole, June 10, 1774, Thomas Wharton Letterbook, Historical Society of Pennsylvania, Philadelphia.

[8] Baldwin to Mr. Howe, June 11, 1774, Baldwin Family Papers, Sterling Library, Yale University, New Haven.

Convinced that the Port Act threatened fundamental liberties, Americans were even more angered by the terms of a second law, the Massachusetts Government Act, because it ordered permanent changes in the government and thus attacked the colonial political structure.[9] Parliament revised the provincial charter granted Massachusetts Bay in 1691 in order to give the British government more direct control over the province. The act provided that the Council of the colony, previously elected by the lower house and the outgoing Council with the approval of the royal governor, would henceforth be appointed by the king and hold office at his pleasure. Another provision allowed the governor to appoint judges without the consent of the Council (even though the latter had been restructured to bring it more under the influence of the king), tightening executive control over the provincial courts. The act further empowered the governor, again without consent of the Council, to appoint the county sheriffs, who were in turn authorized to select jury members—an elective position under the old charter.

The Government Act also curtailed the activities of the town meeting, long considered a prime source of democratic ferment by the British government, allowing only one session each year unless special permission was obtained from the provincial governor. The act noted that town meetings had been misused to treat matters of the "most general concern" rather than dealing only with local business. In the future such meetings were to confine themselves to the election of town officers and other matters expressly approved by the governor. In this, as in its other provisions, the Massachusetts Government Act substantially limited popular participation in the government of the colony and enhanced the authority of the Crown and its representatives.

In many ways the Government Act posed a more ominous threat than the Port Act. Parliament's assumption that colonial charters could be altered by legislative fiat threatened to undermine an institution the colonists had long considered the foundation of self-government in America. Even colonies without charters had come to view established procedures of government as unalterable—at least by parliamentary decree. On this point the Americans found support in a pamphlet written by the Bishop of St. Asaph and widely reprinted in the colonies. The bishop argued, as he had on the floor of the House of Lords, that "to change the Government of a People, without their consent, is the highest and most arbitrary act of sovereignty, that one nation can exercise over another."[10] To be sure, many peo-

[9] The text of the Act for the Better Government of Massachusetts Bay is in Force, ed., *American Archives*, I, 104–12.

[10] *Ibid.*, I, 102.

ple, in both England and the colonies, considered the Massachusetts colony too "democratical" and believed, along with Virginia's Robert Beverley, that its government had come to rest "so entirely with the people that they are perpetually engaged in Tumults & Cabals."[11] Nevertheless, the forms of government in Massachusetts had been long established, and the Government Act, as Beverley was quick to note, represented an extraordinary exercise of power and raised fundamental questions about the nature of the empire.

New England leaders tended to downplay the specific changes made by the Government Act—especially since many of those changes were purportedly aimed only at bringing Massachusetts government more into line with those of the other royal colonies. Instead they concentrated on the threat such alterations posed to the integrity of government in general. Joseph Warren, writing John Adams as the latter was preparing to leave for Congress, gave careful instructions on ways by which the Massachusetts delegates might handle this problem. Warren noted that

the gentlemen from the Royal Governments may possibly think, that, although our council is appointed by mandamus, we are, nevertheless, upon as good a foundation, in that respect, as themselves. But they will consider, that it is not simply the appointment of the council by the King that we complain of; it is the breach thereby made in our charter; and, if we suffer this, none of our charter-rights are worth naming; the charters of all the colonies are no more than blank paper. The same power that can take away our right of electing councillors by our representatives can take away from the other colonies the right of choosing even representatives; and the bill for regulating the Government of Canada shows plainly that it would be very pleasing to the ministry to deprive the Americans totally of the right of representation.[12]

The third of the Coercive Acts passed by Parliament, that for the Better Administration of Justice in Massachusetts Bay, provided that the governor of the colony might, under certain circumstances, transfer a trial from Massachusetts to another colony or even to Great Britain.[13] Whenever a magistrate stood accused of a capital offense committed in the execution of official duties, the governor could remove the trial to a different location if he thought local opinion so inflamed as to cloud the court's ability to arrive at an impartial verdict. Even in cases not involving a magistrate, the governor could order a transfer of trial if the accused had been acting to suppress riots or to support revenue laws under the direction of a magistrate.

---

[11] Beverley to William Fitzhugh, July 20, 1775, Robert Beverley Letterbook, Library of Congress, Washington, D.C. (microfilm, Col. Wmsbg. Foundation).

[12] Warren to J. Adams, Aug. 15, 1774, Richard Frothingham, *The Life of Joseph Warren* (Boston, 1865), p. 340.

[13] The text of the Act for the Better Administration of Justice in Massachusetts Bay is in Force, ed., *American Archives*, I, 129–32.

The ministry anticipated that the act would protect British officials and partisans in the pursuance of official duties and thus encourage a more spirited administration of imperial measures in the colony.

News of the Justice Act heightened American suspicions that the British government was hammering out an all-inclusive plan to fix the authority of Parliament over the colonies. George Washington referred to the statute as the "Murder Act" because he thought it would give British officials free reign to harass Americans without fear of being brought to justice. The Virginia leader argued that transporting offenders into other colonies or to Great Britain made it "impossible from the nature of the thing that justice can be obtained."[14] Indeed the provisions of the Justice Act did raise serious questions about established procedures of jury trial. Although the statute provided that witnesses be reimbursed for expenses encountered in a journey to some other province or to England, many colonists would have found it extremely difficult to leave their homes and businesses for several months in order to bear witness at a trial on the other side of the Atlantic. Moreover, Bostonians pointed out with considerable justification that the trial given the British officers involved in the Boston Massacre in 1770 had been scrupulously fair. Citing such examples, they rejected the ministry's contention that the new act was necessary to insure justice.

The questions raised by the Justice Act illuminate the conflict between American and British definitions of the needs of the empire and illustrate the tensions that plague any colonial relationship. Some of the laws passed in the interests of an imperial power must inevitably threaten the perceived interests of its colonies. These laws can be effective only if local judicial systems owe allegiance to the central authority. Great Britain's dilemma was real. It could not enforce unpopular laws or protect its officials in courts responsive to the demands of local pressure groups; yet its efforts to restructure the judicial system led to increased tensions. The colonists, on the other hand, could argue that trials conducted three thousand miles from the scene of the crime interfered with established concepts of judicial process, which since Magna Charta had included trial by vicinage. Whereas Parliament considered the Justice Act necessary to protect British officials in the pursuit of their duties, Americans viewed the same act as a shield between such officials and the orderly processes of civil government. Since the act could have served either purpose, or both, the colonists were being asked to trust a government in which they had increasingly less confidence, a government which had demonstrated its own lack of faith by its enactment of the statute.

[14]Washington to Bryan Fairfax, July 4, 1774, John C. Fitzpatrick, ed., *The Writings of George Washington*, III (Washington, D.C., 1931), 228.

The fourth, and last, of the acts resulting from British irritation over the Boston Tea Party was the Quartering Act, aimed at solving long-standing problems concerning the housing of British troops in America.[15] Previous measures had proved ineffective. New York at one point had simply refused to cooperate, and the British government had suspended the colony's legislature until it lived up to its supposed obligations. Massachusetts had provided housing for the troops but had done so at Castle William, far enough from Boston to render the troops stationed there useless in case of civil disorders in the metropolis. The Quartering Act of 1774, which applied to all the colonies, allowed officers to refuse unsuitable housing and to demand a more convenient location. In the event that local authorities did not satisfy such a request within twenty-four hours, the act empowered the governor to order any uninhabited buildings prepared for the use of the king's troops. The act did not, as has often been asserted, provide for billeting soldiers in private homes.[16]

In view of the earlier, often bitter controversies over the problem of housing troops, American reaction to the Quartering Act appears surprisingly restrained. The colonists protested its passage but clearly did not consider it so objectionable as the other statutes, and the delegates to the First Continental Congress finally decided not to insist on its repeal as one of the conditions for restoring trade relations with the mother country. The act was, in fact, much less important as an irritant than a fifth statue, the Quebec Act, which had been under consideration before the Tea Party and owed its inclusion among the Coercive Acts more to chances of timing than to events in Massachusetts Bay.[17]

The Quebec Act, or Canada Act as it was sometimes called, did not develop out of British concern over the riots in Boston, but its provisions made it seem as much a part of Parliament's plan for colonial reorganization as any of the other statutes.[18] The bill extended the boundaries of Quebec to include all the area north of the Ohio River, the Northwest Territory. Inhabitants of the old French colony were to "have, hold, and enjoy, the free exercise of the religion of the Church of Rome," and the Catholic clergy was authorized to receive its accustomed dues and rights from those who professed Catholicism. Although the act established English criminal law in

---

[15]The text of the Quartering Act is in Force, ed., *American Archives*, I, 170.

[16]For a defense of the British legislation, see Jack M. Sosin, "The Massachusetts Acts of 1774: Coercive or Preventive?" *Huntington Library Quarterly*, XXVI (1963), 235–52.

[17]For the statement of grievances listed in the Continental Association, see Worthington C. Ford, ed., *Journals of the Continental Congress, 1774–1789*, I (Washington, D.C., 1904), 79–80.

[18]The text of the Quebec Act is in Force, ed., *American Archives*, I, 216–20.

Canada, it permitted the continuance of French civil law, a code excluding the right to trial by jury. Moreover, since the British government deemed it inexpedient to establish an elective Assembly in a province so heavily populated by foreign-speaking inhabitants, the Quebec Act provided for a legislative Council consisting of seventeen to twenty-three members appointed by the king. This body, with the consent of the governor, exercised complete authority over the colony.

The Quebec Act aroused a wider variety of complaints than any of the other four statutes. The establishment of a government without a representative Assembly and the continuation of a legal system not allowing in all cases for jury trial seemed to provide final proof that Parliament had no regard for the traditional rights of British subjects. If Britain could alter a charter, as she had done in the Government Act, and if she preferred colonial governments without representative assemblies, as the Quebec Act implied, then the end of responsible government seemed in sight. As if that were not enough, the act took a large area of land claimed by the original colonies and transferred it not only to a nonrepresentative government but to a feudal system of land tenure. This provision alienated both the land speculators who had hoped to reap a fortune through the purchase and sale of western lands and the individual settler who preferred not to live under such a system.

If the colonists professed concern over the economic and political provisions of the Quebec Act, they were nearly apoplectic over its religious aspects. By providing for the Catholic religion in Canada, the statute raised the specter of an established church. Ezra Stiles, a dissenting minister in Rhode Island, was horrified. He found it "astonishing that King, Lds. & Commons, a whole protestant Parliament should expressly establish Popery over three Quarters of their Empire."[19] Only two explanations were possible, both equally threatening. Either Parliament intended to introduce a more centralized ecclesiastical system into the colonies—perhaps by means of an Anglican bishop—or the Quebec Act signaled Britain's intention to confine the American colonies to the eastern seaboard and to prepare a pacified Canada as a base of operations in case of armed conflict. The First Continental Congress later endorsed this second explanation, charging that the Quebec Act had been designed to enlist the sympathy of the Canadians on the side of the mother country in preparation for civil war.[20]

Because of the many different interest groups affected by the Quebec Act, the statute probably irritated more Americans than did any other single piece of legislation. Thomas Wharton, Sr., concluded that

[19] Franklin B. Dexter, ed., *The Literary Diary of Ezra Stiles,* I (New York, 1901), 455.
[20] Force, ed., *American Archives,* I, 913–14.

the colonists "from One End of this Continent to the Other" considered the act "the greatest departure from the English Constitution of any ever yet Attempted; And fear that its Meant & Intended to keep the Body of Inhabitants of that Province as Auxilaries, to Reduce both the Laws & people of every other colony."[21] When James Duane tried to persuade the First Continental Congress that it should not insist on repeal of the Quebec Act because it did not apply directly to any of the colonies represented in that body, a number of delegates replied that it was the most objectionable grievance of all.[22] William Fitzhugh, recently appointed commissary general of Maryland, thought that "Matters Appeared to go on with more Moderation & afforded a Greater Prospect of a Happy reconciliation before the Canady Bill for Establishing Popery was Published." That act ended the chances of reconciliation. Fitzhugh thought that it had "given a General Alarm to all Protestants, as well Churchmen as Dissenters, & has raised a Universal flame."[23]

The Coercive Acts of 1774 proposed significant changes in the government of Massachusetts and were in many ways as innovative and threatening as the colonists believed them to be. Although George Bancroft made similar observations more than a century ago, recent emphasis on the peculiarities of the colonial mind as an explanation of the American reaction has somewhat obscured the nature of the threat posed by the British legislation. Certainly the colonists' response was intensified by the distinctive ideological framework within which they viewed the acts, but the statutes themselves represented a sweeping and regressive attempt to reorganize the empire unprecedented since the establishment of the Dominion of New England in the 1680s.

If the Americans tended to overstate the role of ministerial "conspirators" in the formulation of British policy, they were nevertheless correct in concluding that the Coercive Acts were intended to force colonial recognition of the unlimited authority of Parliament. It is not necessary to search obscure records for hints and innuendoes about the objectives of the ministry. The Declaratory Act of 1766, the retention of the tea tax in 1770, and the debates in Parliament during enactment of the Coercive Acts speak with clarity. The British government intended to rule the colonies "in all cases whatsoever," intended to do so without constitutional restriction, and was prepared to resort to military force in pursuit of those objectives if necessary.

[21] Wharton to Thomas Walpole, Aug. 20, 1774, Thomas Wharton Letterbook, Hist. Soc. Pa.

[22] Duane, "Notes on Debates," Edmund C. Burnett, ed., *Letters of Members of the Continental Congress,* I (Washington, D.C., 1921), 77–78.

[23] Fitzhugh to James Russell, Oct. 18, 1774, James Russell Papers, Coutts and Company, London (microfilm, Col. Wmsbg. Foundation).

In adopting the Coercive Acts the British government accepted a calculated risk which can be understood only in light of political changes that had occurred in the decade since repeal of the Stamp Act. By 1773 the British cabinet was composed almost entirely of ministers who viewed that repeal as a major blunder and favored the adoption of a colonial policy which would recover lost ground. Convinced that an overly permissive attitude had characterized earlier British policy, these men insisted that conciliatory efforts by the mother country had encouraged the colonists to increase their demands. Foremost among the defenders of this position was King George III. Even after it had become clear that the war was lost and the colonies were gone, George continued to argue that repeal of the Stamp Act had been the single most important error in British policy.[24]

The attitude of the king and his ministers is best exemplified by a government-approved pamphlet from the pen of Dr. Samuel Johnson entitled *Taxation No Tyranny*. Johnson argued that "there must, in every society, be some power or other from which there is no appeal; which admits no restrictions." Thus, he argued, the colonists must choose either to acknowledge the unlimited control of Parliament or to separate from the empire.[25] Unwilling, or perhaps unable, to consider any alternative to this definition of sovereignty, the British gave but little attention to the practical problems of ruling a politically mature people situated three thousand miles from the seat of government. Meanwhile the colonists, conditioned to believe that "the foundation of English liberty, and of all free government, is a right in the people to participate in their legislative council," considered it impossible "from their local and other circumstances" to obtain representation in the body that ruled the empire.[26] It was a problem to tax the abilities of the best of governors, and the British ministers did not fit that category. Johnson's pamphlet attested to the bankruptcy of the government's policy by suggesting that Americans who wished to vote in parliamentary elections had perfect freedom to move to Great Britain and purchase an estate![27]

Even granting British arguments that Parliament would have used

[24]For a careful study of British policy in 1774–75, see Bernard Donoughue, *British Politics and the American Revolution: The Path to War, 1773–75* (New York, 1964). See also Charles R. Ritcheson, *British Politics and the American Revolution* (Norman, Okla., 1954).

[25]James Boswell reported that Johnson wrote the pamphlet *Taxation No Tyranny* at the "desire of those who were then in power" (Boswell, *The Life of Samuel Johnson* [London, 1904], p. 590).

[26]See the Statement of Rights and Grievances endorsed by Congress, Ford, ed., *Journals Cont. Cong.*, I, 68–69.

[27]A defense of Johnson's argument is in Donald J. Greene, *The Politics of Samuel Johnson* (New Haven, 1960), pp. 212–19.

its power with caution, the assertion of an authority "from which there is no appeal; which admits no restrictions" can be labeled despotic. The problem may indeed have been insoluble. Parliament demanded recognition of its supreme authority as the foundation stone of the imperial relationship; the Americans considered any structure built upon such a foundation a political prison designed to stifle their rightful liberties. Whether a particular colonist objected to British authority on economic, religious, political, or ideological considerations, the basic issue remained the same, the extent of parliamentary power. Samuel P. Savage of Middletown, Connecticut, put it succinctly when he wrote in May 1774 that the dispute between England and America involved but one question, "Whether we shall or shall not be governed by a British Parliament."[28]

The ministry's determination that America should be governed by Parliament naturally colored its response to the Tea Party. No doubt the unpleasant affair in Boston angered the ministers, but it also provided a propitious opportunity for the adoption of a more rigorous colonial policy. It offered, in fact, the desired occasion for restoring order to America. Massachusetts—or at least Boston—had responded more violently to the attempted sale of duties tea than any other American city. Thus, according to the British point of view, the New England port could be isolated and punished with a minimum risk of raising overall colonial opposition. Since many persons, both in England and America, considered Massachusetts the center of dis-affection, chastisement of that colony seemed the obvious step toward pacification of the colonies in general.

Moreover, the Tea Party had caused a general outcry against the colonies in Great Britain. Many who had been sympathetic with American demands now agreed that the time had come to "try the issue" with the colonists. Had not the Bostonians destroyed a considerable amount of private property? Had they not struck a blow at the very basis of British control by forcibly nullifying an act of Parliament? How long could reasonable men expect a government to tolerate such lack of respect for its laws and the property of its citizens? Benjamin Franklin reported from London that "the violent Destruction of the Tea seems to have united all Parties here against our Province, so that the Bill now brought into Parliament for shutting up Boston as a Port till Satisfaction is made, meets with no Opposition."[29]

United though the British government may have been, its task was a difficult one, and the policy adopted contained a serious flaw. The

[28]Savage to Wemsley Hobbey, May 26, 1774, Samuel P. Savage Papers, Massachusetts Historical Society, Boston.
[29]Franklin to Thomas Cushing, March 22, 1774, Albert Smyth, ed., *Writings of Benjamin Franklin*, VI (New York, 1906), 223.

ministry hoped to punish Boston as an example and at the same time to prevent the other colonies from making common cause with the refractory city. The dilemma was clear. Boston had not stood alone in refusing to permit the sale of dutied tea; New York, Charleston, and Philadelphia had been equally adamant. Implementation of British efforts to reorganize colonial government might begin in Massachusetts Bay, but as Edward Shippen of Lancaster, Pennsylvania, charged, there was every reason to believe that the acts contained the names of the other colonies "written with lime juice & only want the heat of the fire to make them legible"; .. "have we not acted as rebelliously, nay more so than the Bostonians?"[30] Other colonists also noted the threat posed by the Coercive Acts. From the Virginia House of Burgesses, Richard Henry Lee wrote that "the shallow Ministerial device was seen thro instantly, and every one declared it the commencement of a most wicked System for destroying the liberty of America."[31] Washington, who had expressed serious reservations about the Boston Tea Party, asked whether it were not now "as clear as the sun in its meridian brightness, that there is a regular, systematic plan formed to fix the right and practice of taxation upon us?"[32]

Colonial suspicions of British intentions were intensified by a barrage of letters and instructions from correspondents in Great Britain. Edmund Burke informed the New York Assembly's Committee of Correspondence that the punishment of Massachusetts "had been from the Beginning defended on their absolute Necessitys not only for the purpose of bringing that refractory Town and province into proper Order, but for holding out an Example of Terrour to the other Colonies."[33] Arthur Lee, then in London, wrote his two brothers in Virginia warning them that if they did not unite in support of Massachusetts all would be lost. As early as March 1774 Lee urged a general resistance or "every part will in its turn feel the vengeance which it would not unite to repel."[34] Ominous reports also came from David Barclay, an English Quaker who, along with Dr. John Fothergill, represented Lord Dartmouth in a series of semiofficial negotiations with Benjamin Franklin. Barclay wrote to James Pemberton of Philadelphia that certain "noble lords" had told him that the government intended not only to enforce the act altering the charter of Massachu-

---

[30]Shippen to James Burd, June 28, 1774, Shippen Family Papers, Hist. Soc. Pa.

[31]R. H. Lee to Arthur Lee, June 26, 1774, James C. Ballagh, ed., *The Letters of Richard Henry Lee* (New York, 1911–14), I, 114.

[32]Washington to Bryan Fairfax, July 4, 1774, Fitzpatrick, ed., *Writings of Washington*, III, 228.

[33]Burke to the Committee of Correspondence for the New York General Assembly, Aug. 2, 1774, *The Letters and Papers of Cadwallader Colden*, VII (New York, 1939), 232.

[34]A. Lee to R. H. Lee, March 18, 1774, and Lee to F. L. Lee, April 2, 1774, Force, ed., *American Archives*, I, 229, 237.

setts Bay but to take similar steps with respect to the colonies of
Connecticut and Rhode Island.[35]

Great Britain can no more be faulted for resisting what she saw as
a colonial drift toward independence than the Americans can be
blamed for disputing Parliament's assertion of unlimited authority.
Each side felt that it was maintaining a position that was both logical
and necessary. In a sense both were right. The gradual disintegration
of the British Commonwealth during the nineteenth century seems to
support the contention of the North ministry that sovereignty is in-
divisible. On the other hand, the exploitation of India, or that of Ireland, appears to bear out the American claim that a free people can
ill afford to submit to the unlimited authority of another, even if the
other is well intentioned. Since the colonists could not be "properly
represented" in Parliament, they would have had to engage in a great
"leap of faith" in order to heal the breach in the empire. It was as
unlikely that America would have agreed to submit to the authority
of Parliament in the hope that it would be used benevolently as it was
that Britain would have admitted the claim of the American legislatures to an equality with Parliament in the expectation that common
ties of language and culture would bind the empire together. Neither
policy was logical, and in the long run neither would have worked.

Many writers during the tumultuous summer of 1774 noted the
parallels between that year's events and the crisis that had engulfed
the empire at the time of the Stamp Act. The similarities were
obvious, but there was also an important difference, one of which the
colonists were not yet aware. By 1774 Great Britain was prepared, as
it had not been at the time of the Stamp Act, to force its policies on
the colonies. In the earlier crisis, although George Grenville had
understood that the colonists might complain of his taxation measures, the ministry had not anticipated so great an outcry as that
which occurred. Unprepared for such a storm of abuse from America
and faced with serious difficulties at home, the British government
of 1766 had retreated.[36]

By 1774 times had changed. The rulers of Great Britain, most of
whom had been involved in government at the time of the Stamp Act
crisis, had learned what they considered to be the lessons of history.
They realized that the Coercive Acts might precipitate a confrontation, and they naturally hoped to avoid so dangerous a possibility.
On the other hand, they were determined that if such a crisis did
arise, they would not repeat the mistakes of the past. This time the
government would stand firm. No doubt the colonists, once they

[35]Barclay to Pemberton, March 18, 1775, Pemberton Family Papers, Hist. Soc. Pa.
[36]For an excellent study of the Stamp Act, see Edmund S. and Helen M. Morgan,
The Stamp Act Crisis: Prologue to Revolution (Chapel Hill, N.C., 1953).

realized that the ministry intended to pursue its point, would acknowledge the supremacy of Parliament and avoid a military conflict which they had no chance to win. All that was needed, or so it seemed, was determination.

CHAPTER II

Heeding Boston's Plea

No ASPECT of eighteenth-century politics is more difficult to grasp than the significance of the lengthy delays occasioned by the primitive state of communications. For example, although Parliament responded with unusual speed to the Boston Tea Party, nearly five months passed before reliable reports about the government's decision arrived in New England. Throughout the winter and early spring of 1775 the Bostonians speculated about the probable result of the December crisis, but as time passed so too did the excitement and urgency of the moment. By the time news of the Coercive Acts arrived in Boston, tempers had cooled and the events of the past winter seemed remote.

The Boston Port Act shocked the colonists. Many, even among those who had previously criticized Boston for its excesses, now turned their criticism against the British. The New England port, often condemned as a troublemaker, suddenly appeared in the role of martyr suffering for the common cause. The Boston Committee of Correspondence took full advantage of this change in attitude, exerting every effort to keep the plight of the city constantly before their fellow colonists. The committee lamented the ruination of industrious merchants, raised the specter of starving multitudes, condemned the arrogant presence of British redcoats, and whispered of the threat posed by a standing army to the virtue of New England womanhood.

From Nova Scotia to Georgia, Americans responded to Boston's plea by rushing food, money, and supplies to the beleaguered city. These contributions buoyed the spirits of the Boston patriots, and they provided the committee with yet another opportunity for propagandizing. No donation was so small that it did not elicit a note of appreciation. Sam Adams himself worked late many a night writing and correcting the carefully worded pieces of propaganda and gratitude.

Though Boston's bid for sympathy must have raised a few skeptical eyebrows, it more often achieved the desired effect. Who could deny the gallantry of the little city's refusal to bow to the dictates of the most powerful legislative assembly in the world? George Washington and Benjamin Franklin were among those who, having expressed reservations about the Tea Party, swung strongly to the defense of Boston following adoption of the Coercive Acts. Mrs. William Ship-

pen, Jr., of Philadelphia, offered a characteristic response when she
confided to John Adams upon his arrival at the First Continental
Congress that she believed only the influence of a "Superiour Power"
could have enabled the people of Boston to behave so well "through
their Tryals."[1]

Whether Mrs. Shippen's "Superior Power" watched over Boston
in the form of God or Sam Adams might have been a matter for con-
jecture in some circles, but the efficacy of the city's well-publicized
martyrdom as a rallying point cannot be denied. Within days of the
arrival of official confirmation of the Port Act, meetings in Providence, Hartford, Philadelphia, Newport, New York, Annapolis, Williamsburg, and Charleston had called for united action in support
of Massachusetts Bay. By the end of June nine colonies had endorsed
proposals to hold a continental congress, a decision so rapid and
spontaneous that it has defied the efforts of historians to credit any
town or province with having originated the suggestion.[2]

This is not to suggest that the call for the First Continental Congress issued without direction. Even spontaneous movements require
leadership, and there were many leaders waiting to thrust themselves
forward in a situation like that presented by Parliament's enactment
of the Coercive Acts. Sam Adams, though the best known of the prerevolutionary leaders, had his counterpart in every major colonial
city. These men had long since established contact by correspondence, and their response to news of the Boston Port Act was
suspiciously uniform. New York's Isaac Sears and Alexander
McDougall, Philadelphia's Thomas Mifflin and Charles Thomson,
and Virginia's Richard Henry Lee and Patrick Henry moved in precisely the same direction as Adams, calling for a trade embargo
against Great Britain and a continental meeting to coordinate colonial efforts.

Hopes for American solidarity were, of course, based on more than
the personal correspondence between these few men. Patriot leaders
had established a widespread system of correspondence committees
which now assumed a vital role in organizing resistance to the Coercive Acts. Sam Adams had initiated the movement in 1772 when he
persuaded the Boston town meeting to appoint a committee for the

---

[1] L. H. Butterfield *et al.,* eds., *The Diary and Autobiography of John Adams,* II (Cambridge, Mass., 1961), 120.

[2] A number of historians have credited Virginia with issuing the call for the First
Continental Congress, but the suggestion was made in a number of colonies before
any word was heard from the Old Dominion. See, for example, Alexander McDougall,
Political Memorandums Relative to The Conduct of the Citizens on the Boston Port
Bill, Alexander McDougall Papers, New-York Historical Society, New York City;
and J. R. Bartlett, ed., *Records of the Colony of Rhode Island and Providence Plantations in
New England* (Providence, 1856–65), VII, 280.

express purpose of maintaining a regular correspondence with other towns in the Bay Colony. During the next two years a substantial number of Massachusetts towns responded either by appointing special committees or by instructing their selectmen to answer the Boston letters.[3] Then, in March 1773 Virginia's House of Burgesses improved upon the Massachusetts idea, expanding it from a provincial to a continental system of communication. The Virginia Assembly appointed a provincial committee of correspondence, wrote each of the other colonies suggesting that they do the same and then began systematic communication with the several committees as they were established.[4] The resulting network formed the recognizable basis of a colonial confederation. Whereas Massachusetts, as George Bancroft observed, "organized a province; Virginia promoted a confederacy."[5]

In the twelve months preceding Parliament's adoption of the Coercive Acts, almost as if in anticipation of the approaching crisis, eleven colonies had followed Virginia's suggestion and established provincial committees of correspondence. Pennsylvania, the thirteenth colony, had not taken official action, but the election of a committee in the capital city of Philadelphia kept the chain unbroken. The colonists were neither innocent of the system's potential for advancing colonial unity nor secretive about their objectives. Virginia cited the British appointment of a commission to investigate the burning of the *Gaspée* in Rhode Island as the immediate impetus behind her call for a system of corresponding committees, but the Old Dominion openly advocated a permanent network with more comprehensive objectives. Other colonies, in appointing their committees, responded in kind. The Speaker of the New Hampshire Assembly wrote that "the proposed method of Union in all the Colonies hath ever appeared to us to be absolutely necessary, for which purposes this house adopted the Resolves of the very Respectable House of Burgesses."[6] Connecticut's committee, adopting a similar tone, defended the system as a "basis on which the most lasting and beneficial Union may be formed and supported." It even proposed that the newly created committees actively promote the union of the colonies by adopting, wherever pos-

---

[3] See the Boston Committee of Correspondence Papers, New York Public Library, New York City, for the correspondence between Boston and other towns in Massachusetts.

[4] Charles Washington Coleman, "The County Committees of 1774–1775 in Virginia," *William and Mary College Quarterly*, V (1896–97), 94–95; and J. P. Kennedy, ed., *Journals of the House of Burgesses*, XIII (Richmond, 1905), x–xii, 28, 39–43, 135–140, 287.

[5] George Bancroft, *History of the United States of America*, (Boston, 1876), IV, 259.

[6] John Winthrop to the Speaker of the House of Representatives in Connecticut, Feb. 7, 1774, Samuel Blachley Webb, *Correspondence and Journals*, ed. Worthington C. Ford, I (New York, 1893), 21.

sible, a common code of laws. The group predicted that "were the Laws of the Colonies respecting their Currencies, and other general Concerns, of one tenor so far as particular local Circumstances would any Way admit, it might have a most happy Tendency towards forming and strengthening that union of the Colonies on which their safety and Happiness depends."[7]

The creation of a committee system thus contained a promise (or threat, depending on one's point of view) that more than mere correspondence might be in the offing. It is therefore hardly surprising to find that even before adoption of the Coercive Acts, many colonial observers had begun to discuss a continental meeting of committees. In 1773 Ezra Stiles predicted that "the Resolutions and Measures, proposed by the Virginia Assembly, in March last ... will undoubtedly become universal ... [and] *these Assembly Committees will finally terminate in a general Congress.*"[8] Writing during the summer of the same year, the Reverend William Gordon cautioned Lord Dartmouth that the Virginia proposals pointed in the direction of colonial union. He predicted that efforts to disband the committees would "only convince the country of their importance ... & hasten a kind of congress."[9] Massachusetts's Governor Hutchinson shared the fears expressed by Gordon. He reported to John Pownall in October 1773 that the leaders in the Bay Colony were calling openly for a continental meeting.[10] Indeed, a month earlier, on September 13, the Boston *Gazette* had carried two letters demanding united colonial action; and the following March a writer in the Boston *Evening Post* specifically proposed a general congress to "complete the system for the American Independent Commonwealth."[11]

In addition to providing a basis for developing American union, the committees of correspondence enjoyed, at least in the royal colonies, a decided advantage over the regularly established institutions of government. Whereas royal governors could dissolve or prorogue the provincial assemblies, the committees generally insisted on their right to function whether or not the assemblies that had created them remained in session. The committee system thus provided an alternative method of mobilizing colonial opinion in the face of official efforts to thwart such unity by dissolving the legislatures. Governor William

[7] Conn. Comm. of Corres. to the Va. Comm. of Corres., Mar. 8, 1774, Kennedy, ed., *Journals of Burgesses*, XIII, 144.

[8] Abiel Holmes, *The Life of Ezra Stiles* (Boston, 1798), 167–68.

[9] Gordon to the Earl of Dartmouth, June 16, 1773, *The Manuscripts of the Earl of Dartmouth* (Historical Manuscript Commission, *Fourteenth Report*, [London, 1894–1923], Pt. X), II, 156. Appendix

[10] Hutchinson to Pownall, Oct. 18, 1773, Richard Frothingham, *The Rise of the Republic of the United States* (Boston, 1873), 332n.

[11] March 14, 1774.

Franklin of New Jersey tried unsuccessfully to disband that colony's Committee of Correspondence by arguing that his dissolution of the provincial Assembly should have a similar effect on all committees created by that body. John Murray, Earl of Dunmore and governor of Virginia, experienced similar problems when he dissolved the House of Burgesses only to find that the Committee of Correspondence carried forward the business of communicating with other provinces about the possibility of calling a continental congress. Elsewhere committees of correspondence convened provincial congresses, supervised the election of local committees, and in Connecticut even elected delegates to the First Continental Congress.

The British must have surmised that their policies would provide the seeds of American resistance, but they could not have guessed that those seeds would fall on such fertile ground. In adopting an unpopular program at the moment when the growth of the committee system had focused attention on colonial union, Parliament brought to fruition the anticipated meeting of an intercolonial congress, which was from the beginning designed to deal not only with immediate grievances but with the whole structure of the British Empire.

The Americans had problems also. Behind the general agreement on the utility of calling an intercolonial congress they carried on heated debates about the specific plan of action such a body might propose. The most acrimonious arguments concerned the pros and cons of instigating a boycott of British trade. Some wanted the boycott, some wanted it only after other methods had failed, and some did not want it at all.

Boston was the center of the movement for an embargo. Leaders there soon realized that the most effective opposition to the boycott would come, not from those who opposed it altogether, but from those who sought the moderation of delay. In particular, the Bostonians feared that the call for a continental meeting would work to their disadvantage. Under the best of circumstances such a meeting could not have convened before the end of the summer, and Boston's port was to be closed on June 1. Moreover, once Congress assembled, valuable weeks would pass in debate, and even more time in the implementation of any measures on which the group agreed. Additional weeks would elapse before the effects of the boycott were felt in Great Britain. Such delayed assistance, no matter how well intentioned, might well arrive too late to benefit the city. If, as a majority of Bostonians believed, commercial coercion alone could provide effective resistance to the Port Act, then a congress would waste crucial time. Better to adopt the embargo first and talk about it later.

Spearheading events in Massachusetts Bay was, once again, Sam Adams. He had foreseen that a general congress would assemble and immediately realized that the proposal might provide an excuse to postpone adoption of trade restrictions. Consequently, during the three days intervening between the arrival of the Port Act on May 10 and the appearance of the newly appointed governor, General Thomas Gage, on Friday May 13, Adams and his supporters laid plans to commit the colonies to an embargo. Their immediate goal was to consolidate Massachusetts backing for the proposed measure before calling on the other colonies for support. Accordingly, the Boston town meeting appointed a special committee to consult with representatives of the two neighboring ports, Salem and Marblehead, while the Committee of Correspondence convened a meeting with delegates from eight surrounding towns.[12] Having obtained pledges of support from these neighboring communities, the Bostonians turned their efforts toward securing the approval of parts more remote.

Early on Saturday morning, May 14, Paul Revere rode out of the Massachusetts capital carrying with him to New York and Philadelphia the resolutions of the town meeting. As Revere made his way south he had reason to be optimistic. Boston had obtained the support of several major towns in Massachusetts Bay—including Salem and Marblehead, her two most important commercial rivals—and had friends in both New York and Philadelphia who had already begun to agitate for measures similar to those adopted by the town meeting. It may have been this expectation of support that had persuaded the little city to be so outspoken. Mincing no words, Boston had proposed an immediate embargo, predicting that "if the other Colonies come into a joint Resolution, to stop all Importations from *Great Britain* and Exportations to *Great Britain,* and every part of the *West Indies,* till the Act for Blocking up this Harbor be repealed, the same will prove the Salvation of *North America* and her Liberties."[13]

Sam Adams was, of course, much too adroit a political leader to rest his hopes on official channels alone. Still concerned that proposals for a continental meeting would delay the adoption of sanctions on trade, he utilized his extensive contacts throughout the colonies to lobby for the Boston proposals. On May 18 he wrote Silas Deane, chairman of the Connecticut Committee of Correspondence, explaining that although Boston favored an intercolonial convention, she feared that "a Conference of Committees of Correspondence from all the Colonies, cannot be had speedily enough to answer for the present Emergency." He urged the Connecticut leader to persuade local merchants to suspend trade with Great Britain beginning on

---

[12] Force, ed., *American Archives,* I, 331 and n.; Boston Comm. of Corres. to Charlestown, Brookline, Newton, Cambridge, Roxbury, Medford, and Lynn, May 11, 1774, Boston Comm. of Corres. Papers, N.Y. Pub. Lib.

[13] Force, ed., *American Archives,* I, 331 and n.; Kennedy, ed., *Journals of Burgesses,* XIII, 147-48.

June 14. Adams sanguinely predicted that "one year's virtuous forbearance wd. succeed to our wishes."[14] Two weeks later he used the same argument in an effort to build a fire under the middle colonies, writing Philadelphia's Charles Thomson that "a Congress is of absolute Necessity in my Opinion, but from the length of time it will take to bring it to pass, I fear it cannot answer for the present Emergency."[15]

Despite widespread sympathy for Boston and the indefatigable efforts of Samuel Adams, promoting an immediate embargo of British trade was to prove a Herculean task, even in New England. Those who attempted to push for an immediate cessation of commerce were, in one sense, hampered by their own logic, having argued on previous occasions that the colonies must above all else present a united front. One can imagine the chagrin of the Boston leaders as they read a rehash of their own earlier position in Connecticut's noncommittal, even condescending, response to the suggestion that nonimportation begin on June 14. Deane, writing for the Connecticut committee, explained that the "resolves of merchants, in any individual town or province, however generously designed, must be partial; and when considered in respect to the whole of the colonies, in one general view, at best defective." A congress, on the other hand, would "carry weight and influence on the minds of the people, and effectually silence those base insinuations which our enemies are ever ready to throw out, of interested motives, sinister views, unfair practices and the like."[16]

Then the Connecticut committee, admitting that the urgency of Boston's predicament did indeed present problems, suggested a solution that was for practical purposes no solution at all. It proposed that rather than endorse an immediate embargo the colonists hold two separate meetings: one to include the provinces as far south as Virginia and to convene at the earliest possible date, the other to meet later, after the Carolinas and Georgia had been given adequate time to join the movement. Since Deane admitted that even the earlier of the two meetings could not be held before the last of July, the Boston leaders must have found it difficult to understand exactly how the suggestion would have worked to their advantage.[17]

The reluctance of Connecticut notwithstanding, Boston might well

[14] S. Adams to Deane, May 18, 1774, Harry A. Cushing, ed., *The Writings of Samuel Adams* (New York, 1904–8), III, 115.

[15] S. Adams to Thomson, May 30, 1774, *ibid.*, III, 123–24.

[16] Deane to the Boston Comm. of Corres., June 13, 1774, Samuel B. Webb Papers, Sterling Lib., Yale Univ.; Bartlett, ed., *R. I. Records*, VIII, 294.

[17] Deane to Boston Comm. of Corres., May 26, 1774, Boston Comm. of Corres. Papers, N.Y. Pub. Lib.; Deane for the Conn. Comm. of Corres. to the N.J. Comm. of Corres. *et al.*, June 4, 1774, and Deane to the Boston Comm. of Corres., June 13, 1774, Webb Papers, Sterling Lib., Yale Univ.

have secured New England's support for the embargo if the city could have gained backing in the middle or southern colonies. Hope centered at first on New York and Philadelphia, the most important population centers in the middle colonies, but both responded to Boston's plea with a noticeable lack of enthusiasm for restrictions on trade. Local whigs had, as anticipated, proposed the adoption of an embargo in those two cities, but without success.

Isaac Sears had begun to lay plans for committing New York to the embargo as early as May 12, even before the Boston town meeting had adopted its resolutions. Sears's plan called for a meeting of the city's merchants at the Exchange, where he hoped they would propose colonial adoption of a nonimportation agreement similar to that enforced at the time of the Townshend duties. No doubt Sears realized that his fight would be uphill, for he also planned to suggest the "nomination of a Committee of Correspondence, to bring about a Congress." Nearly three hundred persons met on the appointed day, but despite Sears's entreaties and the assistance of such supporters as Alexander McDougall, the gathering refused to take specific action "until the Sense of the other Colonies Should be Known." The meeting did agree to appoint a new committee of correspondence, but the Sears-McDougall faction suffered a further setback when they attempted to reduce the size of the proposed committee from fifty members to twenty-five. The arrival of Paul Revere the day after the conference at the Exchange had but little effect on the situation, and New York, despite continued factional maneuvering, refused to endorse the Boston resolutions.[18]

Events in Philadelphia closely resembled those in New York, except that the group supporting nonimportation in the city of brotherly love handled matters with greater finesse and avoided much of the bitterness that marked developments in the old Dutch colony. Charles Thomson, Thomas Mifflin, and Joseph Reed—leaders of the more aggressive faction in Philadelphia—anticipated the city's reluctance to adopt the militant measures of Boston and instead urged the endorsement of more moderate methods which, they correctly believed, would ultimately achieve the desired results. Recognizing the importance of a united front, the militants managed by carefully laid plans to secure the support of the immensely popular Pennsylvania Farmer, John Dickinson. Then, at a meeting on May 20 the Mifflin-Thomson-Dickinson organization secured the appointment of a Committee of Fifteen to conduct affairs in Philadelphia and initiated a petition to Governor John Penn calling for a special session of the Assembly. Mifflin, at least, seems to have assumed that Penn would

---

[18] McDougall, Political Memorandums Relative to the Conduct of the Citizens on the Boston Port Bill, McDougall Papers, N.-Y. Hist. Soc.

refuse to convene a session of the Assembly. The Pennsylvania leader predicted that his colony would then call a provincial congress and join with the other colonies in support of a general embargo.[19] This cautious procedure did not please Massachusetts. To Bostonians, both New York and Philadelphia appeared lamentably complacent about the British threat.

These were dark days for Boston. Nathaniel Coffin, a tory (as those who opposed resistance to the Coercive Acts were already being called), reported that the apparent coolness of New York and Philadelphia had combined with actual implementation of the Port Act to reduce support for the "Party" even in Boston. He wrote that some of the merchants had been emboldened to rescind their earlier endorsement of the embargo and had voted that "those . . . who had signed a non-importation Agreement lately put abt. should be released from their engagement, as the other Colonies would not come into it." Encouraged by these developments, the conservative faction in Boston had gathered its forces for a frontal assault, proposing to the town meeting that it condemn and disband the Committee of Correspondence. This attempt failed. Coffin reported bitterly that the patriot leaders had gained such influence over "the minds of this poor deluded people" that they could have led them "into the very Jaws of Hell, & even when they had all the horrors of this scene full in view they could persuade them they were leading them into Paradise."[20]

Despite this incursion by conservative forces within the very citadel of resistance to the Port Act, the battle for the embargo was not yet lost. No colony had actually rejected Boston's appeal for an immediate curb on trade with Great Britain, and the provinces south of Philadelphia had yet to respond. Maryland was poised to revive the cause.

On May 25 an express arrived in Annapolis bearing the resolutions of the Boston town meeting and a forwarding letter from the recently elected Philadelphia committee. These dispatches probably included the resolutions adopted in New York as well, for the Philadelphia letter referred to the measures endorsed by that city.[21] Later that afternoon, with astonishing alacrity, about eighty "Inhabitants" met to consider the proposals from the northern colonies.[22] Within twenty-four hours, they had adopted resolutions, appointed a committee to

[19] Force, ed., *American Archives*, I, 321; *Pennsylvania Gazette* (Phila.), June 8, 1774; Mifflin to S. Adams, May 21, 1774, Samuel Adams Papers, N.Y. Pub. Lib.

[20] Coffin to Charles Steuart, July 6, 1774, Steuart Papers, Nat'l. Lib. of Scotland (microfilm, Col. Wmsbg. Foundation).

[21] Va. Comm. of Corres. to the Md. Comm. of Corres., May 31, 1774, Samuel Purviance Papers, Maryland Historical Society, Baltimore (microfilm, Col. Wmsbg. Foundation).

[22] Force, ed., *American Archives*, I, 353.

correspond with other communities, and written and posted letters to the several counties in Maryland as well as to the Virginia House of Burgesses.

The resolutions adopted in Annapolis went far beyond anything suggested in Philadelphia or New York. The Annapolis residents, like their Boston counterparts, called for an immediate halt to both importation and exportation. Moreover, they suggested that the embargo be incorporated into a written association signed on oath and advocated a boycott of trade with any colony that refused to adopt similar measures. In one area the Annapolis meeting even went further than Boston, proposing that "the Gentlemen of the Law in this Province bring no Suit for the Recovery of any Debt due from any Inhabitant of this Province to any Inhabitant of Great Britain until the said act be repealed."[23] This latter suggestion proved too radical for most communities, but on other points the deliberations of Annapolis foreshadowed, if they did not determine, the response of the southern colonies to the Coercive Acts.

Within a matter of days it became evident that most of the Maryland counties were willing to support the Annapolis call for an embargo on British trade. The Baltimore committee, having suspended its own deliberations in order to await the reaction of "our Friends in Annapolis," subsequently convened a county meeting which on May 31 endorsed the proposed boycott of trade and suggested specific dates for its implementation.[24] During the following two weeks five additional counties—Frederick, Charles, Harford, Anne Arundel, and Queen Anne—called similar meetings and approved the proposed suspension of trade.[25] Although most of these counties hedged the issue by stipulating that the proposed boycott should not go into effect until endorsed by other towns throughout America, Maryland had clearly pronounced itself ready to follow the lead of Annapolis and endorse Boston's call for an immediate suspension of trade with the mother country.

Added to the Maryland backing, the support of Virginia would have provided an almost irreversible momentum to the movement for an immediate embargo. As the oldest, largest, and wealthiest colony, the Old Dominion exercised considerable influence. The Philadelphia committee had recognized this leadership, writing in June that "all America look up to *Virginia* to take the lead on the present oc-

[23] John Hall *et al.* to Peyton Randolph *et al.*, May 25, 1774, Purviance Papers, Md. Hist. Soc. (microfilm, Col. Wmsbg. Foundation).

[24] Baltimore Comm. of Corres. to the Alexandria, Va., Comm. of Corres., May 25, 1774, *ibid.*; Force, ed., *American Archives*, I, 366–67.

[25] Resolutions from all of these counties may be found in Force, ed., *American Archives*, I, 366, 384, 402, 403, and 410, as well as in the *Maryland Gazette* (Baltimore) for 1774.

casion.... You are ancient, you are respected, you are animated in the Cause."[26] Thomas Wharton, Sr., was even more emphatic, writing a friend that "we shall shortly know the sentiments of the Virginians, As their Assembly is sitting, They are Certainly a Sensible & Wealthy people—& the part they shall take in this Affair will have a great Influence on their Sister Colonies."[27]

Recognizing the influence Virginia would exercise, the Annapolis committee took careful steps to prod its more prestigious neighbor to the proper position. The committee addressed a letter to "Peyton Randolph & Other Gentlemen of Williamsburg," knowing that Randolph, as Speaker, would bring it before the House of Burgesses. The Annapolis residents began with a deferential reference to the past leadership of the Old Dominion and an apology for presuming to suggest a course of action to the highly respected Virginia Assembly. The Marylanders explained that only the necessity of proposing immediate action had prevented their awaiting "with Pleasure your Resolutions, which we cannot doubt will be formed on the same generous Principles, which have hitherto actuated your Colony on every late Attempt against American Liberty." They respectfully requested that the House of Burgesses respond to the resolutions adopted in Maryland.[28]

The letter composed in Annapolis on May 25 made no reference to the origin of the proposed resolutions or to the authority by which the committee transmitted them to Virginia. The letter bore the signatures of John Hall, Charles Carroll, Thomas Johnson, Jr., William Paca, Matthias Hammond, and Samuel Chase, all of whom except Carroll were also members of Maryland's provincial Committee of Correspondence. These signatures gave the letter the appearance of an official communication, and Peyton Randolph, Speaker of the House of Burgesses, made a natural mistake in assuming that the letter came from the Maryland committee and that it represented, in some degree, the attitude of that colony's Assembly. It is difficult to believe that Randolph's correspondents in Annapolis had not intended that he make that error. They knew that the House of Burgesses had initiated the appointment of the several provincial committees of correspondence and that the body treated communications from such groups with considerable respect. Certainly a letter from the provincial committee in Maryland would carry more weight than one from an impromptu gathering in a single town. Why else would the Annapolis committee have avoided explaining that both the resolutions they proposed and the authority under which they acted

[26] Kennedy, ed., *Journals of Burgesses*, XIII, 152.

[27] Wharton to Thomas Walpole, May 31, 1774, Wharton Letterbook, Hist. Soc. Pa.

[28] John Hall *et al.* to Peyton Randolph *et al.*, May 25, 1774, Purviance Papers, Md. Hist. Soc. (microfilm, Col. Wmsbg. Foundation).

stemmed from the meeting on May 25? Indeed, the entire proceedings of this newly formed organization suggest a deliberate attempt on the part of a select few "Inhabitants" of Annapolis to counteract the moderating influence that the resolutions of New York and Philadelphia had had on the movement for an embargo of trade. Deliberately or not, the proceedings in Annapolis were to have a crucial effect in Williamsburg.

News of the Port Act, arriving directly from England, had reached Virginia about the same time that the dispatches from Philadelphia had been delivered in Annapolis. The timing of the arrival had thrust the Virginia Assembly into something of a quandary. There was a great deal of local business before the Burgesses, and it was feared that a precipitate stand in opposition to British policy might provoke Governor Dunmore into an early dissolution of the House, thereby preventing the adoption of important legislation. But if the Assembly refused to act, their reticence might be viewed in the other colonies either as a failure of will or perhaps even as an endorsement of the British measures. In attempting to straddle this difficulty the Burgesses had, before the arrival of the Annapolis letter, fallen between two stools.

Shortly after first news of the Port Act arrived, Thomas Jefferson met privately with such kindred spirits as Richard Henry Lee, Patrick Henry, Francis Lightfoot Lee, and a few others to consult upon the proper means of arousing the community's concern without unnecessarily irritating the governor. The method they devised to focus the attention of Virginia on the plight of its sister colony was one that the Massachusetts Puritans had often used to promote civic solidarity: a day of fasting. To avoid any suspicions their association with this pious proposal might arouse, the group prevailed upon Robert Carter Nicholas to suggest the motion because, according to Jefferson, his "grave and religious character was more in unison with the tone of our resolution." Nicholas readily agreed, and on May 24 the House of Burgesses unanimously voted to set aside June 1, the day on which the Port Act took effect, as a "day of Fasting, Humiliation, and Prayer, devoutly to implore the divine Interposition, for averting the heavy Calamity which threatens Destruction to our civil Rights, and the Evils of civil War; to give us one Heart and one Mind firmly to oppose, by all just and proper Means, every Injury to *American* rights."[29] Having thus recorded its opposition to the Port Act, the Assembly put aside further resolutions until they completed the country business.

The House of Burgesses clearly intended to adopt further, more

[29]Julian P. Boyd *et al.*, eds., *The Papers of Thomas Jefferson*, I (Princeton, N.J., 1950), 106n.

explicit measures later in the session. Richard Henry Lee wrote that he had prepared several resolutions for presentation to the House but had delayed introducing them at the request of "many worthy members, who wished to have the public business first finished."[30] Whatever plans the Virginians may have had for the remainder of the legislative session were to remain in limbo, however, for their efforts to avoid the wrath of the governor failed. On May 26 Lord Dunmore called the House into the Council chamber and, holding a copy of the fast day proclamation in his hand, read the message of dissolution.[31]

Dunmore had made an adroit political move. Despite Landon Carter's professed surprise that anyone should take offense at a proposal to pray for the king, the governor had accurately assessed the intentions of the burgesses and had thrown a sizable roadblock in the path of those who wished to commit Virginia to a forward stand against British policy.[32] Dunmore did not expect his dissolution to prevent action by the Virginia Assembly, but he hoped that by depriving the burgesses of their official status he could force them to proceed with greater moderation. This ploy at first proved quite successful. Richard Henry Lee reported that when Speaker Randolph convened the recently dissolved legislature in the Apollo Room of the Raleigh Tavern on May 28, the burgesses "made a distinction between their then state, and that when they were members of the House of Burgesses" and refused to adopt the resolutions Lee had previously composed.[33]

In part because of Dunmore's dissolution and in part because the resolutions from Boston had not yet arrived in Virginia, the meeting at the Raleigh Tavern proceeded cautiously. The group not only failed to endorse a general nonimportation agreement, they even rejected Lee's motion to issue an explicit invitation for the meeting of a continental congress. Instead, the delegates voted to enter a limited agreement binding themselves to refuse only those British goods imported by the East India Company, and even that list was reduced by the exception of "saltpetre and spices." In addition, the members of the dissolved Assembly "recommended" that the provincial Committee of Correspondence write the several colonies in America concerning the "expediency" of appointing an annual congress to meet on "those general measures which the united interests of America may from time to time require."[34] So unexpectedly moderate were

[30] Lee to S. Adams, June 23, 1774, Force, ed., *American Archives*, I, 446.

[31] Kennedy, ed., *Journals of Burgesses*, XIII, 132.

[32] Greene, ed., *Diary of Landon Carter*, II, 818–19.

[33] Gov. Dunmore to the Earl of Dartmouth, May 29, 1774, Force, ed., *American Archives*, I, 352; Lee to S. Adams, June 23, 1774, S. Adams Papers, N.Y. Pub. Lib.

[34] Boyd *et al.*, eds., *Jefferson Papers*, I, 107–8.

these measures that the Baltimore committee subsequently chided Virginia for having fallen "far Short of that Spirit & Zeal by which the Gentlemen of Your Colony have ever been distinguished." Boston's Committee of Correspondence seconded Baltimore's disapproval, expressing surprise that the burgesses had not appeared "more warmly engaged to bring the matter, to a speedy and determined issue."[35]

Many contemporaries (as well as later historians) credited Virginia with originating the invitation for the First Continental Congress in the letters written by the Committee of Correspondence on May 28 at the instruction of the Raleigh Tavern meeting. The committee did solicit suggestions from other colonies on the advisability of holding an annual congress, but the burgesses clearly viewed that suggestion as the logical outcome of their earlier call for establishing committees of correspondence, rather than as a response to the Boston Port Act. Richard Henry Lee made that point explicit in a later letter to Sam Adams criticizing the dissolved burgesses for having made "much too feeble an opposition." The Virginian queried Adams as to whether the Boston leaders wanted the Old Dominion to issue an invitation for the convening of an intercolonial congress.[36] Adams, receiving Lee's letter several weeks after the appointment of delegates had actually begun, must have reflected with some amusement on Virginia's supposed leadership in calling the meeting.

It is now clear that Virginia owes her reputation for leadership in the summer of 1774 partly to her past record and partly to the timely arrival of the letter from those "gentlemen" in Annapolis. That letter, delivered to Peyton Randolph on May 29, prodded Virginia into a much more radical stand. Randolph called an emergency meeting of those burgesses who had not yet left the capital, and the twenty-five members who responded to that invitation injected new life into the movement for an embargo.

The May 30 meeting took a much more vigorous stand in opposition to the Boston Port Act than had any previous Virginia gathering. The participants had before them the proposals from Boston, the resolutions from Maryland, and the letter from Philadelphia—all of which had been forwarded by the committee in Annapolis.[37] Some of the members noticed that the Marylanders had not included a copy of the resolutions from New York, but as there was no im-

---

[35] Baltimore Comm. of Corres. to the Norfolk and Portsmouth Comms. of Corres., June 17, 1774, Purviance Papers, Md. Hist. Soc. (microfilm, Col. Wmsbg. Foundation); Boston Comm. of Corres. to the Baltimore Comm. of Corres., July 16, 1774, Boston Comm. of Corres. Papers, N.Y. Pub. Lib.

[36] Lee to S. Adams, June 23, 1774, S. Adams Papers, N.Y. Pub. Lib.

[37] Va. Comm. of Corres. to the Md. Comm. of Corres., May 31, 1774, Purviance Papers, Md. Hist. Soc. (microfilm, Col. Wmsbg. Foundation).

mediate remedy for that omission, the point was passed over. The effect of that omission was to place before the assembled burgesses letters from two provinces calling for a suspension of trade and only one, that from Philadelphia, expressing reservations about the boycott.

Some of the more aggressive Virginia leaders, sensing an opportunity to commit the Old Dominion to support the proposals from Boston, moved the immediate adoption of nonimportation and nonexportation against Great Britain. This proposal garnered considerable support, and most of the assembled burgesses agreed that a general nonimportation was now inevitable; but the proposal to interdict exports to the mother country was less popular. Several members insisted that so precipitate a move would have a devastating effect on the economy of a colony that lived on its overseas sales of tobacco. In any event, so small a meeting ought not to adopt measures that would vitally affect the entire province. A more proper course of action would be to call a provincial congress in early August and allow that body to detail the terms of an embargo on trade.[38]

Had it not been for the dispute over nonexportation, Virginia might well have added the weight of its influence to the call for immediate sanctions against British trade. According to a broadside sent those members of the Burgesses not at the May 30 meeting, "most gentlemen present seemed to think it absolutely necessary" to extend the recent nonimportation association to include a stoppage of all British imports, but "we were divided in our Opinions as to stopping our Exports."[39] The broadside therefore instructed the members of the late House of Burgesses to collect the sense of their constituents and to return to Williamsburg on August 1 for the purpose of deciding the issues at hand.

Had the twenty-five burgesses who met in Williamsburg on May 30 thrown their support to Boston, as some wanted to do, trade restrictions might have begun before, rather than after, the meeting of the First Continental Congress. Even as it stood the Maryland and Virginia resolutions gave impetus to the move for an embargo and dealt the voices of moderation in New York and Philadelphia a strong blow. Although the dissolved burgesses had admittedly stopped short of endorsing an immediate embargo, they had publicly expressed approval of nonimportation and had arranged for the meeting of a provincial convention that would soon adopt a detailed plan for halting commerce with Great Britain. The battle had in fact been decided. With Maryland and Virginia committed to measures similar to those

[38] *Ibid.*

[39] A copy of this broadside, issued May 31, 1774, is in the University of Virginia Library, Charlottesville.

recommended by Boston, the efforts of the conservative merchants in the middle colonies were doomed to failure. Nathaniel Coffin, who had earlier entertained hopes that the "Party" in Boston might lose the initiative, now admitted that Massachusetts had "lately received great Encouragement from Charleston, Williamsburg, and Annapolis . . . whose Resolves have increased the Flame at New York and Philadelphia."[40] That increased flame would soon illuminate an impressive victory for Boston: the decision to call a congress had delayed but by no means averted the implementation of an economic boycott. Equally important, the delay had solidified American opinion. Even those who had raised a plea for colonial unity as a means of avoiding nonimportation would soon find themselves committed by their own eloquence to support the very measure they had sought to defeat.

[40]Coffin to Charles Steuart, July 6, 1774, Steuart Papers, Nat'l. Lib. of Scotland (microfilm, Col. Wmsbg. Foundation).

CHAPTER III

The Debate on Nonimportation
Why the Tories Failed

I N TIMES of crisis the man of conservative temperament labors
under serious handicaps. His proposals tend toward a policy of
"wait and see" while the spirit of the times demands action. His
supporters must be gathered from among the ranks of those who are
accustomed to upholding the status quo and are therefore ill-
equipped to organize and pursue measures that demand active in-
volvement in political controversy. Finally, the conservative is reluctant to join in extralegal activities. Though he may participate in
such activities for the purpose of exercising a moderating influence,
he may as often withdraw from all political activity in an effort to
avoid conflict with either side. Leadership often goes by default to
those who are active rather than passive, those who are radical rather
than conservative.

Such were the problems that faced the conservative leadership in
the colonies during the summer of 1774. Looking toward the meeting
of the First Continental Congress as a platform from which to divert
the movement leading Americans toward a confrontation with Great
Britain, they found instead that the battle was decided even before
the delegates began to arrive in Philadelphia. When, during the second week of Congress, Richard Henry Lee moved the adoption of a
nonimportation agreement, the delegates adopted the proposal after
only a few hours' debate and without a dissenting vote.[1] The conservatives had failed so thoroughly in their efforts to organize an opposition to the restriction of trade that no member of Congress dared
raise his voice against the proposal.

Any thorough exploration of the conservative failure would necessitate an analysis of events in individual colonies far beyond the scope
of this narrative. Nevertheless, a brief comparison of factional maneuvering in four major colonies—Virginia, Massachusetts, Pennsylvania, and New York—can provide some interesting suggestions
about the weakness of the tories in the crisis generated by Parliament's adoption of the Coercive Acts. These colonies have been
chosen not only because of their size and importance but because
they represent two extremes of the political spectrum. A majority of
the delegates from Virginia and Massachusetts have usually been

---

[1]Ford, ed., *Journals Cont. Cong.*, I, 41; see also chapter 6 below.

grouped with the radical faction in Congress, while those from
Pennsylvania and New York allegedly provided a bulwark for the
more conservative wing.

No colony evidenced greater unity during the summer and fall of
1774 than Virginia. Governor Dunmore's attempt to halt the movement for a congress by dissolving the House of Burgesses failed miser-
ably, as meetings in county after county elected delegates to an extralegal convention to meet in Williamsburg during the first week of
August. Without exception these meetings condemned Parliament,
promised support for Boston, and called for a boycott of British
trade.[2] The ineffectiveness of the Virginia conservatives is evident
not only in the tone of the resolutions adopted by the counties but in
the paucity and weakness of attempts to modify them.

Among those who tried unsuccessfully to alter the trend in Virginia was Robert Beverley of Essex County. Beverley's regard for
private property made it difficult for him to accept Boston's destruction of the East India Company's tea, and his prejudice in favor of
government by the elite left him with the uneasy feeling that the
Massachusetts Bay charter did indeed permit a dangerous excess of
democracy. At the same time he agreed with the general consensus
that the ministry had acted "tyrannically & oppressively" in adopting the Coercive Acts, and he firmly believed that Americans should
resist Parliament's asserted right of taxation. Caught like many
colonists between two extremes, Beverley worked throughout the
summer to devise a solution which would appeal to both sides. "Do
you not think," he wrote Landon Carter in June, "it is in the Power
of Wisdom to project such Terms of Accommodation, that by moderate Concessions on each Side, a Line may be drawn so as to prevent any Disputes or Animosities for the future. Carter thought no
such thing, and correspondence between the two became strained
and then ceased altogether.[3]

As the crisis deepened, Beverley's increasing frustration with the
course of events in Virginia led him to attempt an alteration in public
opinion. When it came time for Essex County to meet and instruct
its representatives to the August Convention, he wrote and moved
the adoption of several conservative resolutions. He proposed that the
colonists make no effort to coerce the mother country until other
measures had failed, suggesting in particular that a delegation be sent
to Great Britain to present the grievances of America before the king.
Beverley asked that the Essex County representatives be instructed

[2]Resolutions from many of these county meetings may be found in Force, ed.,
American Archives, I, as well as in the *Virginia Gazette* (Williamsburg) for 1774.

[3]Beverley to Carter, June 9, 1774, and Beverley to Carter, Aug. 28, 1774, (and enclo-
sure), Landon Carter Papers, Virginia Historical Society, Richmond (typescripts, Col.
Wmsbg. Foundation).

to oppose both nonimportation and nonexportation at the meeting in Williamsburg.[4] His attempt failed. The freeholders of Essex summarily rejected his proposals, voting instead to "stop all exports to, and imports from *Great Britain* and the *West Indies,* and all other parts of the world, ... if such a measure shall be deemed expedient by the Deputies at the general Congress."[5]

Other Virginia conservatives who attempted to slow the move toward trade restrictions found themselves similarly isolated and ignored. In Fairfax County, Bryan Fairfax entertained ideas similar to those of Beverley. He considered standing for election to the Convention but withdrew when he found that "there are scarce any at Alexandria [site of the Fairfax County meeting] of my opinion."[6] Neither Beverley nor Fairfax suggested that the colonists submit to the Coercive Acts, only that they attempt to petition the king before proceeding to economic sanctions; yet not a single town or county in the whole of Virginia endorsed even so mild a deviation from the general consensus.

Proposals like those advanced by Beverley and Fairfax had little appeal in Virginia, in part because of a prevailing belief that petitions had had but little effect on British policy in the past. Even an individual of such generally conservative a temperament as George Washington gradually came to the conclusion that only action could persuade the ministers to alter their course. The Virginia leader had lamented the excesses of the Boston Tea Party but he was exasperated by the Coercive Acts and convinced that Great Britain had determined to force the colonies into an abject recognition of Parliament's unlimited authority. From his plantation at Mount Vernon he tried to convince Fairfax that the time for conciliatory measures had passed. Could those who supported delay produce a shred of evidence "to induce a belief that the Parliament would embrace a favorable opportunity of repealing acts, which they go on with great rapidity to pass?" Washington thought not. With increasing irritation he chided Fairfax for his continued faith in petitions even though they had never affected British policy in the past. Surely the colonists could not expect to obtain "redress from a measure, which has been ineffectually tried already."[7]

After the arrival of the Annapolis resolutions at the end of May, Virginia witnessed no serious effort to defeat nonimportation. Those who opposed that measure soon learned to keep their opinions to themselves and focused instead on thwarting more radical measures.

[4]*Ibid.*

[5]Force, ed., *American Archives,* I, 527.

[6]Bryan Fairfax to George Washington, July 3, 1774, Fitzpatrick, ed., *Writings of Washington,* III, 227n.

[7]George Washington to Bryan Fairfax, July 20, 1774, *ibid.,* III, 230–34.

James Parker, a tory merchant from Norfolk reported on the progress of events in Williamsburg. "There was Some violent debates here about the association," Parker wrote on June 17. "George Mason, Pat: Henry, R. H. Lee & the Treasurer [Robert Carter Nicholas], as I am told, were for paying no Debts to Britain, no exportation or importation & no Courts here. Paul Carrington was for paying his debts & Exporting, in this he was joined by Carter Braxton, Mr. E[dmund] Pendleton, Thos. Nelson jun, & the Speaker [Peyton Randolph]." Parker implied that all these men favored the adoption of nonimportation, and although he himself opposed the measure, he had no doubt that the August Convention would endorse it. He did predict, at one point, that the merchants would avoid entering into such agreements because they had decided to "mind their own business," but he later clarified that statement by adding parenthetically, "I mean the British born Merch[an]ts."[8]

Parker's assessment of sentiment in Virginia was accurate. An overwhelming majority supported immediate nonimportation. The only important points of controversy were whether to adopt non-exportation before the harvest of the tobacco crop then under cultivation and the advisability of closing the colony's courts in order to effect a moratorium on the payment of debts. Consequently, when the Convention voted not to close the courts and to postpone non-exportation until the fall of 1775, the decision was hailed as a victory for the moderates. William Reynolds of York, who attended the Convention, wrote that he was "really fearfull they would resolve against Exporting to take place immediately but am happy to find Moderation has guided their Counsels so far as to postpone it till August next."[9] Beverley was similarly gratified. Though he continued to urge sending a delegation to Great Britain with a petition, he declared himself "pleased" with the vote against immediate nonexportation "notwithstanding it might have been supported by the general Concurrence of the People."[10]

The Virginia Association, as the document detailing the plan of embargo was known, may have pleased moderates in the Old Dominion, but it struck Philadelphia's Thomas Wharton, Sr., as "Extraordinary." Wharton undoubtedly expressed the sentiments of many in New York and Philadelphia when he condemned the actions of the Virginia Convention as neither "prudent or just."[11] The Virginia

[8]Parker to Charles Steuart, postscript to a letter of June 7, 1774, and Parker to Steuart, Sept. 29, 1774, Steuart Papers, Nat'l. Lib. of Scotland (microfilm, Col. Wmsbg. Foundation).

[9]Reynolds to John Norton, Aug. 6, 1774, William Reynolds Letterbook, Lib. Cong.

[10]Beverley to Landon Carter, Aug. 28, 1774, Carter Papers, Va. Hist. Soc. (typescripts, Col. Wmsbg. Foundation).

[11]Wharton to Thomas Walpole, Aug. 20, 1774, Wharton Letterbook, Hist. Soc. Pa.

decision had an important psychological effect not only on the movement in other colonies but on the First Continental Congress itself. When the delegates from Williamsburg arrived in Philadelphia, they supported nonimportation with the determination of those who have already moderated their position in the interest of harmony. Little wonder that those who opposed the boycott hesitated to say so in the presence of their illustrious compatriots from the Old Dominion.

The unanimity successfully cultivated by the Virginia planters during the summer of 1774 was conspicuously absent in Massachusetts. There, the existence of a substantial trading community provided the basis for opposition to any measures that might threaten a break with Great Britain. Moreover, while control in Virginia remained, at least for the time being, in the hands of the wealthy and established planters, leaders in Massachusetts often came from less respected backgrounds. Many of Boston's wealthy merchants harbored a bitter antagonism toward these rising political leaders and were eager to see such upstart politicians put in their place. Nathaniel Coffin did "most fervently long to see the Insolence of these people meet with some check," while James Murray urged the immediate dispatch of British regulars to restore order. Murray condemned the previous leniency of the mother country and blamed "Temporizing Councils" for the "Serious Crisis, which may be fatal to many of us."[12] These comments make it clear that the conservatives had little hope, barring assistance from British troops, of altering events in Massachusetts Bay. Nevertheless, opposition to the proceedings of the Boston radicals was well organized and active.

The opening round in the campaign by the Massachusetts "Friends of government" began even before Governor Hutchinson left the colony as a series of circulated petitions expressing approval of his administration and wishing him well on his voyage to Great Britain. Shortly thereafter, encouraged by the temporizing response of New York and Philadelphia to the proposed embargo, the conservatives fired their second shot, calling a meeting of merchants which voted that those who had already signed the nonimportation agreement need not abide by it as the other ports had refused to join.

Although the whigs had belittled the importance of the petitions congratulating Hutchinson, they could not ignore the defection of the merchants from the projected boycott. Having had but little faith in the fidelity of the merchants from the beginning, the whigs now decided that only the threat of economic ruin could keep their prosperous brethren in line, and so they engineered a consumer boycott. Circulation of this pledge not to purchase British goods, known as

---

[12]Coffin to Charles Steuart, Dec. 10, 1774, and Murray to Steuart, Nov. 17, 1774, Steuart Papers, Nat'l. Lib. of Scotland (microfilm, Col. Wmsbg. Foundation).

the Solemn League and Covenant, caused considerable alarm among
the merchants. Coffin reported widespread fear that "if this agreement should be generally inter'd into that all of them who had great
stocks of Goods on hand & who expected large importations in the
Fall would be ruin'd."

The initial success of the Solemn League and Covenant precipitated a major tory offensive in the early weeks of June. A number of
Boston merchants and their supporters appeared in the town meeting
to urge disbanding the Committee of Correspondence, and for a time
it seemed that the move had some chance for success.[13] Joseph Warren
wrote from Salem that the tories there expected Samuel Adams's
defeat and that he feared the party that supported payment for the
tea was "too formidable." Warren urged Adams to attend the town
meeting and defend the committee; this suggestion may have played
a part in the Boston leader's decision not only to attend but to abandon his position as moderator in order to participate in the debate.
When the vote came, after two days of argument, Coffin reported
that "the Hands help up for the motion were abt. one fifth of those
against." This defeat for the conservatives "occasioned a general
Hissing," and the minority group left the meeting without having
offered an intended proposal to pay for the tea. Coffin objected to this
retreat, complaining that a vote on the question of the tea would
at least have given the tories an opportunity to protest the proceedings of the town "in this important particular as they have done
against their proceedings relative to the Committee."[14]

The conservatives made no further attempt to capture control of
the Boston town meeting and probably ceased even to attend. News
of the Government Act and the Justice Act increased the antagonism
toward Parliament, and evidence of support from other colonies reinforced Boston's determination to resist. Especially reassuring were
the contributions of money and produce pouring into the Massachusetts capital, which served both to ease the distress caused by the
Port Act and to bolster flagging morale.[15] The tories, convinced that
they could have no further effect without outside support, retired
from the fray and prayed for the arrival of a military force sufficient
to reassert the authority of Parliament and, not incidentally, of themselves. The abortive attempt to redirect the activities of the town
meeting persuaded them that Great Britain would have to resort to

[13]Coffin to Steuart, July 6, 1774, *ibid.*; for information on the Solemn League and
Covenant see the Boston Comm. of Corres. Papers, N.Y. Pub. Lib.

[14]Warren to S. Adams, June 15, 1774, S. Adams Papers, N.Y. Pub. Lib.; Coffin to
Steuart, July 6, 1774, Steuart Papers, Nat'l. Lib. of Scotland (microfilm, Col. Wmsbg.
Foundation).

[15]For an extensive list of the donations to Boston, see Massachusetts Historical
Society, *Collections,* 2d ser., IX (Boston, 1822), 158–66.

"blows" if she hoped to have "the least shadow of authority over New England." Murray reported that it was the "general Expectation" that there would have to be a "brush" with British troops in the spring and that after that "the Rubbish of their old Constitutions can be cleared to the foundation."[16]

Events in Philadelphia were far more complex than in either Virginia or Massachusetts. The presence of a substantial Quaker population generally opposed to any kind of extralegal activity, the prolonged struggle still in progress between political factions supporting and opposing the proprietary government of the Penns, and the personal antagonism between such leaders as John Dickinson and Joseph Galloway set the stage for a complicated series of maneuvers. For the most part the whig faction seems to have devoted its energies to uniting the province behind a call for a general congress on the assumption that the popularity of this measure would put them at the head of a united front. In particular, the whigs hoped to undermine the political influence of Galloway, the conservative Speaker of the Pennsylvania Assembly, by organizing local committees and calling a provincial convention.

One of the most effective whig organizers in Philadelphia was Thomas Mifflin, a man of less reputation than Charles Thomson (the "Sam Adams of Philadelphia") but equally effective in his careful direction of both men and events. Mifflin was one of the few persons who presumed to instruct Sam Adams on the techniques of manipulation—suggesting that the Bostonian cultivate the support of John Hancock because the movement needed to attract men of wealth—and it was almost certainly Mifflin who persuaded Dickinson to "step forth." Thoroughly familiar with the subtleties of politics in the city of brotherly love, the Philadelphia leader was able to forecast developments there quite accurately. As early as May 21 Mifflin assured Sam Adams that despite appearances to the contrary, events would "end in what you wish." He further predicted that Pennsylvania would soon appoint committees of correspondence "after your model" and cautioned that the Bostonians must "humor us" in calling a congress because that was a necessary step "in order to lead."[17]

The most important and successful strategy developed by the Philadelphia whigs was their decision to court the support of John Dickinson, the moderate leader who had won fame throughout the colonies by his *Letters from a Pennsylvania Farmer*. Dickinson, unlike Mifflin or Thomson, entered the political arena reluctantly. Wealthy, respected, and possessed of a continental reputation, Dickinson had

---

[16]James Murray to Steuart, Nov. 17, 1774, and Coffin to Steuart, Nov. 21, 1774, Steuart Papers, Nat'l. Lib. of Scotland (microfilm, Col. Wmsbg. Foundation).

[17]Mifflin to S. Adams, May 21, 1774, S. Adams Papers, N.Y. Pub. Lib.

much to lose and little to gain from a too precipitate identification with the Philadelphia whigs. His position and wealth provided him with a generally conservative frame of mind which recoiled from the thought of rebellion and in the end prevented him from signing the Declaration of Independence. John Adams, an admirer of the Pennsylvania leader in 1774, later became so exasperated with his moderating influence that he referred to Dickinson as a "piddling genius" whose actions made the Second Continental Congress seem "ridiculous."[18] Nonetheless, Dickinson had long opposed the expanding power of Parliament. Although he opposed the immediate adoption of nonimportation, he had long been a rival of Speaker Galloway and, in part no doubt because the move threatened the influence of his opponent, supported the convening of a provincial congress. Moreover Dickinson considered the Coercive Acts oppressive, agreed that they must be repealed, and thought that the Americans' only hope for success lay in a coordinate and unanimous opposition. He was therefore not unwilling to see Pennsylvania committed to endorsement of any measures adopted by the Continental Congress. This willingness to assume leadership of the opposition to the Coercive Acts, combined with his substantial popularity, made Dickinson a perfect foil to the more conservative endeavors of Galloway.[19]

Once Dickinson accepted leadership of the whig movement in Philadelphia, he worked diligently to unite all factions. Under his leadership the Committee of Fifteen arranged a series of conferences in May and early June with various interest groups in Philadelphia, including a number of the leading Quakers.[20] The purpose of these meetings was to prepare a set of resolutions and to suggest nominees for a new committee; both of these measures were to be presented for approval at a general meeting of the city and county. Dickinson, convinced that success depended upon unity, worked long hours to effect a united front, modifying proposals that were too radical for the Quakers and using his influence to prevent the mechanics from drawing up separate, more radical, resolutions at a meeting of their own.[21] Reconciling these conflicts caused such delay that the general

[18]Adams to James Warren, July 24, 1775, Charles Francis Adams, ed., *Works of John Adams* (Boston, 1850–56), I, 179.

[19]Mifflin to S. Adams, May 21, 1774, S. Adams Papers, N.Y. Pub. Lib.; Charles Thomson to William Henry Drayton, "The Thomson Papers," New-York Historical Society, *Collections,* XI (1878), 275; Charles J. Stille, *The Life and Times of John Dickinson* (Philadelphia, 1891), 107–8; Force, ed., *American Archives,* I, 392.

[20]James Pemberton to Dr. John Fothergill, July 1, 1774, Etting Collection, Hist. Soc. Pa.; Thomas and John Clifford to Thomas Frank, June 21, 1774, Pemberton Family Papers, Hist. Soc. Pa.; Thomas Wharton, Sr., to Thomas Walpole, May 31, 1774, Wharton Letterbook, Hist. Soc. Pa.

[21]Wharton to Walpole, July 5, 1774, Wharton Letterbook, Hist. Soc. Pa.; Comm. of Mechanicks to Dickinson, June 27, 1774, R. R. Logan Collection, Hist. Soc. Pa.

meeting, originally scheduled for June 15, was postponed until June 18.[22]

The main point of contention between the two factions in Philadelphia concerned the proposed meeting of a provincial congress. Penn, as anticipated, refused the petition for a meeting of the Assembly, and the whigs then called for election of delegates to a provincial convention.[23] No less crafty than their opponents, the tories attempted to thwart whig expectations by proposing that since Penn had rejected the petition, Speaker Galloway should call a special session of the Assembly sometime before August 1. This measure too would have been extralegal, but it appealed to the conservatives because it promised to maintain control in the hands of the more moderate Assembly.

Both sides worked fervently to win their point. The series of conferences between the Committee of Fifteen and other city leaders was dominated by the conservatives, and the committee proposed to the Philadelphia general meeting on June 18 that the Speaker issue a call to convene the Assembly. The meeting modified that suggestion, voting instead that the newly appointed committee should use its discretion about the matter.[24] The end result was that the committee settled for a compromise which may well have come from Dickinson's pen: it accepted both proposals, calling on Galloway to convene the Assembly at the same time that elected county committees met in provincial congress.[25]

This compromise actually worked in favor of the whigs. In the first place, convening a provincial congress presented a serious threat to established governmental institutions and set a precedent which would later serve to facilitate their overthrow. Second, although the Congress remained under the control of the relatively moderate Dickinsonians and went so far as to propose satisfying "all damages done to the East India Company," it was considerably more aggressive than the Assembly. The Congress not only suggested that American commerce should be subject to "no future alterations, without mutual consent"; it also promised that if the Continental Congress adopted a trade embargo, Pennsylvania would abide by the deci-

[22]James Pemberton to Dr. John Fothergill, July 1, 1774, Etting Coll., Hist. Soc. Pa.
[23]Thomas Mifflin to S. Adams, May 21, 1774, S. Adams Papers, New York Pub. Lib., "The Aspinwall Papers," Mass. Hist. Soc., *Collections*, 4th ser., IX (1871), 703.
[24]Broadside submitted by a meeting "of the Committee and a Number of respectable Inhabitants" of Philadelphia on June 10 and 11, Logan Coll., Hist. Soc. Pa. This copy of the broadside has been altered to show the changes made by the public meeting on June 18 in the resolutions prepared at the earlier meeting. See also the Comm. of Mechanicks to John Dickinson, June 27, 1774, *ibid.*
[25]Force, ed., *American Archives*, I, 426–427; Philadelphia Comm. of Corres. to the several counties in Pennsylvania, June 28, 1774, *Pa. Gaz.* (Phila.), July 6, 1774.

sion.[26] Both of these measures counteracted the much more conservative suggestions of the Assembly. Finally, the Provincial Congress recommended the names of three men for appointment to the First Continental Congress—Dickinson, Thomas Willing and James Wilson—but the Assembly refused to consider any of these candidates, further widening the breach between the conservative and moderate factions in Pennsylvania. By the time the Continental Congress met in September, the Dickinson moderates were firmly allied with the more aggressive forces led by Charles Thomson and Thomas Willing. These two groups combined their considerable influence to thwart the efforts of the conservatively oriented Pennsylvania delegation to Congress. Galloway had succeeded in dictating the appointment of the delegates from Pennsylvania but had undermined his position at home and consequently weakened his influence in the Continental Congress.

As the summer progressed the conservative forces in Pennsylvania became more disorganized and, despite their recent victory in the election of delegates, were quite clearly on the defensive. Galloway's headstrong refusal to cooperate with the Provincial Congress had offended the moderates.[27] The Quakers, who had at first attended some of the public meetings in an effort to "hinder any thing from being done that could tend to Inflame or Influence Great Brittain against Us," now began to withdraw from proceedings because of the "Impropriety of any members of our Society meeting in such a matter."[28]

Even as the conservatives grew weaker, the appearance of a radical group on the left made the Dickinson position look increasingly moderate, and consequently more appealing, to many who had previously wavered in their allegiance. On June 27 the mechanics sent a petition to Dickinson condemning his excessive moderation at the general meeting on June 18 and blaming him for the defeat of non-importation, the "one Measure in our Power which has the least Chance for Success." The petition charged that many citizens had given up "their own Judgments in an Instant, and at your Recommendation chose the Men, whom of all others, they most detested & despised. Happy will it be for Pennsylvania, if she weep not Tears of Blood, ere long, for the Respect shown to your Merit that Day."[29]

Because the Continental Congress met in Philadelphia, delegates from other colonies had ample opportunity to learn that the Pennsyl-

---

[26]Force, ed., *American Archives*, I, 555–64.

[27]See *ibid.*, 607n.

[28]Thomas Wharton, Sr., to Thomas Walpole, July 5, 1774, Wharton Letterbook, Hist. Soc. Pa.; James Pemberton to Dr. John Fothergill, July 1, 1774, Etting Coll., Hist. Soc. Pa.

[29]Comm. of Mechanicks to Dickinson, June 27, 1774, Logan Coll., Hist. Soc. Pa.

vania delegation did not enjoy universal support. No sooner did the representatives arrive in town than they were visited by Thomson, or Mifflin, or Dickinson himself, all of whom insisted that Galloway was not to be trusted and that the Pennsylvania delegation did not adequately represent opinion in the colony.[30] They could cite the resolutions of the Provincial Congress to back up their contentions, and those who favored nonimportation undoubtedly made extensive use of that body's promise to enforce a trade boycott if Congress so decided. It must have been apparent to everyone that the Pennsylvania delegates, under fire in the capital of the colony they represented, were not in a good position to oppose measures supported by a majority in Congress. That left only New York.

If the situation in Pennsylvania was complicated, the proceedings of New York were chaotic. From May 16, the day Paul Revere arrived with the Boston resolutions, until the final election of delegates more than two months later, the whig and tory factions struggled almost daily for control of the city. The Committee of Fifty-One which guided affairs in the city was so divided in opinion that each meeting became a parliamentary battle, and the whigs, who were in the minority, finally resigned.[31] Opinion within the committee ranged from that of Alexander McDougall, who sought an immediate endorsement of economic sanctions against Great Britain, to that of Charles McEvers, who opposed even the call for a congress, and Benjamin Booth, who favored a public statement approving alteration of the Massachusetts charter.[32] As in Philadelphia, the mechanics adopted an aggressive position and proved extremely useful to such men as McDougall and Isaac Sears, both of whom continued the fight to commit New York to an embargo of British trade.

Sears and McDougall were to New York what Sam Adams was to Boston and Mifflin and Thomson were to Philadelphia. Resolute, energetic, and persuasive, the two men had begun agitating for nonimportation even before New York received Boston's plea for assistance. On May 14 Sears proposed a meeting of the merchants to plan for a congress, and the next day he and McDougall composed and dispatched a letter to Boston promising that New York would join New England in a boycott of British trade. The Committee of Correspondence in Boston subsequently wrote the Committee of Fifty-

[30]William Bradford, Jr., to James Madison, Aug. 1, 1774, William Bradford, Jr., Letterbook, Hist. Soc. Pa.; Burnett, ed., *Letters Cont. Cong.,* I, 1, 5, 34, 74.
[31]Roger Champagne, "New York and the Intolerable Acts," *New-York Historical Society Quarterly,* XLV (1961), 195–207; Force, ed., *American Archives,* I, 293–330; Comm. of Mechanicks in New York to Boston Comm. of Corres., Aug. 1, 1774, Boston Comm. of Corres. Papers, N.Y. Pub. Lib.; McDougall Papers, N.-Y. Hist. Soc.
[32]Booth to James & Drinker, Philadelphia, Aug. 31, 1774, James & Drinker Business Papers, Hist. Soc. Pa.

one thanking them for their support, but the latter group denied any knowledge of the Sears-McDougall letter and renounced the suggestion that New York supported an immediate embargo.

In New York, as in other colonies, opposition to nonimportation came primarily from the mercantile elements. Interruption of trade would have had an immediate effect on the merchants and was everywhere unpopular with that particular group. Moreover, the merchants tended to be among the wealthier classes, and whether in New York, Philadelphia, Boston, or Norfolk, they considered the Massachusetts government too "democratical" and feared that the emergence of an increasingly vocal faction among the working classes would disrupt the established order. Thus Benjamin Booth, a New York merchant, regularly referred to the whigs as "republicans" and, as a member of the New York Assembly, played a forward part in opposing both the meeting of the Congress and the enforcement of its resolutions.[33] Men like Booth were convinced that the altercation between Great Britain and the colonies might lead to a breakdown of law and order, and like established classes everywhere, they did not view such a development with favor.

The bitterness of the debates that took place in New York City during the summer of 1774 made the divisions in Philadelphia seem insignificant. Fistfights broke out regularly, and Sears himself was the victim of at least one "good drubbing." Perhaps because the tories were more numerous in New York, or the whigs less subtle, or both, the city seemed to one observer "as full of uproar as if it was beseiged by a Foreign Force."[34] One side would hold a public meeting and adopt "unanimous" resolutions only to see a similar meeting by their opponents convene on the following day and just as "unanimously" reject the same proposals. As late as July 25, three days before the final election of delegates, Booth predicted that the "proposed Congress ... would come to nothing, at least with respect to this Province, as we shall never agree on the Persons to be sent as Delegates."[35] Probably because New York's refusal to elect delegates would have served the interests of the tories, the whigs finally agreed to accept the candidates proposed by their opponents. On July 28 Isaac Low, John Jay, James Duane, Philip Livingston, and John Alsop were unanimously elected to represent New York City at the Continental Congress.[36]

Despite Booth's claim that the tories had "obtained a compleat victory over the Republican party, in the appointment of Delegates,"

[33]See Booth's correspondence, *ibid.*

[34]William Sidney to William Samuel Johnson, July 28, 1774, William Samuel Johnson Papers, Connecticut Historical Society, Hartford.

[35]Booth to James & Drinker, July 25, 1774, James & Drinker Business Papers, Hist. Soc. Pa.

[36]Force, ed., *American Archives*, I, 320.

the whigs had in fact won an important concession.[37] For reasons still unclear, the New York delegation published a statement that "at present" they favored a nonimportation agreement.[38] Booth reported a conference between certain members of the New York committee and three of the newly elected delegates—Alsop, Low, and Duane—in terms suggesting that even he had come to expect some kind of embargo. Speaking of nonimportation, he wrote with apparent satisfaction that the delegates "were entirely of our opinion, that such an agreement should extend to every European Commodity, and that all Smuggling should be stopped."[39]

Whatever success the conservative factions in New York and Pennsylvania might claim dwindled to insignificance beside the perfunctory regularity with which other colonies endorsed an embargo on trade. Virginia had led the way, and even though its Convention had voted to delay nonexportation until the fall of 1775, this minor alteration in the proposals from Boston could hardly have soothed conservative spirits in New York or Philadelphia. North Carolina followed Virginia's lead, adopting an almost identical plan of embargo at a convention held in defiance of Governor Eden's efforts to prevent it. Before Congress met, Massachusetts, Maryland, Connecticut, New Jersey, Delaware, and Rhode Island had also given tangible evidence of support for commercial nonintercourse with Great Britain. Some colonies (New Jersey is one example) convened provincial meetings similar to those in Virginia and North Carolina and specifically endorsed nonimportation. Rhode Island, on the other hand, did not hold a convention, but the major towns of Newport, Providence, and Westerly publicly endorsed economic coercion.[40]

[37]Booth to James & Drinker, July 28, 1774, James & Drinker Business Papers, Hist. Soc. Pa.

[38]Force, ed., *American Archives,* I, 319; Comm. of Mechanicks in New York to the Boston Comm. of Corres., Aug. 1, 1774, Boston Comm. of Corres. Papers, N.Y. Pub. Lib.; Booth to James & Drinker, Aug. 1, 1774, James & Drinker Business Papers, Hist. Soc. Pa.

[39]Booth to James & Drinker, Aug. 31, 1774, James & Drinker Business Papers, Hist. Soc. Pa.

[40]For details of the Virginia and North Carolina meetings, see Force, ed., *American Archives,* I, 686–90, 733–37. In Massachusetts the question was not taken up in the Assembly, but almost every major town in the colony supported the trade embargo (see the Boston Comm. of Corres. Papers, N.Y. Pub. Lib.). New Jersey endorsed nonimportation at a provincial congress on July 21, as did the Delaware convention that met on Aug. 2 (Force, ed., *American Archives,* I, 624–25, 667–68). The Provincial Convention in Maryland on June 22 specifically instructed its delegates to effect a plan "operating on the commercial connexion of the colonies with the mother country" (Ford, ed., *Journals Cont. Cong.,* I, 22–23). The resolutions of the Connecticut and Rhode Island towns in favor of nonimportation may be found in the Boston Comm. of Corres. Papers, N.Y. Pub. Lib., the *Connecticut Courant* (Hartford), the Newport *Mercury,* the Providence *Gazette,* and the several newspapers published in Boston. For the resolutions of Providence, Westerly, and Newport, R.I., see Force, ed., *American Archives,* I, 333, 336–37, 343–44.

There is no reason to suspect that more than a handful of delegates elected to Congress opposed, even in private, the adoption of non-importation. The conservative merchant firm of James and Drinker in Philadelphia reported on September 8 that if rumors from Congress proved accurate, "there are at least nine in Ten of their Number for an immediate nonimportation agreement."[41] The radicals had indeed won a resounding victory. Congress would soon commit itself to an embargo of British trade for which even the two most reluctant colonies, Pennsylvania and New York, would cast their votes.

Many of the reasons for the failure of the conservatives to grasp the initiative during the summer of 1774 are evident in the proceedings of the four colonies described above. In the first place, the enormous unpopularity of the Coercive Acts created an American consensus, evident in the comments of representatives from every class in every colony. From Fredericksburg, Virginia, the merchant Charles Yates estimated that not one person in fifty would hesitate to "risque their lives" in opposition to parliamentary taxation. William Fitzhugh, who owed his recent appointment as commissary general of Maryland to his influence with British officials, thought the colonies "Desperately resolved" to oppose the "Power of Taxation," and Philadelphia's Joseph Reed wrote Lord Dartmouth that there was "scarcely a man in this country ... in or out of office, not of immediate appointment from England, who will not oppose taxation by the British Parliament."[42] These are but a few examples. Perhaps the best testimony came from Governor Penn of Pennsylvania who wrote, also to Dartmouth, that "the resolution of opposing the *Boston* Acts, and the Parliamentary power of raising taxes in *America* for the purpose of raising a revenue, is, in a great measure, universal throughout the Colonies, and possesses all ranks and conditions of people."[43]

The unanimity with which the colonists rejected parliamentary legislation forced the conservative elements in America into a most unenviable position. Those who actually supported the Coercive Acts found their views so unpopular that they refrained from voicing them publicly. On the other hand, those who agreed with the whigs in condemning the Coercive Acts could only argue weakly that the mode of opposition was improper and that the colonists should first petition the king for a redress of grievances.

[41] James & Drinker to Benjamin Booth, Sept. 8, 1774, James & Drinker Business Papers, Hist. Soc. Pa.

[42] Yates to Henry Fletcher, Feb. 16, 1775, Charles Yates Letterbook, UVa. Lib. (microfilm, Col. Wmsbg. Foundation); Fitzhugh to James Russell, Nov. 24, 1774, Russell Papers, Coutts and Co. (microfilm, Col. Wmsbg. Foundation); Reed to the Earl of Dartmouth, July 25, 1774, William B. Reed, *Life and Correspondence of Joseph Reed* (Philadelphia, 1847), I, 72.

[43] Deputy Gov. Penn to the Earl of Dartmouth, Sept. 5, 1774, Force, ed., *American Archives*, I, 773.

The supporters of petition themselves often realized that their position was lacking in dynamic appeal, especially in light of the fact that Britain had surrounded Boston with an armed force. The tories constantly had to answer the charge that petitions would only waste time while "the People of Boston are suffering in the meanwhile." Edward Burd of Pennsylvania attempted to reply, warning that the colonists ought not "thro' Consideration of the trivial Loss which they [the Bostonians] must sustain upon this Occasion endanger the Happiness & the Safety of all America," but the warning was in vain.[44] Most Americans did not consider the problem at Boston "trivial" and insisted that relief for the New England port should take precedence over all other considerations.

Moreover, in proposing to petition the king, the conservatives had to admit that such measures had not been effective in the past, whereas many colonists credited nonimportation for repeal of both the Stamp Act and the Townshend Duties. Once again, the conservatives found themselves on the defensive. Robert Beverley of Virginia spoke to the point rather more convincingly than most; yet his arguments reveal the weakness of the conservative position.

It has been urged that we have petition'd & remonstrated without Effect— True we have, but let it be remembered in what Manner their Affairs have been conducted—Our Petitions have usually been transmitted to an insignificant Agent, or committed to the Care of a Governor—In both cases they have fallen into the Hands of Ministers, & never been suffer'd to approach Majesty itself—Would it not be supposed that a numerous & respectable Delegation, supported by all the Influence arising from a Connexion with us, which might be very readily collected together, avowing what were to be our ultimate Resolutions in Case of not obtaining Redress, be a more probable Means of effectually answering our Purpose, than the Schemes hitherto proposed by the Patriots of this Country.[45]

Beverley may have believed in the distinction between the king and his ministry, but an increasing number of Americans did not, and the arguments based on that distinction point up another of the weaknesses in the conservative position. In contending that either the king or Parliament would respond favorably to a decent and humble petition, the tories were proposing a "wait and see" policy which depended entirely on some kind of favorable reaction in Great Britain. But Parliament continued to pass, and the king to sign, measures that increased discontent in the colonies. If anything, the efficacy of petitions in altering British policy seemed to have decreased. The Philadelphia merchants Thomas and John Clifford reported in early September that "many of the most moderate Americans who were for

---

[44]Burd to Edward Shippen, June 4, 1774, Shippen Family Papers, Hist. Soc. Pa.
[45]Beverley to Landon Carter, Aug. 28, 1774, Carter Papers, Va. Hist. Soc. (typescripts, Col. Wmsbg. Foundation).

remonstrating & Petitioning have now changed their Sentiments, all thoughts of those measures seem to be laid aside on presenting since the Reception the Lord Mayor and Aldermen of London met with on presenting their Petition."[46]

A further weakness of the conservatives stemmed from their lack of organization. When the Coercive Acts forced Americans to begin consideration of means for opposing British authority, the Boston Committee of Correspondence had immediate access to a communications network spread throughout colonial America. Within days of the arrival of the Boston Port Act, Sam Adams had contacted, and been contacted by, leaders in Connecticut, Rhode Island, New York, Philadelphia, Virginia, and South Carolina.[47] Those who shared a fundamental aversion to nonimportation had no existing apparatus for organizing their opposition. Beverley in Virginia voiced opinions quite similar to those of Burd in Reading, Pennsylvania, William Samuel Johnson in Stratford, Connecticut, Booth in New York, and Galloway in Philadelphia; but these men had no established lines of communication.[48] Moreover, some of them chose not to become involved, a decision which probably reflects a fundamentally conservative turn of mind and suggests another problem plaguing those who opposed the more aggressive elements in the colonies. Johnson, for example, refused to accept a nomination to attend the Continental Congress as a delegate from Connecticut because he feared the meeting would prove too radical. In making this decision, he not only deprived the conservatives of a potential vote in Congress, he undermined his influence in his own colony.[49] A similar observation might be made about the Quakers in Pennsylvania. Although their withdrawal from politics reflected religious conviction, it certainly deprived the conservative forces of a considerable body of active supporters. It is notable that many Quakers who endorsed the whigs did not feel a similar compulsion to refrain from giving the movement their active support.[50]

Another major fault of the conservative faction was its inability to form coalitions with other groups. Perhaps because many of the tories came from the wealthy class, they seem to have been better equipped to command than to persuade. They often appeared stiff-necked in their contacts with other interests. Galloway's disagreements with

[46]Thomas & John Clifford to Thomas Frank, Sept. 16, 1774, Thomas & John Clifford Letterbook in the Pemberton Family Papers, Hist. Soc. Pa. For the petition of the lord mayor and city of London on the Quebec Act, and the king's reasons for not replying to the same, see Force, ed., *American Archives*, I, 215–16.

[47]S. Adams Papers, N.Y. Pub. Lib.

[48]See previous references to the suggestions of Beverley, Burd, Galloway, and Booth. For letters of William Samuel Johnson see the Johnson Papers, Conn. Hist. Soc.

[49]Johnson to Benjamin La Trobe, July 25, 1774, Johnson Papers, Conn. Hist. Soc.

[50]Stephen Collins is a good example. See the Stephen Collins Papers, Lib. Cong.

Dickinson illustrate this point. Dickinson's relatively conservative outlook offered ample ground for compromise between himself and the Galloway supporters, but the latter made no such attempt. Had Galloway approved Dickinson's appointment to the Continental Congress, as proposed by the provincial convention, he might have forged a conservative-moderate alliance and given the Pennsylvania delegation a firm basis of support from which to wage its battle against nonimportation.

The weaknesses undermining the conservatives in 1774 were exacerbated by the widely accepted belief that the colonists could defeat Parliament if they maintained a united front. The conservatives themselves had encouraged this point of view in contending that no decision should be made on nonimportation until an intercolonial congress was convened. Thus the conservative minority was forced, both from personal conviction and prior commitment, to support nonimportation publicly once Congress gave its endorsement. An example of this is contained in a letter from Maryland's Thomas Johnson, Jr., to New York's James Duane, written shortly after they had both returned home from Congress. Johnson thought that although both he and Duane had been "equally distressed on particular Points . . . as things are now circumstanced if the Proceedings of the Congress come before the Assemblies I am affraid a Disapprobation of any Article might be of infinite Mischief to our Cause."[51]

Finally, the measures proposed by the so-called radicals during the summer of 1774 were not, from the point of view of many Americans, particularly radical. The colonists had engaged in boycotting British trade on two previous occasions, neither of which had resulted in drastic changes for either America or the mother country. Few colonists had any reason to suspect that conditions had altered, and a majority probably expected that nonimportation, supported by the most impressive assembly ever gathered on the North American continent, would soon convince Parliament of its error.

Historians have long looked toward the First Continental Congress for evidence of a last-ditch stand by those who opposed adoption of trade restrictions in retaliation against the Coercive Acts. The evidence is not there. It has been fabricated from the subsequent writings of Joseph Galloway, an overemphasis on the significance of his Plan of Union, and in some cases, a determined disregard for the facts. There were those who opposed nonimportation during the summer of 1774, but they achieved, at best, a stand-off in Pennsylvania and New York and were soundly defeated in most of the remaining colonies. In so far as there was an attempt to divert the move toward an embargo of British trade it took place before Congress convened, and it was entirely unsuccessful.

[51]Johnson to Duane, Dec. 16, 1774, James Duane Papers, N.-Y. Hist. Soc.

CHAPTER IV

Beyond Tea and Taxes
The Constitutional Crisis

THREE distinct problems faced the members of the First Continental Congress as they gathered in Philadelphia in September
1774. They were to formulate a statement or plan that would define a
viable constitutional framework binding the colonies to the British
Empire; they were to decide precisely which acts of Parliament vio-
lated the rights of America; and they were to devise a means for obtaining repeal of the most objectionable of those statutes.

In order to clarify the proceedings of the Congress, I have adopted
a topical rather than a chronological approach. This chapter isolates
the constitutional debate and focuses on the efforts of the delegates
to propose a plan for future regulation of the empire. Chapter V deals
almost exclusively with the grievances of the Congress, and chapter
VI with what the delegates called a "mode of redress." To come to a
clearer understanding of the workings and the importance of the First
Continental Congress, it is essential to note that the members were
themselves clearly aware of the distinctions between these three tasks.
Consequently they were able to prevent the rather heated arguments
over constitutional issues from affecting discussion of the other
problems.

Most of the disputes that divided Congress could have been
avoided if the members had confined themselves to the issues at
hand—obtaining repeal of the Coercive Acts and an end to parliamentary taxation. Instead, Congress sought to achieve the impossible; the delegates devoted fully half of their time to a futile effort to
solve constitutional problems that had plagued the empire for one
hundred and fifty years and would for one hundred and fifty more. It
was not the Coercive Acts, taxation, or even the adoption of a trade
embargo that caused conflict in Congress, but the effort to define the
nature and extent of Parliament's right to regulate imperial trade.

Congress's determination to deal with the complex and potentially
divisive constitutional issues grew out of the prevailing belief that
to consider only immediate grievances would be to cure symptoms
without eradicating the disease. Since 1764 a series of crises had
threatened the connection between Great Britain and America, and
in each case the settlement of one problem had led only to the rise
of another. The Sugar Act, Stamp Act, Townshend duties, and now
the Coercive Acts had followed one after another because the imperial

question remained unresolved: What were the limits of parliamentary authority in the American colonies? William Bradford, Jr., a student at Princeton, expressed this general concern in his letters to James Madison. If Congress did no more than satisfy the needs of Boston, "they will not reach the root of the disorder: they may procure a repeal of the present acts, but that like repeal of the stamp act will be but a temporary relief."[1]

Although repeal of the Coercive Acts was the primary objective of Congress, most Americans shared Bradford's opinion and hoped that the delegates would be able to define a viable constitutional framework binding the colonies to the British Empire. The debate on that question, both in and out of Congress, provides a great deal of insight into the state of opinion in the colonies on the eve of the American Revolution. It attests to the sincerity of American claims that they wanted to remain united to the mother country, but it also indicates that they expected the ties binding the empire to remain loose. On the constitutional issue, almost all Americans could have been labeled radical.

James Parker of Norfolk, Virginia, provides a good example. British by birth and by inclination, Parker had achieved considerable success as a merchant, if not much popularity in Virginia. His mercantile endeavors provided him with more than his share of the comforts in life, and he was understandably interested in upholding both the sanctity of private property and the imperial ties on which his trade depended. News of the Boston Tea Party did little to assuage his fears on either point. The wanton destruction of the East India Company's tea made him fear for his own property and confirmed his suspicion that the Massachusetts government had been weakened, perhaps incapacitated, by the pernicious influence of the lower classes. Nor was he encouraged by the sympathy for Boston's action expressed by some of his Virginia neighbors—including not a few who should have known better. When news of the Coercive Acts arrived, Parker applauded Parliament's decision as a justifiable step toward reasserting the authority of government, and when war later broke out he joined the British army and fought against the Americans.

Despite Parker's unquestioned sympathy with the mother country, his criticisms of British efforts to extend her authority over the colonies are scarcely distinguishable from those of his less conservative compatriots. Horrified by the "rash madness" of the Boston mob, Parker nevertheless placed much of the blame for the dissatisfaction on Britain's efforts to rewrite the imperial constitution. He thought that matters had gone quite satisfactorily in America as long as

[1]Bradford to Madison, Aug. 1, 1774, Bradford Letterbook, Hist. Soc. Pa.

Parliament had contented itself with the "entire Command of the Trade of the Colonies, & the uncontrolled power of imposing any dutys on any Commoditys p[aya]ble in Britain." As late as 1774 the Norfolk merchant thought that the problem was a fundamental defect in the imperial constitution. He complained that "it was no part of the original plan of Settlement that a Briton should lose part of his liberty by moving to any part of the Empire." Parker realized that it might be impossible to find a solution to the imperial conflict and confessed that the man who could suggest a plan to "unite the Colonies to our Country [Britain]" would "merit a Crown of Glory."[2]

Others of a conservative persuasion echoed Parker's criticism. James Duane and Joseph Galloway, while attending the Congress, also spoke of a "manifest defect in the Constitution of the British Empire with respect to the Government of the Colonies." This defect had "arisen from the Circumstances of Colonization which was not included in the System of the English Government at the time of its Institution nor has been provided for since."[3] Duane was to go along with Congress reluctantly and Galloway would reject its work, but both men agreed that constitutional revision was essential to the protection of American liberties.

Despite the unanimity with which the colonists called for a revision of the imperial constitution and the high hopes with which Congress undertook the task, the effort was doomed from the beginning. Congress agreed on the need for revision but could not unite on a solution. Some delegates favored a complete reorganization of the empire along lines leading toward the development of an American Parliament. Galloway was the best-known proponent of this suggestion, but the very meeting of an intercolonial congress was a step toward the realization of some such plan. Other delegates opposed so drastic a revision, favoring instead an explicit statement of American rights which would define the precise limits of parliamentary authority and grant the colonies a free hand to legislate for themselves in other areas.

Both of these suggestions presented problems. The creation of a permanent American Congress would entail a complete revision of the institutions of imperial government; it would have to be accepted not only by each of the several colonies but by the British Parliament. Some colonies would be called upon to give up charter rights, and Britain would have to concede virtual independence to the colonists on all but a few limited matters. The second proposal, an explicit definition of rights, seemed less drastic, but there were

[2]Parker to Charles Steuart, June 7, 1774, Steuart Papers, Nat'l. Lib. of Scotland. (microfilm, Col. Wmsbg. Foundation).
[3]Resolves intended to be offered by Galloway and seconded by Duane, Duane Papers, N.-Y. Hist. Soc.

irreconcilable differences of opinion over the provisions to be included. Some delegates believed that the colonists must explicitly
recognize Parliament's right to regulate colonial trade; others feared
that the recognition of any parliamentary right invited abuse. Some
proposed that since Parliament would be denied the right of taxation,
the colonists ought to contribute to defray the expenses of empire;
others argued that the mother country was sufficiently compensated
through the advantages it reaped from the Acts of Trade and Navigation.

Despite these obvious difficulties, the delegates were determined to
settle the constitutional problem once and for all. They began their
work in Philadelphia by taking up the issue that most threatened to
divide them—the respective rights of Britain and the colonies. A
committee of twenty-four was appointed—soon to be known as the
Grand Committee—and assigned three tasks: (1) formulating a statement of American rights, (2) compiling a list of grievances, and
(3) devising the "mode of redress," or a plan for securing Britain's
acquiescence. At its first meeting the Grand Committee decided to
facilitate its work by dividing into even smaller groups, and the members accordingly separated into three subcommittees. Each of these
groups was expected to concern itself with one of the three tasks.
They were to meet in sequence rather than simultaneously, for it was
generally agreed that the subcommittee on a "mode of redress" could
not work effectively without a list of the grievances for which they
sought redress and, in turn, that the men dealing with grievances
must await the statement of rights before they could list violations.
For nearly three weeks all other activity ceased while a group of about
ten delegates worked over a resolution defining the "proper" connection between the colonies and the mother country.[4]

If, as Galloway later charged, the First Continental Congress
bogged down in debate and was unable to proceed with business for
several weeks, the issue was unquestionably the effort to prepare a
statement of American rights.[5] The subcommittee and the Grand
Committee struggled with the problem until the end of September
and then turned a proposal over to Congress where it generated so
much controversy as to force an additional three-week postponement.

The attempts to formulate a statement of rights illustrate the broad
areas of agreement among the delegates. The conservative Galloway,
during committee debates, agreed with the radical members on
fundamental constitutional issues. He admitted that it was the "es-
sence of the English constitution" that no laws were binding unless

[4]See the notes of James Duane, J. Adams, and Samuel Ward in Burnett, ed., *Letters Cont. Cong.*, I. Note also that Ford, ed., *Journals Cont. Cong.*, I, indicates repeated
adjournments of the Congress during the first weeks of September.
[5]*Examination of Joseph Galloway before the House of Commons* (London, 1780), pp. 60–61.

made by the "consent of the proprietors." Consequently, Congress could, in theory, legally deny the validity of any act passed by Parliament "since the emigration of our ancestors."[6] But the Pennsylvanian hastened to add that he did not favor so extreme an assertion of right. A denial of all laws passed since the settlement of the colonies would "tend to an independency." Galloway proposed instead that Congress remedy this constitutional defect by including in its statement of rights an explicit acknowledgment of Parliament's authority in limited areas.[7] Such a statement would provide a constitutional basis for binding the colonies to the mother country and would thus remedy the defect deplored by commentators on both the left and the right—James Parker, William Bradford, Jr., James Duane, John Adams, and Galloway himself. Superficially, at least, the delegates seemed during the early meetings of the committee to be agreed on the importance of some such solution to the constitutional crisis.

Unfortunately the consensus did not extend to more practical considerations. Whenever the delegates turned to specific proposals they confronted the question of Parliament's right to regulate colonial trade. Galloway and Duane considered such an acknowledgment essential, others viewed it with skepticism. Few wanted to deny the validity of existing statutes affecting trade, but many opposed a blanket recognition of Great Britain's right to enact future legislation in the area. Thomas Lynch, for example, spoke for many when he argued that the admission of parliamentary right in this one instance would weaken the denial of it in others. Lynch professed a willingness to grant Parliament certain controls over colonial trade but objected to admitting that the authority was a right because Parliament could determine the limitations of that right and thus gradually extend it.[8] A different group, of which Galloway and Duane were the most outspoken members, insisted that Congress must accept parliamentary authority over the commerce of the empire or abandon all hope of reconciliation.[9] It was the heated nature of the debate and the nearly equal divisions on this issue that convinced the delegates to shelve the question temporarily and concern themselves instead with the "mode of redress." On September 24, Congress dissolved the Grand Committee, voted to delay consideration of the Report on Rights and Grievances, and turned to discussion of the less controversial question of an embargo on British trade.

This decision bothered Galloway. He noted the relief with which Congress had turned to the question of embargo, and when on Sep-

[6] J. Adams, "Notes of Debates," Burnett, ed., *Letters Cont. Cong.*, I, 22.

[7] *Ibid.* See also James Duane, "Address before the Committee to State the Rights of the Colonies," *ibid.*, I, 23–26.

[8] James Duane, "Notes of Debates," *ibid.*, I, 72.

[9] *Ibid.*

tember 27 the delegates unanimously approved nonimportation of British goods, he began to suspect that they might adjourn without endorsing Parliament's right to regulate trade. Consequently he decided to try a different tack. If Congress would not approve an adequate statement of Britain's authority over trade, perhaps the delegates would consider a proposal to reorganize the empire. On September 28, the day after Congress adopted the trade embargo, the Pennsylvanian attempted to turn attention back to the constitutional issue by introducing his Plan of Union.

Galloway's proposal, in brief, called for a reorganization of the imperial ties along lines suggested by a number of Americans during the years preceding the Revolution, most notably by Benjamin Franklin at the Albany Congress in 1754. An American Congress would be established as an "inferior branch" of the British legislature, and the colonial body would have equal authority with Parliament over such imperial issues as trade regulation and taxation. No law would be binding on the colonies unless approved by both the American Congress and the British Parliament, and the colonies would each retain control over internal matters. Each colony would have a number of representatives in the Grand Congress proportional to its wealth and population, and the king would appoint a governor general to preside over the assembly and exercise the veto power.

Historians have frequently touted Galloway's Plan of Union as the conservative alternative to the radical proposals for nonimportation, but it is apparent that the plan was a substitute, not for the trade embargo, but for the sidetracked statement of rights. In the first place, Galloway did not present his proposal to Congress until debate of Parliament's right to regulate trade had bogged down, and the delegates had approved nonimportation. Moreover, in arguing for adoption of his proposal, Galloway pointedly referred to the failure of Congress to agree on a statement recognizing Britain's authority and implied that his plan would alleviate that problem. James Duane also based his support for the proposal on Congress's failure to admit Parliament's right to regulate trade. The New Yorker expressed his disappointment that the delegates had "departed" from their original intention to formulate a statement of constitutional right, and he reminded Congress that New York expected the meeting to "lay a plan for a lasting accommodation with Great Britain."[10] In a letter written after adjournment, Duane stated that he had endorsed the Galloway Plan only because Congress had failed to recognize the authority of Parliament "in any terms which could give Satisfaction or even elude suspicion."[11]

[10]J. Adams, "Notes of Debates," *ibid.*, I, 53.
[11]Duane to Samuel Chase, Dec. 29, 1774, *ibid.*, I, 88.

The attention paid the Galloway Plan of Union has far exceeded its practical importance. Congress clearly expected repeal of the Coercive Acts to precede or accompany any plan of accomodation, and this expectation would have been ignored even if the British government had given serious consideration to the plan itself. Nor is it likely that the plan would have had much affect in England. Benjamin Franklin showed a copy of the proposal to Lords Chatham and Camden and reported to Galloway that they had found "the Idea ingenious, but the Mode so new as to require much attentive Thought before a Judgement of it could be formed."[12] If these friends of the colonies viewed the Galloway Plan with caution, more hostile spirits would certainly have remained unimpressed.

Galloway's later efforts to publicize his proposal brought it to the attention of future generations, but Congress gave it short shift. Having postponed debate on rights and grievances, the members did not relish beginning another prolonged argument over what was essentially the same issue. They considered the plan for a day and then voted 6 to 5, with one colony abstaining, to let it lie on the table.[13] Galloway later charged that the radicals had barely managed to defeat his proposal by the margin of one vote and that they had been so frightened by it that they ordered it expunged from the record.[14] But there is, first, no evidence to suggest that Congress came within one vote of adopting Galloway's proposal. The 6-to-5 division suggests rather that a bare majority was willing even to consider the plan at a future time and that five colonies wanted to reject it immediately. When the delegates returned to the proposal on October 22, they were in the final rush of completing business. Five of the members from Virginia, including the president of Congress, Peyton Randolph, had departed for home. In all probability Galloway asked for an extra day to debate and defend his plan, and Congress, in the rush to adjourn, rejected the request. The only contemporary reference to a final vote on the issue is an entry in the diary of Samuel Ward of Rhode Island for October 22, which simply states that Congress met, "dismissed the plan for a union, etc; (Mr. Hopkins for the plan, I against it), read several letters, etc."[15] No other delegate made any reference to this final, supposedly narrow, decision. The fact that Congress had earlier delayed consideration of the proposal by a vote of 6 to 5 in no way proves a similar division on its final rejection. Nor does the former vote show that six colonies favored adop-

[12]Franklin to Galloway, Feb. 5, 1775, William L. Clements Library, Ann Arbor, Mich. (photostat at Yale).

[13]Samuel Ward, "Diary," Burnett, ed., *Letters Cont. Cong.*, I, 51.

[14]Galloway, *A Candid Examination of the Mutual Claims of Great Britain, and the Colonies* (London, 1780), p. 64; Galloway, *Examination before the House of Commons*, p. 48.

[15]Ward, "Diary," Burnett, ed., *Letters Cont. Cong.*, I, 80.

tion, only that they wanted to give the plan further consideration. George Bancroft may well have been accurate in his assertion that only one colony voted for the plan on October 22.[16]

Galloway's second charge, that Congress struck all references to his suggestion from its journal in order to hide evidences of disagreement, is similarly misleading. Charles Thomson, secretary of the Congress, had earlier adopted the policy of including in his formal notes only those measures ultimately approved.[17] He undoubtedly did this to minimize the evidence of disputes in Congress, but there is no reason to suppose that he singled out the Galloway Plan for special treatment. A number of controversial issues that were discussed do not appear in the record, including suggestions for the arming of colonial troops and the report from a committee appointed to investigate acts affecting trade and manufacturing.

The postponement of debate on the right of Parliament to regulate trade on September 24 did not, of course, resolve the issue. Congress avoided the question for several weeks while it debated the specifics of the embargo, but eventually, on October 12, Congress once again took up the Statement of Rights and once again found itself divided on the question of trade regulation. John Adams reported the two sides exactly even. Five colonies favored Parliament's right, five opposed, and two (Massachusetts and Rhode Island) were unable to vote because of split delegations.[18]

If Adams's later recollections are accurate, Congress finally agreed to endorse the proposals originally submitted by the Grand Committee's first subcommittee, primarily because the delegates found it impossible to agree on anything else.[19] Incorporated as the fourth section in the Statement of Rights and Grievances, the article stated that:

the foundation of English liberty, and of all free government, is a right in the people to participate in their legislative council: and as the English colonists are not represented, and from their local and other circumstances, cannot

[16] According to a note in the hand of James Duane appended to the copy of Galloway's Plan now filed among the Duane Papers in the New-York Historical Society, New York seconded and supported the proposal. There is no other reference to the final vote except Ward's statement that Rhode Island was divided. Bancroft probably referred to the Duane notation, but it is possible that he had access to some information since lost (*History of the United States,* IV, 304). It would be logical to assume that Pennsylvania supported the proposal, but it is at least plausible that the colony changed its position after Dickinson was added to the delegation in October. Dickinson had never been enthusiastic about either the plan or its author, and his influence, combined with that of Thomas Mifflin, could have determined the issue among his colleagues.

[17] Lewis R. Harley, *The Life of Charles Thomson* (Philadelphia, 1900), pp. 95–96.
[18] J. Adams, "Diary," Burnett, ed., *Letters Cont. Cong.,* I, 74.
[19] C. F. Adams, ed., *Works of J. Adams,* II, 373–77.

properly be represented in the British parliament, they are entitled to a free
and exclusive power of legislation in their several provincial legislatures,
where their right of representation can alone be preserved, in all cases of
taxation and internal polity, subject only to the negative of their sovereign,
in such manner as has been heretofore used and accustomed. But, from the
necessity of the case, and a regard to the mutual interest of both countries,
we cheerfully consent to the operation of such acts of the British parliament,
as are bona fide, restrained to the regulation of our external commerce, for
the purpose of securing the commercial advantages of the whole empire to
the mother country, and the commercial benefits of its respective members;
excluding every idea of taxation, internal or external, for raising a revenue
on the subjects in America, without their consent.[20]

At first glance this statement seems to authorize parliamentary
control over American trade, but a closer reading suggests a different
conclusion. What, for example, did Congress mean by "bona fide,"
and who was to decide which acts of Parliament fit that description?
Congress had attempted to meet the argument that Great Britain
might abuse the right to regulate trade by drafting a careful definition of the limits of parliamentary authority. The result was an ambiguous statement that did nothing to clarify the question, and may
even have further confused it. The delegates had carefully avoided
any reference to Parliament's right to regulate trade, promising only
that they would "cheerfully consent to the operation of such acts"
as might fit the conditions set down in the Statement of Rights.

Many delegates must have been disappointed over the failure of
their efforts to "lay a plan for a lasting accommodation with Great
Britain." Some were no doubt surprised at the determination with
which others had resisted the acknowledgment of so limited a parliamentary authority as the right to regulate imperial trade. Certain of
the delegates, both radical and conservative, must also have recognized that the differences between American and British ideas of the
imperial tie were irreconcilable. Galloway went back to Pennsylvania to denounce the work of Congress, and there is every reason to
believe that Sam Adams went back to Massachusetts convinced that
the end of the British Empire was in sight.

Still, a majority of the Congress hoped that the crisis would pass,
that Parliament would repeal the most objectionable colonial legislation. Disagreements over the constitutional issue had undoubtedly
lowered morale, but the general consensus that existed on grievances
and the "mode of redress" encouraged the delegates. Surely, if Congress was moderate in its demands for redress and united in its support of a trade embargo, Britain would take some steps toward effecting an accommodation.

[20] Ford, ed., *Journals Cont. Cong.*, I, 68–69.

CHAPTER V

Listing American Grievances
A Rationale for Resistance

H UMAN beings are notoriously prejudiced in their own cause, and
as historians are well aware, those prejudices are usually exag-
gerated in documents intended for public consumption. Twentieth-
century scholars, influenced by the insights of Marx and Freud, have
been especially reluctant to credit either the public or the private
observations of creatures so frail as man. Such caution, when carried
to extremes, can obscure the value of much important historical evidence. The First Continental Congress is hardly immune to charges
that its members doctored their public statements with an eye on
their use as propaganda. But, despite the subjectivity of these documents, the grievances listed have provided the most reliable contemporary explanation of the causes of the American Revolution.
Unlike later congresses, the members who gathered in the fall of
1774 were more interested in clarifying colonial expectations than in
justifying new escalations of American resistance. The anticipated
adoption of trade restrictions designed to force British concessions
convinced the delegates that they must clearly and carefully explain
colonial demands. Parliament could hardly meet conditions for restoring trade with America unless those conditions were specifically
and judiciously enumerated.

Congress spent considerable time in debating and revising its list
of grievances, and the delegates gave careful consideration not only
to philosophical questions but to the specific acts to be included in
the list. These discussions resulted in substantial alterations; a number of grievances named in earlier documents were dropped before
Congress prepared its final statement of demands.

The first narrowing of grievances mirrored Congress's failure to
settle on a satisfactory statement of Parliament's right to regulate
trade. To compile a list of acts violating that right was, of course,
impossible if Congress could not agree that it was a right. The most
prudent solution, and the one Congress adopted, was to pass over
the issue entirely. The decision to sidestep debate of these particular
grievances came during the same stormy session in which Congress
postponed debate on the Statement of Rights. The resolution was
couched in somewhat devious terms. Rather than specifically admit
the validity of statutes affecting trade and manufacturing, or even

make mention of the controversial subject, Congress simply voted not to concern itself with acts of Parliament adopted before 1763.[1]

Restricting grievances to the period after 1763 eliminated a wide variety of controversial issues. Not only could Congress debate colonial grievances without reopening the question of Parliament's right to regulate trade, but it could skirt another touchy subject. If Congress had suggested that the colonists intended to reject legislation regulating trade and manufacturing, they would have succeeded only in alienating their few friends in Parliament. Sam Adams, never one to miss so promising an opportunity to consolidate a political alliance, spoke of these dual benefits even as Congress debated the 1763 limitation. In a letter to Joseph Warren, written the day after adoption of the resolution, Adams noted that "it is of the greatest importance, that the American opposition should be united, and that it should be conducted so as to concur with the opposition of our friends in England."[2]

Politically advantageous, the 1763 limitation was also a valid reflection of colonial priorities. Even before Congress met the colonists had repeatedly asserted that their objections to British control stemmed primarily from recent legislation. In Pennsylvania the Provincial Convention had provided a precedent for a selected list of grievances. The Quaker colony was particularly sensitive to legislation restricting manufacturing, and her August Convention initially called for repeal of both the Hat Act of 1732 and the Iron Act of 1750. The convention then admitted that the Continental Congress might not be able to obtain "all the terms above mentioned" and proceeded to outline a second list of demands characterized as minimal. This modified statement proposed that the colonies accept, if necessary, all existing statutes for both the regulation of manufacturing and the taxation of particular imported items. Such a concession seemed acceptable to the Pennsylvanians provided that Parliament would take immediate steps to redress more important grievances by, among other things, repealing the Coercive Acts and promising not to enact additional taxes.[3]

Despite the advantages of ignoring parliamentary statutes adopted before 1763, the decision did not go uncontested. The South Carolina delegates, for example, argued that Britain had illegally expanded the jurisdiction of admiralty courts before that date, and they insisted that their constituents would be offended if Congress failed to condemn so serious an infringement of American rights.[4] At the other

[1] Ford, ed., *Journals Cont. Cong.*, I, 42.

[2] S. Adams to Warren, Sept. 25, 1774, Burnett, ed., *Letters Cont. Cong.*, I, 47.

[3] Force, ed., *American Archives*, I, 560–62.

[4] Christopher Collier, ed., "Silas Deane Reports on the Continental Congress," Connecticut Historical Society *Bulletin*, XXIX (1964), 5–6.

extreme stood those members who favored the 1763 restriction but considered it inadequate. The question raised by these delegates once again concerned the right of Parliament to regulate trade. New York's Isaac Low condemned Congress for its continued failure to confirm Britain's control over commerce and insisted that the error would be compounded by the vagueness of the 1763 limitation. The delegates must not just ignore legislation passed before that year; they must explicitly confirm its legality. If they did not intend to admit Parliament's right to control commerce, surely they must at least promise not to contest previously enacted legislation in that area.[5]

Low's point was well taken. If Congress was to avoid future conflicts with Parliament, it should clearly state its stand on all issues. Joseph Galloway was later to insist that the delegates had prepared a secret list of grievances to be presented in case Great Britain agreed to its original conditions.[6] This accusation, though it distorts the delegates' intent, was to a certain extent true. Galloway no doubt was referring to the unrecorded report from a committee appointed to review statutes affecting trade and manufacturing.[7] The report, which has never been located, might well have provided the basis for future colonial demands.

Congress, by rejecting Low's proposal to confirm the validity of all statutes passed before 1763, kept its options open. John Adams assured the delegates that failure to demand repeal of a particular act did not foreclose the possibility of taking it up at some future time. Indeed, the Statement of Rights and Grievances conceded the possibility of future escalation by referring to the "many infringements and violations of the foregoing rights, which, from an ardent desire, that harmony and mutual intercourse of affection and interest may be restored, we pass over for the present."[8] The colonists were not yet prepared to demand an end to British control of their commerce and manufacturing, but if the activities of the First Continental Congress are an indication of prevailing sentiment, the demand for complete autonomy might not have been far in the future.

Were the colonists shortening their list of grievances only to be politic? Was their professed desire for a restoration of "harmony and mutual intercourse" merely propaganda? As the congress progressed, the delegates continued to debate the reasons for colonial discontent, and in the end they eliminated a large number of their original de-

---

[5] *Ibid.*

[6] Galloway, *Historical and Political Reflections on the Rise and Progress of the American Rebellion* (London, 1780), 90.

[7] Ford, ed., *Journals Cont. Cong.*, I, 26. When Congress decided not to complain of acts passed before 1763 the report of this committee, which had at first been handed to the Grand Committee for consideration, became irrelevant.

[8] *Ibid.*, I, 71.

mands. This process becomes especially clear when the complaints noted in the Statement of Rights and Grievances, adopted on October 14, are compared with those enumerated several days later in the Continental Association. The comparison sheds considerable light on contemporary efforts to explain the causes of what would soon become the American Revolution.

The Statement of Rights and Grievances listed thirteen specific acts of Parliament, plus the practice of stationing troops in the colonies during peacetime, as intolerable. Repeal of these statutes was described as "essentially necessary in order to restore harmony between Great-Britain and the American colonies."[9] Included were the Currency Act of 1764, the Revenue Acts of 1764 and 1766, the Post Office Act of 1765, the unrepealed portions of the Townshend duties, the act of 1767 creating a customs board in America, the act of 1768 extending jurisdiction of the admiralty courts, and the Dock-Yards Act of 1772 providing in certain cases for the trial of colonial offenders in other parts of the empire. In addition Congress demanded repeal of the acts that had occasioned its meeting: the Boston Port Act, the Massachusetts Government Act, the Justice Act, the Quartering Act, and the Quebec Act.[10] This list omitted all mention of statutes passed before 1763 but included most of the major pieces of parliamentary legislation enacted since that date. Two major exceptions were the Tea Act of 1773 and the Declaratory Act of 1766.[11]

The omission of the Declaratory Act and the Tea Act reflected considerations similar to those prompting the 1763 restriction: a desire to avoid conflict within Congress and a determination to promote cooperation with the opposition party in Great Britain. The Tea Act dealt primarily with methods of shipping and selling that controversial article, and the colonists contended that their objections focused rather on the Townshend duty than on the provisions of the act of 1773. In demanding repeal of the tax, Congress rendered the Tea Act innocuous without becoming entangled in the problem of trade regulation. At the same time, it left the monopoly aspects of the Tea Act unopposed despite the almost universal protests of the colonial merchants. This decision, like several others made in Philadelphia, raises some interesting questions about the amount of influence wielded by the mercantile interests in the First Continental Congress.

Conditions in Great Britain probably dictated elimination of the Declaratory Act. Many of the Rockingham Whigs in Parliament, the group among whom the Americans reckoned their most numerous

[9] *Ibid.*

[10] *Ibid.*, I, 71–73.

[11] Both of these acts are listed as grievances in several other documents prepared by Congress. See, for example, the Memorial to the Inhabitants of the British Colonies, *ibid.*, I, 92, 98.

supporters, had engineered adoption of the Declaratory Act and
would have recoiled from a demand for its repeal. Since the statute
had no immediate application, Congress no doubt considered it a
point worth sacrificing to the interests of political expediency. Several
years earlier Benjamin Franklin had contended in a letter to Galloway that the colonists could well afford to ignore the Declaratory
Act. "We shall consider it in the same Light with the Claim of the
Spanish Monarch to the Title of King of Jerusalem."[12]

The demands included in the Statement of Rights and Grievances
were intended to be definitive, at least for the time being, but the
delegates had become so involved in the imbroglio over defining
rights that they had all but ignored the grievances portion of the
document. The consequences of this neglect became apparent during
the debate over the Continental Association—the agreement that was
to bind Americans to a boycott of British trade. Since the embargo
was to remain in effect until Parliament met the conditions set by
Congress, it was essential that those conditions be subjected to a
more discriminating review that they had previously been given. The
result was a further reduction in the scope of American demands.

Whereas the Statement of Rights and Grievances had called for
the repeal of thirteen acts and the practice of stationing troops in the
colonies during peacetime, the Continental Association listed only
five statutes and referred to portions of four others. Those specified
in toto were the Dock-Yards Act of 1772, the Boston Port Act, the
Massachusetts Government Act, the Justice Act, and the Quebec
Act.[13] In addition to demanding repeal of these five acts in their en-
tirety, the Association also bound the colonists to observe the trade
boycott until

such parts of the several acts of parliament passed since the close of the last
war, as impose or continue duties on tea, wine, molasses, syrups, paneles,
coffee, sugar, pimento, indigo, foreign paper, glass and painters' colours, imported into America, and extend the powers of the admiralty courts beyond
their ancient limits, deprive the American subject of trial by jury, authorize
the judge's certificate to indemnify the prosecutor from damages, that he
might otherwise be liable to from a trial by his peers, require oppressive
security from a claimant of ships or goods seized, before he shall be allowed
to defend his property, are repealed.[14]

This paragraph had reference to portions of the Revenue Acts of 1764
and 1766, the unrepealed sections of the Townshend Act of 1767, and
the act of 1768 establishing new courts of vice-admiralty in the colonies. Congress dropped entirely five of the grievances named in the

12 Quoted in Esmond Wright, *Fabric of Freedom* (New York, 1961), 71.
13 Ford, ed., *Journals Cont. Cong.*, I, 80.
14 *Ibid.*, I, 79–80.

Statement of Rights and Grievances: the Currency Act of 1764, the Post Office Act of 1765, the act of 1767 creating an American board of customs commissioners, the Quartering Act of 1774, and the practice of stationing troops in the colonies.

This reduction of grievances took place on October 15 and 17. There are almost no records of these debates, and they can be reconstructed only from the most scattered of references.[15] The changes are nonetheless intriguing, and they may, in part, provide a key to the rationale behind American demands and expectations in the fall of 1774.

One reason for the changes was the all-pervasive question raised by the effort to delineate the bounds of parliamentary authority. James Duane reminded Congress that it had decided not to complain of acts passed before 1763 and argued that it was a breach of that resolution for the delegates to demand repeal of acts that only modified or extended legislation adopted prior to that date. The Post Office had been in existence long before 1763. Was it not unreasonable and duplicitous to attack it simply because the most recent statute affecting it had passed in 1765?[16] Congress readily agreed that consistency called for eliminating the Post Office Act from the Association's list of intolerable grievances, and similar considerations probably influenced the decision to abandon demands for repeal of the Currency Act, the Quartering Act, and the act establishing an American board of customs commissioners.

The reduction of grievances also reflected the sincerity of efforts to avoid petty or impossible demands. Realizing that the Association would commit the colonists to continue the boycott until Parliament repealed every act named therein, Congress eliminated those which seemed trivial. Once again Duane played the gadfly. He insisted that the delegates consider each grievance separately and ask themselves if they would consider that particular act sufficient justification for continuing the boycott in the event that all others were repealed.[17] Presumably, so innocuous a statute as the Post Office Act failed this rigorous test.

Finally, Congress narrowed the list of grievances to preserve its argument that the real issues were constitutional. The delegates contended that Americans would have tolerated British abuses had they not detected the clear outlines of a "wicked" plan to deprive them of their British rights. Congress insisted that the grievances retained in the Continental Association dealt exclusively with constitutional issues and fell into one of three categories: (1) acts affecting established traditions of trial by jury; (2) taxes imposed on the colonists

[15] Nearly all of these are in Burnett, ed., *Letters Cont. Cong.,* and Collier, ed., "Silas Deane Reports."

[16] J. Adams, "Notes of Debates," Burnett, ed., *Letters Cont. Cong.,* I, 53.

[17] Duane, "Notes of Debates," *ibid.,* I, 77.

without their consent; and (3) measures designed to punish Massachusetts Bay in the wake of the Boston Tea Party. A review of parliamentary legislation had made it "clear beyond a doubt" that these particular acts constituted vital links in a general plan to deprive the colonists, and indeed all Englishmen, of their constitutional rights. Such statutes had been found "not only to form a regular system, in which every part has great force, but also a pertinacious adherence to that system, for subjugating these Colonies ... to the uncontroulable and unlimited power of Parliament."[18]

Congress insisted again and again that it was demanding repeal of only those acts aimed at forcing American submission to the arbitrary fiat of Parliament. Its Address to the People of Great-Britain contained twenty-five references to this nefarious plan, its Memorial to the Inhabitants of the British Colonies mentioned the scheme sixteen times, and its Address to the Inhabitants of the Province of Quebec included ten such allusions.[19] Having so often insisted that only the fear of "impending destruction" forced them to resist the authority of Great Britain, the delegates felt compelled to reflect that fact in their demands for redress. In petitioning the king, Congress professed to trust "in the magnanimity and justice of your majesty and parliament ... for a redress of our other grievances."[20]

The phrasing of the Continental Association reflects in several particulars the care with which the delegates justified their demands as an outgrowth of concern over constitutional rights. They were especially concerned to avoid any hint of an effort to nullify acts regulating trade. For example, both the Statement of Rights and Grievances and the Association complained of a provision in the Revenue Act of 1766 authorizing judges "to indemnify the prosecutor from damages." The latter document, however, included an additional clause basing American objections on constitutional rather than economic grounds. The clause noted that if the prosecutor were indemnified as provided for in the Revenue Act, the result would be to protect him "from damages, that he might otherwise be liable to from a trial of his peers."[21]

So minor an addition can only be explained in light of the determined effort to root colonial demands in constitutional issues. The method of listing grievances indicated the same concern: The Statement of Rights and Grievances enumerated a list of objectionable statutes; the Continental Association appended a paragraph specifying the objectionable clauses of each act. The alteration made it clear

---

[18] Memorial to the Inhabitants of the British Colonies, Ford, ed., *Journals Cont. Cong.*, I, 94.

[19] All these documents are printed in *ibid.*, I.

[20] The Petition to the King, *ibid.*, I, 120.

[21] Compare the Statement of Rights and Grievances with the Continental Association, *ibid.*, I, 71, 80.

that except for the Coercive Acts, each demand pertained exclusively to sections dealing either with taxation or with changes in the judicial process.

Only in the case of the Quebec Act did Congress refuse to eliminate a grievance not easily characterized as a threat to fundamental constitutional rights. Duane argued in a lengthy address on October 17 that Congress could not justify demanding repeal of the Quebec Act. The New Yorker agreed that the statute should be mentioned as an irritation in the Petition to the King, but he contended that Congress ought not make its repeal "operate upon our commercial intercourse with G[reat] B[ritain]." He feared that "if we demand *too much* we weaken our efforts—lose the chance of securing what is *reasonable* and may get *nothing*."[22] On the other hand, Richard Henry Lee thought it one of the most objectionable statutes ever passed by Parliament, probably because it threatened Virginia's land claims in the West, although he stressed the dangerous precedent of granting liberties to Roman Catholics and condemned the absence of an elective assembly.[23] Thomas McKean supported Lee, arguing that the "magnitude of the law" made it impossible to ignore. McKean also noted that the Americans might profit by demanding repeal of the act due to its apparent unpopularity in the mother country.[24]

The delegates appear to have found it impossible to ignore Duane's arguments. It was indeed difficult to demonstrate that the Quebec Act threatened Americans with "impending destruction," unless that label could be applied to statutes that threatened land hunger and religious bigotry. Congress's solution was ingenious and suggests something about the lengths to which men will go to justify doing what they are determined to do. The Association insisted on repeal of the Quebec Act because it constituted an effort of Parliament "by the influence of civil principles and ancient prejudices, to dispose the inhabitants to act with hostility against the free Protestant colonies, whenever a wicked ministry shall chuse so to direct them," in other words, because the statute posed a military threat to the colonies represented at Philadelphia. No mention was made of other points raised in debate: the supposed establishment of the Catholic church, the closing of the Ohio Valley, or the provision for a government without a representative assembly or the guaranteed right of trial by jury.[25]

Still, the Quebec Act stands as an exception. For the most part the delegates were consistent, deliberate, and moderate in their demands. More important, they were united. Conflict over statutes for the

---

[22] Duane, "Notes of Debates," Burnett, ed., *Letters Cont. Cong.*, I, 77–78.

[23] *Ibid.*

[24] *Ibid.*

[25] The Continental Association, Ford, ed., *Journals Cont. Cong.*, I, 76.

regulation of trade and the restriction of colonial manufacturing had in no way marred the consensus on more important grievances. The delegates did not even debate their decision to insist on repeal of the Coercive Acts, parliamentary taxation, or statutes affecting the right to jury trial. They all agreed that to admit the validity of such legislation would be to submit to the "unlimited" power of Parliament, and that was a concession they were determined not to make.

CHAPTER VI

Resistance Short of War
The Continental Association

THE third problem facing Congress—defining a "mode of re-dress"—was complicated by the growing tension in Massa-chusetts Bay. The delegates realized that they were pitted in a race against time; they must find a peaceful solution for a situation which threatened momentarily to break out into open warfare. The most sanguine member must have realized that it would take at least six months for nonimportation to affect British policy. What, in the meanwhile, was Massachusetts to do? With its principal port block-aded by the British navy, its legal government in shambles, its courts of law inoperative, and its citizens threatened by an ever-expanding British army, who dared hope that conflict might be postponed even for a week, let alone the several months necessary to test the efficacy of an embargo? Who knew but that the next mail from Boston might bring to the ears of Congress the "clash of resounding arms"?

September 6 was a warm day in Carpenters' Hall. The sun shone hotly through the fan window at the front of the room, and the de-bate over proportional representation for the larger colonies had brought beads of perspiration to the brows of the participants. In the middle of this debate, at about 2:00 P.M., a messenger rushed into the hall and approached the president's desk. Within moments Congress was in an uproar. Israel Putnam had just arrived in Philadelphia with reports that the British had attacked the provincials in Massa-chusetts and that "troops and fleets [were] cannonading the town of Boston."[1] Consternation and confusion swept the floor as delegates rushed to assure the New England members that America would sup-port Massachusetts in resisting this cowardly attack. Some seemed stunned, first by the news of the attack and then by the shouts of "war! war!" that echoed through the chamber.[2] The confusion was so great that Congress was forced to adjourn temporarily in order to await further reports and to allow men time to settle their thoughts.[3]

Not for forty-eight hours did reports arrive to contradict the ru-mored bombardment of Boston, and for two days Congress labored under the assumption that war had actually begun in New England.

[1] Samuel Ward, "Diary," Sept. 6, 1774. Burnett, ed., *Letters Cont. Cong.*, I, 19.
[2] J. Adams to his wife, Sept. 18, 1774, *ibid.*, I, 34.
[3] Congress reconvened about 5 P.M. See Burnett, ed., *Letters Cont. Cong.*, I, 10, 11, 16, 19.

The effect of this rumor was profound. Church bells tolled throughout the city for the supposed destruction of New England's principal
port, and people could talk of little else. Was the city burning? Had
there been bloodshed? What would the other colonies be called upon
to do and how would they respond? The first additional reports
seemed to confirm the original rumor. The Massachusetts delegates
were of course fearful for their families and friends, but they also
perceived an opportunity to assess the attitudes of other delegations—
perhaps even to influence them. John Adams was buoyed by the
realization that "every gentleman seems to consider the bombardment of Boston as the bombardment of the capital of his own province." Writing his wife after the rumor was contradicted, Adams
predicted that "if it had proved true, you would have heard the
thunder of an American Congress."[4]

The report of an attack on Boston undoubtedly affected the subsequent debates. It probably contributed to the later endorsement of
the supposedly radical resolutions submitted by Suffolk County, and
it certainly reminded the members of Congress that almost any in-
cident might touch off events that could lead directly to war. This
reminder persuaded a few delegates that before leaving Philadelphia,
Congress should suggest ways in which the colonies could defend
themselves if necessary.

Among those who attempted to convince the delegates that America should arm was Virginia's Richard Henry Lee. Lee suggested
that Congress encourage each colony to ready its militia and adopt
measures necessary to provide this citizens army with "ammunition
and proper arms."[5] Patrick Henry wholeheartedly supported the
proposal, insisting that "preparation for Warr is Necessary to obtain
peace." Suppose that nonimportation and nonexportation fail, Henry
suggested. What was to be the next step? Surely the answer was
clear: "Arms are a Resource to which We shall be forced a Resource
afforded us by God & Nature, & why in the Names of both are We
to hesitate providing them Now whilst in Our power."[6]

Henry's arguments were logical and persuasive. It was unquestionably hazardous for Congress to adopt measures that might lead to
conflict while refusing to make preparations for that possibility.
Moreover, the worsening situation of Massachusetts made it difficult
to ignore the possibility of war. Since the Bay Colony had refused to
accept the changes ordered by the Government Act, and General
Gage would not meet with the newly elected Assembly until it did so,
chaos threatened. Reports from Massachusetts brought news of a

---

[4] J. Adams to his wife, Sept. 18, 1774, *ibid.*, I, 34.

[5] Collier, ed., "Silas Deane Reports," p. 3; Ford, ed., *Journals Cont. Cong.*, I, 54n.

[6] Collier, ed., "Silas Deane Reports," pp. 3–4.

growing sentiment in the colony to take up the original charter of 1629 and elect a governor fo supplant Gage. Such a step could lead to armed conflict, and few doubted that a clash in Massachusetts would throw the entire continent into war.

But Congress adamantly refused to recommend arms. A majority continued to hope that the situation in New England would remain stable until the nonimportation agreement could force a relaxation of British policy. They admitted, according to John Adams, that it was impossible for 400,000 people to live without a legislature or courts of justice; yet "nothing is done." Adams explained to William Tudor that "you see by this what they are for; namely, that you stand stock still, and live without government or law, at least for the present, and as long as you can."[7]

Standing "stock still" did not appeal to the Massachusetts delegation. The men from Boston were determined that Congress should deal with the plight of their unhappy metropolis. The conspiratorial hand of Sam Adams is evident in the multitude of resolutions, petitions, and pleas for assistance that arrived from the beleaguered colony. On September 14 the delegation presented Congress with the proceedings of a convention held in Middlesex County, and three days later they read similar resolutions from Suffolk, and asked Congress to take action on them. The emphasis placed on the latter resolves presumably reflected the expectation that Congress would be more sympathetic to the decisions of Suffolk County because Boston lay within its confines.

Congress endorsed the Suffolk Resolves, thereby giving the first indication of the temperament of the delegates. The members unanimously approved Massachusetts's refusal to abide by the terms of the Coercive Acts, thus condoning overt resistance to an act of Parliament. Congress even encouraged the Bay Colony to continue in its opposition, and by so doing served notice that the rest of the continent would support Massachusetts in its present policy. Small wonder that John Adams's diary entry for September 17, the day the resolves were endorsed, recorded it as "one of the happiest Days of my Life."[8]

For a few weeks the problems of Massachusetts slipped into the background as Congress debated its proposed Statement of Rights and Grievances. Then, on October 6 messengers arrived from New England with alarming news that again forced Congress to confront the possibility of armed conflict. General Gage had begun building fortifications on the neck of land connecting Boston with the mainland, which, according to the town meeting, would enable him to

[7] J. Adams to Tudor, Sept. 29, 1774, Burnett, ed., *Letters Cont. Cong.*, I, 60.
[8] J. Adams, Sept. 17, 1774, Butterfield, ed., *Diary and Autobiography*, II, 134.

block access to Boston "both by sea & land." The citizens feared that Gage intended to hold them hostage and had consequently decided to ask Congress for advice. So critical did the situation appear that the town meeting was prepared to recommend a mass evacuation of the city if Congress approved. Boston also asked the delegates to suggest some course of action in light of the problems plaguing the colony as a result of the prolonged absence of legally constituted government.[9]

These new reports touched off another lengthy debate. It was well enough to list American grievances and propose a boycott of British trade as a means of obtaining redress, but what if relief did not come or if it came too late? What if Gage should attempt to enforce the Coercive Acts with the British army and so precipitate a military engagement with the provincials similar to that rumored in early September? Or, on the other hand, what if the Bay Colony should force a showdown by attempting either to elect a governor or to drive the British from the city of Boston? Congress knew that its deliberations would be to little effect unless Massachusetts remained calm.

As they debated the Boston letter for several days, the delegates considered a number of alternatives. Two of the more conservative delegates, Joseph Galloway and George Ross, proposed that Congress leave the Bay Colony to its own devices. They wanted Congress to suggest that Massachusetts assume the responsibility for the situation at Boston but to warn the New Englanders that although they might take whatever measures seemed necessary, they must also proceed at their own risk.[10] More militant delegates recommended that the Bostonians be encouraged to abandon the city; others wanted to threaten Gage with armed attack and to demand that he pull down the fortifications under construction at once.[11]

Once again Congress held to a middle course. On October 7 Congress appointed Thomas Lynch, Samuel Adams, and Edmund Pendleton to prepare a letter to General Gage informing him that "the town of Boston, & province of Massachusetts-bay, are considered by all America as suffering in the common cause." The committee was further instructed to entreat Gage to halt the building of fortifications on Boston Neck and to restrain his troops from their alleged abuses of the citizenry.[12] Sam Adams, who no doubt considered these instructions timid at best, prepared the first draft of the letter to Gage and, as might have been expected, minced no words. The proposed

[9] Ford, ed., *Journals Cont. Cong.*, I, 55–56.

[10] J. Adams to Edward Biddle, Burnett, ed., *Letters Cont. Cong.*, I, 87.

[11] Ford, ed., *Journals Cont. Cong.*, I, 59n. John Drayton stated that Christopher Gadsden had proposed an attack on Boston before Gage could be reinforced but was overruled (Drayton, *Memoirs of the American Revolution*, I [Charleston, S.C., 1821], 165).

[12] Ford, ed., *Journals Cont. Cong.*, I, 57–58.

letter insisted that Gage cease his fortifications or face "Consequences of the most serious Nature," and it openly referred to the
"Horrors of a civil War." The delegates refused to adopt so militant
a stand and modified the letter significantly before sending it.[13]

Although Congress rejected the belligerent tone expressed in
Adams's letter, the delegates had been thoroughly alarmed by Gage's
apparent threat to Boston. For the first time they adopted resolutions
containing an explicit threat of civil war. They approved the "opposition by the Inhabitants of the Massachusetts-bay, to the execution of
the late acts of Parliament" and resolved that if Gage attempted to
effect the acts by force, "all America ought to support" the threatened New England colony.[14] In this resolution, and in the debates
accompanying it, Massachusetts had its answer. If the colony acted
only on the defensive, Congress promised that the other colonies
would support any measures taken to repulse a British attack. In
adopting this resolution, Congress promised support in a situation
similar to that which was to occur a few months later at Lexington
and Concord.

Having promised to defend Boston in case of open attack, Congress
took advantage of the opportunity to plead that the New Englanders
themselves avoid measures that might lead to war. The delegates advised the Bostonians not to attempt an evacuation of the city unless
the Provincial Congress of Massachusetts judged it absolutely necessary. Congress also took a moderate position on the problems of
government in Massachusetts Bay, arguing that if the courts could
not meet in a legal and peaceable manner, the colony must get along
temporarily without them. The delegates were determined, however,
that conciliation not be confused with weakness, and they repeated
their insistence that Massachusetts should under no circumstances
submit to the Coercive Acts or accept any change of government
dictated by Parliament. They further resolved that any citizen who
accepted a commission under the Massachusetts Government Act
should be held in detestation as a tool of the "despotism" that was
poised to destroy the liberties of America.[15]

These resolutions illustrate the dilemma of those delegates, and
colonists, who opposed a military solution to the crisis facing America. By encouraging Massachusetts to oppose enforcement of the
Coercive Acts, Congress was, whether consciously or not, increasing
the possibilities of war. The British ministry had committed itself to
implementation of the Coercive Acts, it had sent an army and a
navy to Boston, and it was determined not to retreat. There could be
no stand-off. Either Massachusetts would be governed by the new

---

[13] Cushing, ed., *Writings of S. Adams,* III, 159; Ford, ed., *Journals Cont. Cong.,* I, 60–61.
[14] Ford, ed., *Journals Cont. Cong.,* I, 58.   [15] *Ibid.,* I, 59–60.

establishment created by Parliament, or it would not. If the colony refused (as Congress now urged it to do), then Great Britain must decide between admitting defeat or ordering the army to take the field. Many delegates believed, or at least hoped, that Britain would not choose military action unless forced to it by the Bostonians. They therefore believed that by promising Boston support in exchange for moderate opposition to the Coercive Acts, they had lessened the possibility of war. They had not, but for the time being, the fears of many of the more conservative Americans were assuaged.

Amid the continued interruptions of messengers bearing bad news from Boston and the frustrations that had attended the debate on the Statement of Rights and Grievances, Congress turned to the "mode of redress" with a sigh of relief. The delegates had postponed their bitter arguments on rights and grievances precisely because they expected to reach easy agreement on the terms of the embargo, and that expectation proved, for the most part, justified. New York's John Jay expressed the general agreement of Congress when he stated that "war is, by general consent, to be waved at present. I am for negotiation and suspension of commerce."[16]

On September 27 Congress voted unanimously to adopt nonimportation of British goods as one means of securing a redress of colonial grievances (which they had as yet been unable to enumerate). Eight colonies had previously endorsed the measure, and Congress had already warned colonial merchants not to order goods from Great Britain because of the probability of its adoption.[17] If any of the members privately opposed restricting trade with the mother country, they apparently had found themselves in such a minority as to make dissent not only useless but impolitic. Jay and James Duane, both of whom were known for their generally conservative outlook, stated on the floor of Congress that they supported the embargo of trade.[18] It seems probable that even Galloway voted for the measure, since his opposition to so universally popular a resolution would have been noted by at least one of the delegates in a private letter or diary. Certainly no one raised an objection on the floor of Congress.

Most of the decisions concerning the embargo of trade followed with a similar lack of difficulty. None of the records, public or private, indicate any opposition to either nonexportation or nonconsumption, and both measures were adopted after a quick debate. Excepting the full day Congress devoted to discussing Galloway's Plan of Union, the major planks of economic restriction were completed within four days. Congress began formal consideration of

---

[16] J. Adams, "Notes of Debates," Burnett, ed., *Letters Cont. Cong.*, I, 50.
[17] See chapter 3, n. 40; Ford, ed., *Journals Cont. Cong.*, I, 41.
[18] J. Adams, "Notes of Debates," Burnett, ed., *Letters Cont. Cong.*, I, 53.

nonimportation on September 26 and on the 30th appointed Thomas Cushing, Isaac Low, Thomas Mifflin, Richard Henry Lee, and Thomas Johnson, Jr., "to bring in a plan for carrying into effect, the non-importation, non-consumption, and non-exportation resolved on."[19]

The delegates disagreed only on the precise date for putting that program into effect. The Virginia Association, which served as a model for much that Congress did, had specified that nonimportation should begin on November 1, and nonexportation the following autumn—provided, of course, that Great Britain had not redressed colonial grievances by then. Neither of these dates fully satisfied Congress; the first was attacked as too early and the second as too late. A number of members suggested a short delay in effecting nonimportation because they feared that too early a deadline would alienate the merchants. They argued that the cooperation of the mercantile community was essential to the success of nonimportation and contended that Congress should make every possible effort to conciliate that group. These members proposed that nonimportation begin on December 1, rather than November 1, in order to permit the receipt of orders sent out during the summer. Virginia at first thought this delay unnecessary. Its delegates insisted that the merchants had expected nonimportation since at least the first of June. Pennsylvania's Mifflin agreed, arguing that no "honest orders" had gone out since that date.[20] After a brief debate the Virginians capitulated. One month's delay seemed a small price to pay for advancing colonial unity. Patrick Henry, at first a staunch supporter of the earlier date, soon conceded the point on the grounds that Congress ought not to harm even the "rascals" in America, assuming of course that there were any.[21]

The argument over nonexportation was more heated. The Virginia delegates refused to alter the timetable adopted at their colony's August Convention which had voted to delay the embargo of exports until the present tobacco crop had been marketed. No combination of inducements or threats could alter its stand. Both Maryland and South Carolina attempted to persuade the stubborn colony to change its mind, but to no avail. The Carolina delegates even proposed that Congress should go ahead without the consent of Virginia.[22] That proposal failed, not only because Congress was determined to win unanimous support for its program but because other tobacco-producing colonies considered it unfair. Maryland's Samuel Chase

[19] Ford, ed., *Journals Cont. Cong.*, I, 42–53; J. Adams, "Notes of Debates," Burnett, ed., *Letters Cont. Cong.*, I, 48.

[20] J. Adams, "Notes of Debates," Burnett, ed., *Letters Cont. Cong.*, I, 48.

[21] *Ibid.*, I, 50.

[22] C. F. Adams, ed., *Works of J. Adams*, II, 384 and n.; Drayton, *Memoirs*, I, 168, 170.

strongly opposed the South Carolina suggestion, noting that his colony could not think of withholding its tobacco crop unless all others did the same.[23] The delegates finally bowed to Virginia's insistent demands and agreed to continue exporting to Great Britain until September 10, 1775.

Realizing that a delay of nonexportation would substantially reduce the immediate impact of the embargo, and increasingly aware of Boston's urgent need, Congress tried to find effective proposals that Virginia would support. One suggestion was a ban on export of specific articles to go into effect concurrently with nonimportation. Connecticut's Eliphalet Dyer noted Ireland's need for flax seed and pointed out that Britain depended on American naval stores. Why not halt shipment of those two products prior to the general nonexportation? Surely the outcry in both Ireland and England would have a significant effect on the ministry.[24] Several delegates rose to support the idea or to propose additional items for the list. Without American lumber, the West India sugar planters would be unable to ship their produce to Great Britain. Would not an embargo of that item force both the influential sugar planters and British merchants to throw their support behind the demands of Congress?[25]

As late as October 3 Rhode Island's Samuel Ward predicted that Congress would adopt selective nonexportation, but a few days later the effort was abandoned. One objection came from those colonies that thought it unfair to cripple their own commerce while Virginia continued to reap the profits of its tobacco trade. Then too, partial nonexportation threatened to alienate groups who might otherwise support the colonies. Ross of Pennsylvania contended, for example, that to decree the immediate nonexportation of flax seed would be "quarrelling with Ireland before We begin with G. Brittain."[26]

After considerable debate the delegates did find one other way to intensify the trade boycott. A proposal was made to extend nonimportation to include articles from places other than Great Britain if they carried a parliamentary tax. This proposal again raised the delicate question of Britain's authority to regulate trade. Chase insisted that to stop the importation of such goods would be to question this authority.[27] New York's Isaac Low, one of the most conservative delegates in Philadelphia, supported Chase. Increasingly concerned about Congress's inability to agree on a statement authorizing Parliament to regulate trade, Low thought that the proposal

[23] Drayton, *Memoirs,* I, 168; J. Adams, "Notes of Debates," Burnett, ed., *Letters Cont. Cong.,* I, 48.

[24] J. Adams, "Notes of Debates," Burnett, ed., *Letters Cont. Cong.,* I, 50.

[25] *Ibid.,* I, 49.

[26] Collier, ed., "Silas Deane Reports," p. 3.

[27] J. Adams, "Notes of Debates," Burnett, ed., *Letters Cont. Cong.,* I, 63.

gave "too much reason . . . to suspect that independency is aimed at."
The New Yorker also doubted that the colonists would submit to a
total interruption in the supply of such duticd products as rum,
sugar, or molasses.[28]

Once again Congress decided to avoid measures that might seem to
be a denial of Britain's control over colonial commerce. The delegates
agreed to halt the importation of several dutied articles from places
other than Great Britain, but in each instance the taxes on those
articles were clearly revenue measures rather than attempts to regulate trade. On October 6 Congress instructed the committee drafting
the Association to provide for nonimportation of molasses, coffee,
and pimento from the British colonies, wines from Madeira, and all
foreign indigo. The committee itself added tea, syrups, paneles
[brown unpurified sugar], and slaves to the list.[29]

Congress's determination to avoid measures that might reflect on
Parliament's right to regulate trade stemmed from the desire to keep
the door open for reconciliation with Great Britain. For similar
reasons the delegates insisted on accompanying the embargo with a
"humble" petition to the king. There were unquestionably members
who did not expect results from the petition (no doubt some even
doubted the effectiveness of nonimportation), but even the skeptics
saw no harm in petitioning the king, especially if it satisfied the more
conservative members.

Significantly Congress did not petition Parliament—an omission
intended to suggest that the delegates did not recognize any binding
tie to that branch of the British government—nor did they appoint a
committee to petition the king until the day after they had approved
the general outline of the commercial boycott. A curious fact about
this committee was its relatively radical membership. None of the
four members—Richard Henry Lee, Patrick Henry, John Adams,
and Thomas Johnson—were known for conciliatory attitudes or
faith in petitions. Their first draft, predictably, was rejected. On
October 21 Congress suggested that the committee reconsider its
project and appointed a fifth member, John Dickinson. Dickinson,
just elected to Congress to fill a vacancy in the Pennsylvania delegation, was known both for his moderation and his skill with the pen,
and he soon prepared a second draft of the petition which Congress
approved on October 23.[30]

Dickinson's draft was softer in tone but similar in message to that
of the earlier copy prepared by Richard Henry Lee. It asked the king

[28] *Ibid.*, I, 64.
[29] Ford, ed., *Journals Cont. Cong.*, I, 57, 77.
[30] Edwin Wolf 2nd, "The Authorship of the 1774 Address to the King Restudied,"
Wm. and Mary Qtly., 3rd ser., XXII (1965), 189–224.

for relief but informed him that the colonists intended to enforce their boycott until Great Britain redressed their enumerated grievances. Some of the conservative members thought that the petition should be more propitiating, and Jay proposed that Congress offer payment for the tea.[31] The debate on this proposal indicates the vast distance separating the colonies from Great Britain. Even those who supported Jay did so with reservations that Parliament would have found totally unacceptable. Pendleton of Virginia, for example, thought that the colonists might "expressly justify the Town of Boston for destroying the Tea, & offer to pay for the Tea, on Condition that the Town . . . be instantly relieved." Pendleton further proposed that Congress resolve to boycott all East India Company products until the company agreed to refund the money.[32] Even with such modifications the proposal was unpopular, and not a single delegation supported its adoption.[33]

For many members of Congress, the Petition to the King represented little more than a sop to the timid, and the prior adoption of the trade embargo shows that a majority did not expect petitions to have much effect unless accompanied by stronger measures. George Washington had written before he left Virginia that petitions had proved ineffective in the past, and that he could see no reason to expect greater success at the present time.[34] John Adams claimed in later life that he had never "bestowed much attention on any of those addresses" because he considered them but "dress and ornaments rather than body, soul, or substance." At the same time Adams admitted the petitions did give "popularity to our cause, both at home and abroad."[35]

By the second week in October it seemed that the "mode of redress" would be settled without difficulty. Congress had adopted the outlines for nonimportation and nonexportation, and they had agreed to petition the king. One unexpected obstacle remained. The South Carolina delegates refused to sign the Association because they thought the nonexportation clauses unfair. John Rutledge later explained his position to a public meeting in Charleston. He, and other members of the delegation, had favored a total nonexportation—to Europe as well as to England. But the northern colonies had rejected that proposal because they wanted to reap the profits of continued sales to Europe. Philadelphia, for example, carried on an annual export trade of £700,000, but only £50,000 of that went to the mother

---

[31] Collier, ed., "Silas Deane Reports," p. 2.

[32] *Ibid.*, p. 3.

[33] *Ibid.*

[34] Washington to Bryan Fairfax, July 20, 1774, Fitzpatrick, ed., *Writings of Washington*, III, 230–34.

[35] C. F. Adams, ed., *Works of J. Adams*, X, 80.

country. Thus Pennsylvania, like other northern colonies, would be much less affected by nonexportation than South Carolina, whose commerce, Rutledge lamented, would be "almost ruined." Its primary exports, rice and indigo, were enumerated articles and could be sold only to England. Unless Congress were to approve sale of these articles to Europe—a violation of the Acts of Trade and Navigation—nonexportation to England would mean a total cessation of sales. Meanwhile the wheat-producing colonies could continue their trade with Europe and perhaps, if a shortage of rice resulted, even increase their profits.[36]

The South Carolina delegates kept their peace until the last week of meetings. Then, choosing the day Congress had set aside for signing the completed Association, all of the colony's delegates except Christopher Gadsden stalked out of the hall in protest. After weeks of work it suddenly seemed that the carefully preserved unanimity would be shattered. Some of the other delegates were angry, suggesting that if the South Carolinians were determined to remain obstinate, the colony should be excluded from the Association. Gadsden tried to soften the blow by offering to take responsibility for his colony and sign the document without the consent of his fellow delegates.[37] In the end the determination to preserve American unity prevailed. Congress invited the South Carolina delegates back into the hall and then worked out a compromise. The Association was amended in order to authorize the export of rice to Europe, and South Carolina yielded on the article of indigo.

The exact nature of the compromise on rice and indigo remains clouded. Some later commentators have suggested that Congress intended to authorize the continued export of rice to England, but that is unlikely. The most reasonable explanation is that because the Acts of Trade and Navigation forbade exportation of rice to Europe, the delegates intended to authorize South Carolina to ignore that legislation. If that was indeed the intention of Congress, it stands as the only instance in which disobedience of an act of Parliament dealing with the regulation of trade was approved.

On October 20 the Continental Association was formally read before Congress and signed at the table in front of the hall. Every delegate present affixed his signature, and the others did so at a later time.[38] The Continental Association is one of the most important documents of American colonial history. By authorizing the estab-

[36]Drayton, *Memoirs*, I, 168–70; J. Adams, "Notes of Debates," Burnett, ed., *Letters Cont. Cong.*, I, 50.

[37]Drayton, *Memoirs*, I, 169.

[38]Cushing, ed., *Writings of S. Adams*, III, 159; Ford, ed., *Journals Cont. Cong.*, I, 75–81. See also A. W. Farmer [Samuel Seabury], *The Congress Canvassed* (New York, 1774), 6.

lishment of local committees to enforce the embargo of trade, it provided the apparatus that would eventually develop into the government of revolution. By providing for nonimportation and nonexportation as a means of forcing Great Britain to redress colonial grievances, it convinced Parliament that war was inevitable and thus led directly to the engagement at Lexington and Concord. By committing a substantial majority of Americans to support Boston in resisting an act of Parliament, it provided a broad basis of support for the whig position that would contribute substantially to the success of the Revolution.

The Association began with a brief statement of the reasons for American opposition to certain measures of Parliament and a paragraph explaining that Congress had decided on a boycott of trade with the mother country as the "most speedy, effectual, and peaceable measure" for obtaining redress. It included fourteen separate provisions for implementing the embargo and concluded with a list of grievances whose redress Congress considered essential for a restoration of commercial ties. Most of the provisions concerning nonimportation and nonexportation were proposed and debated on the floor of Congress and have already been discussed. A number of other provisions, which did not deal directly with the implementation of the embargo, were presumably written into the Association by the committee appointed for that purpose and then adopted by the Congress without extended debate.[39] Consequently it is impossible to trace the origin of each clause of the document.

The most important sections of the Association dealt with the temporary embargo of trade, of course, but there were substantial portions aimed at permanently reducing the economic dependence of the American colonies on Great Britain. The agreement committed the colonists to "use our utmost endeavours" to increase the number of sheep in America and improve the stock so that the domestic manufacture of woolens might be advanced. It also bound the colonists to "encourage frugality, economy, and industry, and promote agriculture, arts and the manufacture of this Country." The delegates attempted to encourage republican virtue by urging their countrymen to "discountenance and discourage every species of extravagance and dissipation, especially all horseracing, and all kinds of gaming, cock-fighting, exhibitions of plays, shews, and other expensive diversions and entertainments. The Association also called for a freeze on prices and especially warned peddlers and vendors against inflating profits due to the scarcity that was expected to accompany nonimportation.[40]

[39] Ford, ed., *Journals Cont. Cong.*, I, 75–81.
[40] *Ibid.*, I, 78.

No provision of the Continental Association was more important than the establishment of local committees to enforce the program of commercial boycott. Committees were to be chosen in each county, city, or town by all those entitled to vote for representatives in the legislature, and they were to be responsible for observing the "conduct of all persons touching this association." Whenever a committee decided that a violation had occurred, it was authorized by the Congress to publish the name of the offender in some public place so that he might be "universally condemned" as an enemy of American liberty and ostracized. A similar isolation was to be invoked against entire towns, counties, or colonies that refused to enforce the Association.[41]

The Association also contained specific instructions for the disposition of articles imported in violation of the boycott. These provisions illustrate the determination of Congress to pacify the merchants. There was to be a period of grace from December 1 to February 1 during which the owner of imported goods could select one of three alternative means of satisfying the terms of nonimportation. He could have his goods shipped to another port, stored by the local committee until the trade boycott ended, or sold at public auction. If he chose the last alternative, the committee would arrange the auction, reimburse the importer for his costs and the charges of transportation, and then set aside the profits for the poor of Boston.[42] This provision protected the merchant whose shipment was legitimately delayed, as well as those who had sent out last-minute orders in anticipation of the coming shortage. Not until after February 1 did goods have to be returned unopened, a much more costly penalty for the importing merchant.

Congress did not adopt specific instructions on the enforcement of other provisions of the Association but instead left the committees free to adopt whatever measures they might consider necessary. The delegates did, however, authorize one other provision for making the trade boycott more effective. They instructed the existing committees of correspondence in the several colonies to "frequently inspect the Entries of their Custom Houses" and exchange information about what they found as well as "other material circumstance that may occur relative to this association."[43]

The program endorsed by the First Continental Congress was more elaborate and more comprehensive than any previously adopted by an individual town or colony; yet there was little in the Association that had not been previously suggested. In every colony, public meetings had recommended nonimportation and nonexportation and

[41] *Ibid.*, I, 79.
[42] *Ibid.*, I, 78–79.
[43] *Ibid.*, I, 79.

proposed means of enforcement similar to those adopted by the Congress. A number of colonies, including Massachusetts, Maryland, Virginia, and North Carolina, had established local committees similar to those recommended by the Association.

Among the most direct influences on the men who adopted the Continental Association was the Virginia Association, and that in turn owed a great deal to the resolutions adopted in the several counties of the Old Dominion. One of the most influential of these sets of local proposals was that of Fairfax County. The Fairfax Resolves came from the pen of George Mason. George Washington, chairman of the public meeting in Fairfax County, carried the resolutions to the Virginia Convention and the Continental Congress and brought them to the attention of the delegates.[44] Significantly the proposals of Fairfax dealt not just with local and provincial action but outlined a general program for the entire continent. Like Congress, Fairfax County began by objecting to certain enactments of the British Parliament on constitutional grounds and enumerating those acts which it considered unconstitutional. The county meeting further anticipated the provisions of the Association by recommending a boycott of trade, the establishment of local enforcement committees, the nonimportation of slaves, and the isolation of any town or county that did not join the general confederacy.[45]

No doubt the presence of Washington at the Virginia Convention and the Continental Congress meant that the resolutions of Fairfax County had a more direct impact on the Association than the recommendations of other localities. This is not to suggest that one county or one colony dictated the measures adopted in Philadelphia. Annapolis, Maryland, suggested the adoption of an Association similar to that endorsed by Congress some time before Fairfax County did so, and the Maryland community also proposed ostracizing those who refused to join in the common cause.[46] In other areas as well the local committees had begun to act as enforcement agencies of nonimportation before Congress met. Several towns in Massachusetts had assumed that their committees of correspondence would enforce the Solemn League and Covenant circulated there during the summer.[47] There were, in fact, no significant proposals incorporated in the Continental Association that were not contained in the resolutions of at least one town or county in every province.

As Congress put the finishing touches to the Continental Association, the delegates turned again to the question raised by Patrick

[44]The Fairfax Resolutions were also sent to other towns. There is, for example, a copy of them in the Boston Comm. of Corres. Papers, N.Y. Pub. Lib.

[45]Fore, ed., *American Archives,* I, 597–602.

[46]*Ibid.,* I, 352–53.

[47]Boston Comm. of Corres. Papers, N.Y. Pub. Lib.

Henry: What if the trade boycott failed? From the first meetings in Philadelphia it had been assumed that one answer to this question was to arrange for a second meeting of the Congress, and on October 22 the members voted to hold another Congress on May 10 unless grievances were redressed.[48] This date roughly approximated the length of time needed for Great Britain to respond to the measures adopted at the first meeting, and the decision attests to Congress's determination to follow through with its program. The delegates knew that a second session might have to adopt more drastic measures than those contained in the Association, and they realized that such a step would almost certainly involve military conflict. The day after Congress adjourned, Dickinson, one of the more cautious members, wrote Arthur Lee that "the Colonists have now taken such grounds that Great Britain must relax, or inevitably involve herself in a civil war."[49] Dickinson might have added that whatever the decision, a second meeting of Congress had been so timed as to facilitate a proper reply. As it turned out, a number of the delegates to the Second Continental Congress were enroute to Philadelphia when they learned that Britain had decided to dispatch troops to Lexington and Concord.

[48] Ford, ed., *Journals Cont. Cong.,* I, 102.
[49] Dickinson to Lee, Oct. 27, 1774, Burnett, ed., *Letters Cont. Cong.,* I, 83.

CHAPTER VII

A Note on Consensus

As THE delegates to the First Continental Congress left Philadelphia during the last days of October, they congratulated
each other on the remarkable unanimity that had accompanied their
deliberations. Unlike the Stamp Act Congress of 1765, at which two
influential members had refused to endorse the resolutions adopted,
every delegate at the Philadelphia meeting had signed and agreed to
abide by the provisions of the Continental Association.[1] Nor had the
delegates resorted to evasion in order to preserve unanimity. The
Association explicitly listed the acts of Parliament that Congress considered oppressive and endorsed a detailed plan for their repeal. To
all outward appearances the colonies had never been more united in
their opposition to British policy. Yet one of the delegates would
soon label the apparent harmony a sham and charge that the radical
members of Congress had forced adoption of the Association over the
strenuous objections of the minority. In making these charges,
Pennsylvania's Joseph Galloway launched a controversy over the proceedings of the Congress which has dominated accounts of that meeting until the present day.

In a series of pamphlets published after Congress adjourned, Galloway maintained that upon their arrival the delegates had almost
immediately divided into two equal factions: conservatives who
wanted to defend colonial rights within the framework of the empire
and radicals who used "fiction, falsehood, and fraud" to manipulate
the adoption of measures leading to resistance and independence.
The first were men of "loyal principles, and possessed the greatest
fortunes in America; the other were congregational and presbyterian
republicans, or men of bankrupt fortunes, overwhelmed in debt to

---

[1]Three of the 56 members of Congress did not sign the Association: John Haring
of New York, Robert Goldsborough of Maryland, and Samuel Rhoads of Pennsylvania. It is not likely that any of the three were present at Congress when the final
draft of the document was endorsed. Rhoads had been elected mayor of Philadelphia
and apparently was replaced in Congress by John Dickinson. Haring did not arrive
until Sept. 26, and no other mention of him is made in any of the minutes. One New
York pamphleteer stated that every member of the New York delegation signed the
Association except for one, presumably Haring, who was not in attendance. Goldsborough spoke against paying for the tea on Oct. 1, but he is not mentioned again.
Also, he signed none of the documents prepared by Congress.

the British merchants." The conservatives, having no designs to conceal, had conducted themselves in an "open and ingenuous" manner, but the radicals had left "no art, no falsehood, no fraud unessayed" in their attempt to mask their true objectives. This willingness to engage in chicanery provided them with their narrow margin of victory.[2]

Galloway argued that during the first weeks the conservatives had managed to block the adoption of measures tending toward "violent opposition" and that as a result Congress had found itself unable to agree on any proposals at all. Unfortunately, Sam Adams, a man who "managed at once the faction in Congress at Philadelphia, and the factions in New England," stepped forward to break the deadlock by introducing the "inflammatory resolves of the county of Suffolk." Congress's endorsement of those resolutions was a "declaration of war," and "by this treasonable vote the foundation of military resistance throughout America was effectually laid." The Suffolk Resolves had inflamed Congress to the point that the conservatives, "although they knew a great majority of the colonists were averse to the measure, perceived the improbability of stemming the torrent."[3]

In defiance of the adage that the victors write their own history, Galloway's charges against the Continental Congress have set the tone for most twentieth-century accounts of that meeting. Arthur Schlesinger, Sr., in *The Colonial Merchants and the American Revolution* (1918), closely followed the Galloway narrative. He portrayed the Plan of Union as a conservative platform on which the opponents of trade restrictions raised their opposition to the Continental Association, and Schlesinger, like Galloway, referred to the introduction of the Suffolk Resolves as the point at which the radicals "threw off their mask" and managed to turn the tide.[4] In 1941 Edmund C. Burnett published *The Continental Congress*, also describing the meeting of 1774 as a battle between "conservatives, aiming at patching up the quarrel, and radicals, determined upon resistance."[5] By the time John C. Miller published *The Origins of the American Revolution* in 1943, the chronology of events in Congress had been rearranged in order to fit more readily with the picture of factional confrontation.[6]

Recent accounts of the Congress have followed a similar interpretation, although with more sophistication. Lawrence Henry Gipson, in volume XII of *The British Empire before the American Revolution,*

[2]Galloway, *Historical and Political Reflections,* pp. 66–67.
[3]*Ibid.,* pp. 67–69.
[4]New York, 1918, p. 412.
[5]New York, 1941, p. 33.
[6]Boston, 1943. Miller confuses the Suffolk Resolves with a set of resolutions passed later, an alteration which enhances the part played by the former in breaking the deadlock in Congress (p. 384).

conceded that it is sometimes difficult to distinguish "radical from conservative" and cited at least one occasion on which the supposedly conservative Galloway espoused the radical position by denying the legislative authority of Parliament.[7] Merrill Jensen in *The Founding of a Nation* presented a plausible modification of the Galloway narrative but also expressed "surprise" at the breakdown in traditional categorizations of radicals and conservatives. He noted, for example, that the Massachusetts delegation divided over the issue of Parliament's right to regulate trade and that one of the two members from Rhode Island voted for the Galloway Plan of Union.[8]

The most important cause of this confusion is the hitherto ignored distinction between the issues that caused dispute in Congress and those which did not. Despite the debates which arose over Parliament's right to regulate trade and the Plan of Union, the delegates never divided seriously on any of the major provisions of the Continental Association. They argued about the dates on which nonimportation and nonexportation should go into effect, they haggled over inclusion of the Quebec Act as one of the "intolerable" grievances, and they debated at length South Carolina's insistence that it be allowed to export rice to Europe. But these issues were procedural rather than substantive and attest only to the differences of opinion bound to arise in a group of more than fifty delegates from twelve different colonies.

If there was serious opposition to any part of the Continental Association, it came from those who favored more aggressive action rather than from any conservative faction. The most prolonged arguments on the Association concerned the question of nonexportation, and there is every reason to believe that the compromise adopted represented the moderate position. Had it not been for the opposition of Virginia, Congress might have endorsed immediate invocation of that measure instead of delaying it until the fall of 1775. South Carolina's Edward Rutledge, one of those who had suggested an immediate stoppage of trade despite Virginia's opposition, wrote shortly after adjournment that he had fought the delay and still saw no reason "why a non-exportation should not be put on foot immediately."[9] James Weems, a tobacco exporter in Maryland, reported in December that according to rumor, "there was but a very Small Majority in the Continental Congress for continuing our Exports till Sept. next."[10]

[7]New York, 1965, p. 243.

[8] *The Founding of a Nation: The American Revolution, 1763–1783* (New York, 1968), pp. 499, 503.

[9]Rutledge to Ralph Izard, Oct. 29, 1774, Ann Izard Deas, ed., *Correspondence of Mr. Ralph Izard of South Carolina* (New York, 1844), pp. 23–25.

[10]Weems to James Russell, Dec. 7, 1774, Russell Papers, Coutts and Co. (microfilm, Col. Wmsbg. Foundation).

Galloway's charge that the Massachusetts delegation used the radical Suffolk Resolves to batter an unwilling Congress into support for Boston has been widely repeated, and yet the record suggests nothing of the sort. No doubt the representatives from the Bay Colony presented the resolutions from Suffolk County, including the city of Boston, for the purpose of arousing a sympathetic response from their fellow delegates. It is also true that by approving the "wisdom and fortitude" with which Suffolk citizens had resisted the Coercive Acts, Congress condoned measures that the British viewed as rebellious. But the congressional resolutions endorsing the resolves did no more than formalize sentiments universally popular among the delegates; they encouraged the Bostonians not to accept enforcement of the Coercive Acts and at the same time cautioned them to continue to act in a defensive rather than offensive manner.[11] The "radicals" did not have to exert themselves to secure the endorsement; it apparently passed without a dissenting vote. The journals of Congress show that every colony voted for the measure, not excluding the two conservative delegations from New York and Pennsylvania. Silas Deane wrote that Congress had acted "without one dissenting Voice, though all the members were present," and John Adams spoke of "perfect unanimity." Joseph Reed informed Lord Dartmouth that on the question of the resolutions from Suffolk "there was not only unanimity of provinces, but of individual members." Reed himself did not attend Congress, but he was closely associated with several delegates, and his observations were usually accurate.[12]

Simply to show that the traditional emphasis on factionalism in Congress has been an exaggeration leaves a number of questions unanswered. Was there a conscious conservative faction in Congress, and if so, how near did it come to altering the program adopted by that meeting? Or, on the other hand, was there a radical coalition which secured the adoption of measures toward which a majority was, at best, lukewarm? Is there sufficient evidence of block voting to suggest serious factionalization, and if so, which delegates provided the nucleus of the two groups and which provided the swing votes?

Any truly conservative faction in the First Continental Congress would undoubtedly have organized around Galloway, the one dele-

---

[11]Ford, ed., *Journals Cont. Cong.*, I, 39. [Philip Livingston], *The Other Side of the Question* ... (New York, 1774), p. 26, said that by endorsing the Suffolk Resolves the delegates intended to "recommend moderate and pacific conduct, supported by firmness and resolution."

[12]Deane to the Wethersfield Comm. of Corres., Sept. 19, 1774, Webb, *Correspondence and Journals*, I, 39; J. Adams to Abigail Adams, Sept. 18, 1774, Burnett, ed., *Letters Cont. Cong.*, I, 35; Reed to the Earl of Dartmouth, Sept. 25, 1774, W. B. Reed, *Life and Correspondence of J. Reed*, p. 79.

gate who certainly opposed the Association (though perhaps under cover) and subsequently attempted to prevent its enforcement. Galloway had long minimized the dangers involved in an acknowledgment of the authority of the Crown and Parliament, in large part because of his association with that group in Pennsylvania seeking to depose the proprietors and convert the colony into a royal dominion. In 1767, when Parliament enacted the Townshend duties, he had worked to obstruct the adoption of nonimportation in Philadelphia, and he unquestionably, though covertly, opposed the endorsement of similar measures by the Congress of 1774. His identification with the elements in Pennsylvania who opposed the Penns had brought Galloway into conflict with such popular leaders as John Dickinson and Charles Thomson and had gradually undermined his influence in Philadelphia. Nevertheless, he had maintained his seat in the Pennsylvania Assembly as representative from rural Bucks County and, in the summer of 1774, had used his considerable influence as Speaker to insure the election of a conservative delegation to the Congress.[13]

Galloway's effort to control Congress proved futile, both because his previous disputes with Dickinson had weakened his position of leadership in Pennsylvania and because his objectives ran counter to those of an overwhelming majority of the delegates. Two days before Congress convened, he wrote Governor Franklin of New Jersey that he had begun to sound out the delegates and believed they would act with "Temper and Moderation." He implied that he could persuade Congress to offer to pay for the tea and to reject nonimportation, predictions that missed the mark by unanimous votes in both cases.[14] During the first day's debate Congress twice rejected Galloway's leadership, first by voting to sit at Carpenters' Hall rather than accepting his offer of the Pennsylvania State House and then by going outside the elected membership to appoint Thomson as secretary. Deane wrote that these decisions had proved "highly agreeable to the mechanics and citizens in general, but mortifying to the last degree to Mr. Galloway and his party, Thompson [*sic*] being his sworn opposite, as you may say, and by his means prevented being one of the Congress for this Province."[15]

Deane's statement has often been cited as proof of the early factionalization of Congress, but the context in which the Connecticut delegate used the term "party" shows that he was speaking instead

[13] See David L. Jacobson, *John Dickinson and the Revolution in Pennsylvania, 1764–1776*, University of California Publications in History, LXXVIII (Berkeley and Los Angeles, 1965).

[14] Galloway to Gov. Franklin, Sept. 3, 1774, Burnett, ed., *Letters Cont. Cong.*, I, 5–6.

[15] Deane to Mrs. Deane, Sept. 5–6, 1774, *ibid.*, I, 11.

about divisions in Pennsylvania. Deane, like other delegates arriving in Philadelphia, was well aware of the conflict that had taken place in Pennsylvania between the Assembly and the Provincial Convention. His remark clearly refers to events in the city rather than inside Congress. Moreover, the overwhelming majorities with which the delegates chose Carpenters' Hall and elected Thomson would not have provided Deane or anyone else with much evidence concerning congressional factions. Galloway and James Duane, both of whom opposed the two decisions, referred to the "great Majority" in favor and found Thomson's election so popular that they allowed the decision to go uncontested.[16] John Adams noted in his diary that only a "very few" opposed the selection of Carpenters' Hall "and they were chiefly from Pennsylvania and New York."[17]

If Galloway did attempt to organize a conservative faction, his efforts failed. Members of Congress who thought along similar lines naturally tended to vote together on certain issues, but the remarkable fact about the conservative representatives was not their organization but their diversity. Although they generally supported Parliament's right to regulate American trade, they disagreed on other points. Insofar as the fragmentary nature of the record makes an analysis of voting patterns possible, it reveals a clear divergence of opinion among those delegates who have been labeled conservative.

To analyze the voting patterns of the First Continental Congress it must be possible to define the conservative and radical positions on a question with some degree of confidence and there must be sufficient evidence to show how certain members voted. The issues also must have been debated. A number of important decisions, including nonimportation, nonexportation, and the Suffolk Resolves, cannot be used because they were adopted without division. These decisions, of course, support the argument that there was a general consensus among the delegates.

Four important issues do fit the criteria: the Galloway Plan of Union, the proposal made in the Grand Committee to cite natural law as a basis for defining American rights, the question of Parliament's right to regulate colonial trade, and the suggestion that Congress offer to pay for the tea destroyed at Boston. Men of conservative leanings were likely to favor the Plan of Union, the right of Parliament to regulate trade, and the proposal that Congress offer to pay for the tea. They would oppose references to natural law.

Excluding Galloway, four members of Congress are known to have taken a conservative position on at least two of these four issues:

---

[16]Duane, "Notes of Proceedings," *ibid.*, I, 8; Galloway to Gov. William Franklin, Sept. 5, 1774, *ibid.*, I, 9.

[17]J. Adams, Sept. 5, 1774, Butterfield, ed., *Diary and Autobiography*, II, 122.

James Duane, Samuel Chase, John Rutledge, and John Jay. Of these, only Duane voted as expected on all four issues. Chase took the conservative position in opposing the citation of natural law and voting for Parliament's right to regulate colonial trade, but he strongly and consistently opposed the Plan of Union. Jay supported the Plan of Union and favored paying for the tea, and yet, he contended that the delegates should refer to natural law as one of the bulwarks of American rights. Rutledge voted conservatively in opposing the statement on natural law and in supporting the Plan of Union, but he vigorously opposed the motion to pay for the tea. In view of these differences it seems unlikely that the four men had made any significant effort to coordinate their activities.[18]

These statistics are skimpy, but combined with the unanimity that marked other supposedly controversial debates, they suggest a decided absence of factionalization. A closer took at the attitudes of two delegates—Rutledge and Chase—throws additional light on the divisions in Congress. Galloway considered Rutledge one of those members with whom he had most in common, and yet the South Carolinian took an actively radical position on two of the more controversial issues debated in Congress. He opposed the decision not to demand repeal of acts passed before 1763, and he favored immediate implementation of nonexportation.[19] Chase was equally inconsistent. He worked closely with Duane, a conservative leader in Congress, and after adjournment he continued to correspond with the New Yorker about their identical views of parliamentary regulation of trade. Yet Chase refused Duane's pleas that he support the Plan of Union.[20]

A comparison of the positions taken by Duane and Chase at the First Continental Congress illustrates an important point about the attempt to classify Americans as radical or conservative in the crisis of 1774–76. Duane may legitimately be considered a conservative, not because he supported Parliament's right to regulate trade or the Galloway Plan of Union, but because he sincerely believed that Great Britain would respond positively to American demands. The opposite was true of Chase. Like Duane he believed that Congress should admit Parliament's right to regulate trade and was even willing to grant the British legislatuⅰe a limited power of taxation for use in exercising that right. However, his evaluation of conditions in Great Britain convinced him that the mother country would not retreat and that

[18]All voting records have been compiled from notes taken by J. Adams, Duane, and Deane. Most of these are in Burnett, ed., *Letters Cont. Cong.*, I, and Collier, ed., "Silas Deane Reports."

[19]Galloway to Gov. William Franklin, Sept. 3, 1774, Burnett, ed., *Letters Cont. Cong.*, I, 5–6; Collier, ed., "Silas Deane Reports," p. 6; Drayton, *Memoirs*, I, 169–70.

[20]Chase to Duane, Feb. 5, 1775, Duane Papers, N.-Y. Hist. Soc.

the colonists must therefore prepare for war. That attitude made him a radical regardless of how much or how little authority he was willing to concede to Parliament.

Indeed, Parliament's decision to pass and enforce the Coercive Acts had made all Americans radical on the constitutional issue, including Galloway and Duane. Any attempt to classify the delegates to the First Continental Congress is meaningless unless such categorization is based, not on the objectives of the members, but on the means they wished to pursue in achieving them. Thus the radicals favored military preparation and the conservatives hesitated to go beyond petition. It is of utmost importance to note that Congress overwhelmingly rejected both positions.

Turning to the so-called radicals in Congress, it is apparent that they were more numerous and better organized than the conservatives but were not alone responsible for the measures adopted. In fact the more aggressive members of Congress, including Samuel Adams, seem to have concentrated their efforts toward achieving unanimity rather than pursuing the adoption of a particular program. They realized that Congress would endorse nonimportation and that more militant measures would serve only to divide the members. Disagreement would reduce the chances of colonial success, whether political or military. The Connecticut delegates commented at length on this point, writing Governor Jonathan Trumbull that Congress had proceeded with great deliberation because it aimed at "something more than a majority, an unanimity." They explained that "unanimity being in our view of the last importance, every one must be heard, even on those points or subjects, which are in themselves not of the last importance."[21]

In retrospect it appears that the radicals in Congress had come to believe that the most important immediate objective was to maintain colonial unity. Even those who considered military conflict with Great Britain inevitable, and only a few did, realized that they must allow Parliament to assume the role of aggressor. Perhaps the most astute observations on the necessity for unity were made by Joseph Hawley of Massachusetts, writing to John Adams before the latter left for Congress. Both John and Samuel Adams had great respect for Hawley's opinions.

Fearful that this first meeting of Congress would inevitably lead to a break with Great Britain, Hawley urged that the most important concern of the Massachusetts delegation be consolidation of all the colonies' representatives. He warned that "the good issue of the Congress depends a good deal on the harmony, good understanding, and

21Conn. Delegates to the Governor of Conn., Oct. 10, 1774, Burnett, ed., *Letters Cont. Cong.*, I, 69–70.

I had almost said brotherly love, of its members." Hawley referred to the prevailing opinion that the Bostonians did "affect to dictate" and to "assume big and haughty airs" and insisted that Adams and his compatriots avoid conduct that might "beget or strengthen such an opinion." It would be both unnecessary and foolish for the New Englanders to promote measures that might prove divisive.[22]

Both John and Samuel Adams acted in accordance with Hawley's advice. The former wrote his wife, Abigail, that the delegation had tried to steer a delicate course between "too much activity and too much insensibility in our critical, interested situation."[23] To William Tudor he admitted that he thought Congress should offer Massachusetts "more adequate support" than just a boycott of British trade, "but I tremble for fear we should fail of obtaining it." He predicted that the delegates, though "unalterably against your submission to any of the Acts for a single moment," would never support the adoption of offensive measures.[24]

Sam Adams also made an effort to remove "prejudices" and appears to have stayed very much in the background at Congress. On one occasion when he figured prominently in debate, his purpose was clearly to prove the sincerity of the Massachusetts delegates in their efforts at conciliation. Jay and one of the Rutledges had opposed opening Congress with prayer because of the differences of religious convictions among the delegates. Adams, who was hardly known for his tolerant attitude on religious matters, sprang to his feet to insist that he was "no bigot" and could hear a prayer from any gentleman of virtue who was also a friend of his country. The delegates listened with some surprise as the Boston Congregationalist proposed that an Anglican, Jacob Duche, be invited to give the invocation.[25] Joseph Read of Delaware thought the move a "masterly stroke of policy" and told John Adams that it had had "a very good effect" and that the "sentiments of the people here, are growing more and more favorable every day."[26] Other delegates also noted the successful efforts of the Massachusetts delegates to avoid the charge of radicalism. Caesar Rodney concluded that the men from Boston "who (we know) have been condemned by many for their violence are moderate men when compared to Virginia, South Carolina and Rhode-Island."[27]

That the Boston delegates attempted to curry favor with their fellow members of Congress neither proves nor disproves the charge that they were busily promoting radical measures at the same time.

[22]Hawley to Adams, July 25, 1774, C. F. Adams, ed., *Works of J. Adams,* IX, 342–45.
[23]J. Adams to Abigail Adams, Sept. 18, 1774, Burnett, ed., *Letters Cont. Cong.,* I, 35.
[24]J. Adams to Tudor, Sept. 29, 1774, *ibid.,* I, 59–60.
[25]J. Adams to Abigail Adams, Sept. 16, 1774, *ibid.,* I, 32.
[26]C. F. Adams, ed., *Works of J. Adams,* II, 378.
[27]C. Rodney to Thomas Rodney, Sept. 9, 1774, Burnett, ed., *Letters Cont. Cong.,* I, 27.

It is therefore important to reemphasize that neither the men from Boston nor anyone else appear to have persuaded Congress to adopt any proposal not favored by a majority of the delegates before their arrival in Philadelphia. John Adams would have preferred to see Congress encourage Massachusetts to assume its own government until Parliament repealed the Coercive Acts, but he did not dare suggest such a measure. Patrick Henry and Richard Henry Lee did propose that the several colonies take steps to ready the colonial militia, but they also found Congress unwilling to endorse such offensive measures. Congress preferred to test the trade embargo that the members had come to Philadelphia to endorse.

Nor were the radicals in Congress so united as historians have often suggested. On some points, notably the Galloway Plan of Union, the delegates from Virginia and New England seem to have formed an alliance; on others that entente fell apart. The Old Dominion flatly refused to accept immediate nonexportation and so put a stop to one measure close to the hearts of the men from Boston. On the most controversial measure to come before Congress, the right of Parliament to regulate colonial trade, the delegates from Massachusetts found themselves internally divided and had to abstain on the issue.

In light of the general unanimity with which Congress adopted the Continental Association, and the skimpy evidence of factional intrigue, what explains the later emphasis on internal discord? One answer lies in the subsequent writings of Joseph Galloway and John Adams.

Adams, after retirement from public life, wrote many letters recounting his experiences in the American Revolution, including the meeting in Philadelphia during the fall of 1774. In one of these he estimated that "Tories" constituted one-third of the delegates in that Congress, and in another he compared the meeting to the "Council of Nice," noting that decisions approved by one or two votes went out to the world as unanimous through the device of recording the vote by colony rather than by individual delegate.[28]

Passing time and a selective memory had colored Adams's recollections of the problems he faced in 1774. None of the notes he made at the time record significant opposition to decisions he deemed important. His references to the other delegates reflected no particular malice, and he commented favorably on the general disposition of Congress to support Massachusetts Bay. Writing his wife from Philadelphia, he had in fact described the membership of Congress in glowing terms. "There is in the Congress a collection of the greatest men upon this continent in point of abilities, virtues, and fortunes.

---

[28] J. Adams to Thomas Jefferson, Nov. 12, 1813, and J. Adams to Jefferson, Aug. 24, 1815, C. F. Adams, ed., *Works of J. Adams*, X, 79, 172.

The magnanimity and public spirit which I see here make me blush for the sordid, venal herd which I have seen in my own Province.'' He found "such a spirit through the colonies, and the members of the Congress are such characters, that no danger can happen to us, which will not involve the whole continent in universal desolation."[29]

Adams's charge that proposals carried by one or two votes went out to the world as unanimous is also inaccurate. It is true that Congress used the unit rule and made no record of individual votes. Nevertheless, for the vote on an issue to have been recorded as unanimous, and many of the most important were, a majority of at least one in each of the twelve delegations would have been necessary. These twelve ayes alone would have insured more than a three-fifths majority of the full house. Since Rhode Island and New Hampshire sent only two delegates each, not one of the four could have opposed any decision recorded as unanimous. The Massachusetts delegation included four persons; if more than one had voted in the negative on any issue, the colony would have had to abstain. Moreover, Virginia's delegation of seven, one of the largest in Congress, seems to have supported most of the important votes by a lopsided majority. It seems most unlikely that even ten delegates opposed the "unanimous" resolutions adopted by Congress, and twenty nays would have been maximum on such a vote.[30]

Galloway presented a similarly distorted view of the proceedings in Congress. In his later pamphlets he contended that he had voted against many of the measures adopted in Philadelphia and emphasized the efforts of the conservative faction to alter the program adopted there. He claimed to have opposed both the invocation of trade restrictions and the Suffolk Resolves; yet there is no evidence that he spoke or voted against either. He may have argued against nonexportation (though that is not at all certain) since he suggested at one point in the debates that such a measure "would weaken us [the colonies] in another struggle, which I fear is too near."[31] Even

[29] J. Adams to Abigail Adams, Sept. 8, 1774, Burnett, ed., *Letters Cont. Cong.*, I, 19-20. See also J. Adams to Abigail Adams, Sept. 14, 1774, *ibid.*, I, 31.

[30] It is difficult, even in the official records, to tell which votes were unanimous. Endorsement of the Suffolk Resolves and nonimportation are so recorded, as are eight of ten resolutions in the Statement of Rights and Grievances. The vote on nonexportation was not unanimous, but this reflected the objections of those who wanted it to begin sooner, or perhaps South Carolina's dissatisfaction with the original refusal to allow for exportation of rice and indigo. After adoption of the Statement of Rights and Grievances on Oct. 14, Secretary Thomson seems to have forgotten to designate the unanimous votes—at least no others are so recorded. The vote to thank the Pennsylvania Assembly for its hospitality carries no note of unanimity although it seems improbable that any colony voted against it, and the same applies to many decisions made in the last two weeks.

[31] J. Adams, "Notes of Debates," Burnett, ed., *Letters Cont. Cong.*, I, 51.

in dealing with members of Congress whom he considered sympathetic, Galloway made no mention of his apparent wish to see the colonies represented in Parliament, and not a single delegate made contemporary reference to his alleged opposition to the measures adopted.[32] Galloway's comments in debate, as recorded by John Adams, were moderate, and as late as October 10 the usually volatile delegate from Massachusetts referred to him as a "sensible and learned" man.[33]

Galloway's private statements during and after the meeting in Philadelphia contrasted sharply with this moderate pose. After a brief period of optimism just before the meetings began, he informed Governor Franklin that he expected the measures of Congress would be considered "illegal and unconstitutional," and he conceded that he retained "little Expectations of much Satisfaction from the Event of Things."[34] Shortly after Congress adjourned, Galloway wrote that Great Britain must strictly enforce the Coercive Acts if she hoped to retain her colonies, and he called for the king to "bring the Point in Dispute between the two Countries to *a final Decision.*"[35] Galloway's willingness to sign the Continental Association and his support of trade restrictions during the debates suggest the deviousness of his conduct throughout this period. His subsequent attempt to justify signing the Association by arguing that he expected Congress to adopt more conciliatory measures later does not fit with the timing of the official signing which took place near the end of the meeting.[36] Galloway endorsed the final resolutions of Congress, and in doing so pledged himself to abide by the terms of an agreement which he denounced as treasonable almost before the ink had dried.[37]

Galloway cannot be blamed for concealing some of his more unpopular opinions in order to increase his influence in Congress. But his inaccurate reporting of events continued long after Congress adjourned and has played a substantial part in supporting accounts of a determined and significant opposition to the measures adopted in

[32]C. F. Adams, ed., *Works of J. Adams,* II, 396.

[33]Galloway to Gov. William Franklin, Sept. 3, 1774, Burnett, ed., *Letters Cont. Cong.,* I, 5; Gov. Franklin to Galloway, March 12, 1775, W. A. Whitehead *et al.,* eds., *New Jersey Archives,* 1st ser, X (Newark, 1886), 578. Franklin stated in this letter that he was convinced the "most eligible Scheme, for the true and lasting Interest of the whole Empire will be the sending Members to the British Parliament," and he added that he knew Galloway also favored such a plan.

[34]Galloway to Gov. Franklin, Sept. 5, 1774, Burnett, ed., *Letters Cont. Cong.,* I, 10.

[35]Galloway to Gov. Franklin, March 26, 1775, Whitehead *et al.,* eds., *N.J. Archives,* 1st ser., X, 579.

[36]Galloway, *Candid Examination,* p. 62.

[37]The Association pledged those who signed it to abide by its terms; Galloway argued that he had signed the document as a representative of Pennsylvania rather than for himself. See Thomas B. Chandler, *What Think Ye of the Congress Now?* (New York, 1775), p. 11.

Philadelphia. No other delegate reported such an opposition. In fact, one of the few contemporary references to Galloway's conduct takes direct issue with his contention. Joseph Reed, a relatively moderate whig leader in Pennsylvania, commented at some length in January 1775:

> Mr. Galloway's conduct is so various, that it is impossible, I believe, to judge what his sentiments and intentions are. I fear among all their varieties he will never stumble upon those of an honest man or gentleman. He once, in the House of Assembly, I am told, obliquely reflected upon the measures of the Congress, but his dissenting at the time, protest, &c., he concealed so carefully, that no member of Congress knew of it besides himself.[38]

The First Continental Congress was not marked by dissension; it exhibited the extraordinary unanimity with which the colonists began the final confrontation with Great Britain. The Revolution began at the high-water mark of American consensus. Washington of Virginia, Dickinson of Pennsylvania, John Adams of Massachusetts, Chase of Maryland, Richard Caswell of North Carolina all were men of fundamentally conservative temperament who willingly committed themselves and their influence to opposing enforcement of the Coercive Acts. Nor did this consensus result from the manipulation of a few radical leaders. Historians have, for example, asserted that the Massachusetts delegation duped Washington into believing that New England did not favor independence, and they have implied that this deception insured the Virginian's support for the Association.[39] This assertion ignores Washington's prior advocation of a program similar to that adopted by Congress. The Continental Association differed in no significant respect from the resolutions adopted in Fairfax County at a meeting over which he presided.[40]

The unanimity with which Congress endorsed the Continental Association, combined with a prevailing belief that nonimportation had been effective in previous disputes, led an overwhelming majority of colonists to commit themselves to the whig position. If that commitment did not seem particularly radical in 1774, it soon became so by virtue of Parliament's determination to enforce the Coercive Acts. As Great Britain moved to implement its legislation, some colonists found that they had almost unknowingly chosen resistance. Most had believed that Parliament would retreat; when that did not happen they had to choose between military confrontation and backing down. For many Americans the decision to accept the recommendations of Congress and endorse the Continental Association proved to be the point of no return.

[38]Reed to Charles Pettit, Jan. 14, 1775, W. B. Reed, *Life and Correspondence of J. Reed*, I, 91.

[39]Jensen, *Founding of a Nation*, p. 490.

[40]Force, ed., *American Archives*, I, 597–602.

Government by Committee

ALL the colonies represented in Congress endorsed the Continental Association except New York, and even in the latter province local committees saw to the enforcement of its nonimportation sections. Except in Georgia and the occupied city of Boston, purchases from Great Britain stopped entirely. The most outspoken critics of the measure were forced to admit that the boycott had the force of law throughout the colonies.[1] Another, and in the long run more significant, aspect of the Association was the provision calling the election of committees to enforce the trade boycott. Because approval and enforcement of the Association were placed in the hands of local groups rather than provincial assemblies or congresses, these committees became the regulatory agencies of the First Continental Congress.

In almost every colony these local committees began enforcement before any kind of provincial body met. New York City elected a Committee of Inspection which effectively implemented the nonimportation agreement despite the repeated refusal of the provincial Assembly to endorse the program adopted by Congress. A similar situation occurred in Georgia, where the legislature also refused to act on the Association; yet the Parish of St. John's promised to execute the boycott of trade and asked to be accepted by other associating communities.[2] By thus administering nonimportation, the committee system became the first step toward the creation of an American union.

Just as the committees of correspondence had aided in calling the Continental Congress, so they proved almost indispensable in organizing enforcement of the program it adopted. Some of these committees actually took over the task of implementing the Association, and in almost every other case they arranged the election of committees to do so. In New England the towns elected committees, and

---

[1] See, for example, Gov. William Franklin to the Earl of Dartmouth, Dec. 6, 1774, Whitehead *et al.*, eds., *N.J. Archives,* X, 503; Lt. Gov. Colden to the Earl of Dartmouth, March 1, 1775, E. B. O'Callaghan and Berthold Fernow, eds., *Documents Relative to the Colonial History of the State of New York* (Albany, 1853–87), VIII, 543; and Gov. Josiah Martin to the Earl of Dartmouth, March 10, 1775, William L. Saunders, ed., *Colonial and State Records of North Carolina* (Raleigh, 1890), IX, 1155–56.

[2] Force, ed., *American Archives,* I, 1161–62.

the only county organizations that existed took the form of congresses made up of delegates from the several local communities. The southern colonies elected committees at county meetings, as well as in such towns as Wilmington in North Carolina, Charleston in South Carolina, and Williamsburg and Norfolk in Virginia. In the middle colonies a hybrid system prevailed: for example, each Pennsylvania county elected a committee, as did many of the towns and districts within the several counties. In many instances the latter groups seem to have been entirely distinct from the larger county committees.[3]

A typical election took place in James City County, Virginia. The local Committee of Correspondence arranged for the publication of the Association in the *Virginia Gazette* and followed it with a notice announcing "that the above, and all other *resolutions* of the *Congress,* may be carried into *strict execution,* the several freeholders of James City county are desired to meet at eleven o'clock on Friday the 25th instant, if fair, otherwise the succeeding day, at the house of Mr. Isham Allen, in order to elect a *committee* to act *throughout* the said county, and do what is *required* of them by so respectable and august a body."[4] Normally the citizens, whether assembled in town or county meetings, adopted resolutions approving the Association and then proceeded directly to the election of a committee of inspection. In some southern counties the election might be scheduled for an entire day, or even two, to accommodate those who had to travel long distances. Northampton County, Virginia, appointed the sheriff and two others to manage the election and provided that the polls remain open from eleven in the morning until eight at night.[5] Many communities also elected a new committee of correspondence at these meetings, or else instructed the newly appointed Committee of Inspection to designate a certain number of its members for that purpose. In some cases the two committees functioned separately, but it was more common for the same individuals to take responsibility in both areas.

South Carolina was unique in that, with the major exception of Charleston, the Provincial Congress appointed the local committees, arguing the necessity of taking immediate action. The convention recommended that each parish and district meet as soon as possible to approve the appointed committees or to elect different ones if they so desired.[6]

The number of committee meetings varied. In many small com-

[3] The meeting in Philadelphia County in Nov. 1774 appointed a committee to act for the county and at the same time resolved that the committees in the townships be continued. *Pa. Gaz.* (Phila.), Nov. 30, 1774.

[4] Purdie and Dixon's *Va. Gaz.* (Williamsburg), Nov. 17, 1774.

[5] Dixon and Hunter's *Va. Gaz.* (Williamsburg), Feb. 4, 1775.

[6] *South Carolina Gazette* (Charleston), Feb. 20, 1775.

munities—especially in the frontier areas—the committees probably did not meet at all. A town such as Warwick, Massachusetts, did not at first appoint a committee because, as the clerk had written earlier to Boston, "we are a New town and ... have No traders in this town that Sell any merchandise that comes from Great Britain." Nevertheless Warwick wanted to assure Boston that it was firm in the cause, especially since "a Number of people that Call them Selves Baptists have taken unwearied pains to propogate a Story Round the Country that we were all Torrys."[7] In larger towns and in many of the southern counties, the committees met regularly, usually once a month, as well as on special call from the chairman or members who had been authorized to convene them. Committees in seaports met more often than those elsewhere to cope with the time-consuming problems involved in implementing the nonimportation agreement. Philadelphia's committee divided the city into districts and appointed a "sub-committee of Inspection & Observation" for each. These smaller groups then designated two or three of their members to sit each day at the coffeehouse or some other central location and receive reports of incoming cargoes.[8] Similar arrangements prevailed in New York and Charleston. In Boston, of course, the British navy was enforcing a boycott under the provisions of the Port Act.

It is not possible to say exactly who participated in the election of committee members. The Association provided that all those eligible to vote for members of the legislative assemblies should participate in electing the committees; where variations occurred, the suffrage was probably extended. In Harwich, Massachusetts, the town meeting decided that anyone aged twenty-one or over might vote for the local committee.[9] Contemporary accounts noted the attendance of "freeholders and other inhabitants," but it seems unlikely that all who gathered at these meetings actually voted.[10] Nevertheless committees were often elected in public meetings, and this fact may have permitted many to vote for committees of inspection who would not have qualified to participate in the regular colonial elections.

Although Congress had proposed the election of committees for the specific purpose of enforcing the Continental Association, it was apparent from the beginning that such groups might perform a variety of functions. The committees of correspondence had not always confined themselves to correspondence, and there was no reason to

[7] James Ball, town clerk of Warwick, Mass., to William Cooper, town clerk at Boston, Sept. 12, 1774, Boston Comm. of Corres. Papers, N.Y. Pub. Lib.

[8] Philadelphia Committee of Observation Papers, Hist. Soc. Pa.

[9] Josiah Paine, *A History of Harwich* (Rutland, Vt., 1937), p. 310.

[10] See, for example, Force, ed., *American Archives*, I, 388, 392, 417; Gov. Dunmore to Earl of Dartmouth, June 6, 1774, *ibid.*, I, 387.

suppose that the new committees might not do more than inspect. Indeed, the number and size of the committees suggests an objective beyond the simple observance of a trade boycott. New York and Philadelphia may have needed committees of fifty or sixty persons to stop the importation of prohibited cargoes, but why did an interior county in Maryland find it necessary to appoint more than 150 persons to its committee? Why should a frontier town with almost no access to British goods decide to appoint a committee at all? The obvious answer is that the whig leadership in the colonies sought to influence local opinion and strengthen its position by involving the largest possible number of freeholders in active opposition to parliamentary legislation. This effort was eminently successful.

In Virginia and Maryland the records documenting committee membership are particularly complete. At least fifty-one of Virginia's sixty-one counties appointed committees, as did the three towns of Williamsburg, Norfolk, and Fredericksburg.[11] The size of more than forty of these committees is given; the average was just above 21 members each.[12] This calculation, given the magnitude of the sample, can be projected with confidence to the county committees whose size is unknown. After eliminating the ten counties for which no committees were recorded, one can confidently estimate that more than 1,100 freeholders were appointed to committees of inspection in Virginia.

Maryland, though smaller in population than Virginia, appointed nearly as many committee members. At least eleven of the sixteen counties elected committees, and for eight of these counties the number and names of the appointees were recorded.[13] The average size of the committees in Maryland was in excess of 100, and the range was from 20 to nearly 200. After discounting all the counties for which records are unavailable and assuming that the three committees of unknown size were no larger than the smallest of the eight that were known, it is apparent that over 900 persons were named to enforce the Association in the colony.

The figures for Massachusetts, Connecticut, New Hampshire, and

[11] Resolutions of, or references to, most of these committees may be found in the *Va. Gaz.* (Williamsburg) and in Force, ed., *American Archives,* I. It seems probable that every county in the colony appointed committees since the Association called for condemnation of counties which failed to do so, and there are no records of such condemnations.

[12] The largest was Stafford County with 69 and the smallest, Frederick and Dunmore with 6 each (Force, ed., *American Archives,* I, 617, 392, 417).

[13] The eight counties for which records are most complete are Prince Georges, Harford, Anne Arundel, Frederick, Baltimore, St. Marys, Charles, and Calvert. The three that definitely had committees but for which no estimate of size is known are Talbot, Kent, and Cecil. Figures for most of these may be found in the *Va. Gaz.* (Williamsburg) and in Force, ed., *American Archives,* I.

New Jersey are equally remarkable. The Bay Colony appointed at least 160 town committees, and the average size appears to have been just less than 10 members each. These statistics point to a committee membership for the colony somewhere in excess of 1,600.[14] New Jersey counted more than 500, New Hampshire at least 400, Connecticut better than 650, and South Carolina just over 300.[15]

Records in the remaining colonies—New York, Pennsylvania, Rhode Island, North Carolina, and Delaware—are less informative. New York, outside its port city, was not overly enthusiastic in its support of the Association. The minimum number of persons named to committees there cannot safely be set in excess of 150.[16] In Pennsylvania it is possible to get some idea of the size of county committees, but little information exists on the groups in the towns and districts other than references showing that some were appointed. At least nine of the eleven counties in Pennsylvania established committees, with a total membership of about 500.[17] The minimum in Rhode Island can be set at 135, in North Carolina at 200 (although inadequate records make it likely that this number is only a fraction of the actual count), and in Delaware at between 40 and 60.[18]

That the whig leadership deliberately sought to promote this extensive participation in extralegal local governments is indicated not only by the size of the committees appointed but also by their gradual enlargement. Maryland's committees, from the start larger than those in other colonies, increased dramatically in size during the latter part of 1774 and the early months of 1775. Prince Georges County more than doubled the membership of its committee, from 84 in November 1774 to 171 in January of the next year.[19] The Anne Arundel committee grew from 44 to 88 in two months' time, Frederick

[14] The size of committees in Massachusetts ranged from 3 to over 60. I have included the counties of Maine in this estimate.

[15] In South Carolina, where the Provincial Convention appointed the local committee, I have compared the list of convention delegates with committee members and have used a total of the two to estimate the number of persons involved in enforcing the Association.

[16] More communities in New York are known to have rejected the Association than in all the other colonies combined. Only in New York City and in Albany do the committees appear to have been active prior to the engagement at Lexington.

[17] The size of county committees in Pennsylvania ranged from 15 in Berks to 70 in Chester. Nothing is known about committee activities in the two frontier counties of Cumberland and Lancaster.

[18] Two of the three counties in Delaware are known to have appointed committees of inspection before the battle at Lexington. One of these, Kent, elected more than 20, and it seems safe to assume that at least one of the others did as well. Since all three counties sent delegates to the Provincial Congress which endorsed nonimportation before the meeting of the Continental Congress, there seems to be no reason to suppose that any of the three refused to endorse the boycott later.

[19] Force, ed., *American Archives*, I, 1011, 1141.

and Baltimore counties each added 40 new members in January 1775, and Charles County increased the size of its committee by 16.[20] One resident of Baltimore made note of the reason for increasing committee membership there. In a letter to John Dickinson, Charles Ridgley admitted that although the committee had previously consisted of "no less than 70" members, it was enlarged because of the belief that "it wd. engage ye. Country People more warmly if gratified in a more Numerous Appointmt. amongst them."[21]

Other counties and other colonies entertained similar ideas. A broadside in Philadelphia argued in favor of appointing separate committees for the town and the county because, among other reasons, "by interesting people in most remote townships the enforcement will be more effective."[22] County committees in Pennsylvania and New Jersey often encouraged membership expansion by arranging for local districts to elect persons to represent them in enforcing the Association. In Harford County, Maryland, the committee decided to hold its meetings in different locations because "it is Necessary that the good People of this County be Informed of the Proceedings of their Deputies in Committee."[23] In almost every colony there were towns or counties that enlarged their committee membership despite the already total effectiveness of the nonimportation agreement.

Increased participation in government was also provided by the provincial congresses, which were much larger than the regularly established assemblies. The Boston Committee of Correspondence, in discussing plans for the colony's first congress, was "universally of Opinion that tis best to send as many Representatives as the Charter & Province Laws allow," and the Provincial Congress, meeting in Concord, repeatedly called on unrepresented towns to send delegates.[24] The South Carolina General Committee was larger than the Assembly in part because an early meeting of the committee had voted to create additional districts in the colony in order to insure a more equal representation. The *South Carolina Gazette* thought that the new convention was "the most complete Representation of all the whole Colony, that ever was, and perhaps ever will be obtained."[25]

In Massachusetts 279 persons were elected to the Provincial Con-

[20] *Ibid.*, I, 1143, 1173–74, 1082.

[21] Ridgley to Dickinson, Jan. 19, 1775, Logan Coll., Hist. Soc. Pa.

[22] Pinckney's *Va. Gaz.* (Williamsburg), Nov. 17, 1774.

[23] Apr. 5, 1775, Harford County, Maryland, Committee of Inspection Papers, Lib. Cong.

[24] Boston Comm. of Corres. to the Berkshire Co. Comm. of Corres., Sept. 24, 1774, Boston Comm. of Corres. Papers, N.Y. Pub. Lib.; Force, ed., *American Archives*, I, 848, 1007–8.

[25] On Nov. 8 the General Committee voted that the January meeting be composed of six deputies from every parish, "except St. Mark's, which, divided into three Dis-

gress of October 1774, and at least 250 of these appear to have attended.[26] Yet at the last session of the Assembly held in the Bay Colony, only 129 delegates were recorded present.[27] New Hampshire sent 144 members to its Convention in January 1775—more than triple the number of representatives in the Assembly.[28] That same month the Pennsylvania Convention met and, despite the failure of three counties to send delegates, counted almost three times as many members as the Assembly which met the following month.[29] In both New Jersey and Maryland the membership of the provincial congresses were more than twice that of the regular assemblies, and the South Carolina Provincial Congress, with some 180 members, was over three times as large as its Assembly.[30]

Although election to local committee membership or to a position in a provincial congress did not automatically insure active participation, it is significant that not more than half a dozen of the thousands so designated made any public attempt to renounce their appointment. The spring of 1775 found at least 7,000 persons publicly identified as leaders of a movement which the British government had already labeled as rebellion and would soon attempt to suppress forcibly. The success of the whigs in tying so substantial a group of local leaders to the enforcement of the Association was a psychological victory of the first magnitude. Individuals who participated in this first stage of the revolutionary movement, even those who simply allowed the use of their names, must have found it difficult to disassociate themselves later on.

In most cases committees and provincial congresses included many people who had long been active in local government. In Massachusetts towns, the selectmen sometimes acted as a local committee and in other cases met with the committees to concur in making important decisions.[31] Timothy Pickering, running for office in Essex

---

tricts, is to choose ten for each on Account of its great Extent and Populousness; and except Charlestown, the inhabitants whereof are to choose thirty" (*S.C. Gaz.* [Charleston], Nov. 21, 1774, and Jan. 23, 1775).

[26] Force, ed., *American Archives*, I, 830–34; Elbridge Gerry to S. Adams, Oct. 15, 1774, S. Adams Papers, N.Y. Pub. Lib.

[27] Force, ed., *American Archives*, I, 421.

[28] *Ibid.*, I, 1180, II, 519.

[29] *Ibid.*, I, 1169–70, 1280.

[30] Elizabeth Merritt, ed., *Archives of Maryland*, LXIV (Baltimore, 1947), xiii; Force, ed., *American Archives*, I, 438–39, 1031, 1109–10, II, 589, 685. The maximum possible attendance in the lower house of the Maryland Assembly was 58; 4 from each county and 2 from the city of Annapolis. Although the membership of the Congress came close to 100, it too could have been much larger. In May 1775 Harford County elected 16 delegates, Baltimore, 15, and Charles County, 16 (Harford Co., Md., Comm. of Inspection Papers, Lib. Cong.; Charles Ridgley to John Dickinson, Jan. 19, 1775, Logan Coll., Hist. Soc. Pa.; Force, ed., *American Archives*, II, 668).

[31] Selectmen of Acton to the Boston Comm. of Corres., Aug. 10, 1774, Middleborough Town Resolutions, Oct. 17, 1774, Northbridge, Mass., Comm. of Corres. and

County, circulated campaign endorsements signed by the selectmen and the committee from his native town of Salem.[32] From North Carolina, Governor Alexander Martin wrote that because the Convention and the Assembly in that colony were virtually identical in membership, he thought it would be of little use to ask one to condemn the other.[33] When Governor Dunmore dissolved the Virginia House of Burgesses, the counties almost without exception elected the same men to represent them in the Convention.[34] Moreover, a decided majority of the justices of the peace in the Old Dominion were committee members.[35] On the whole it is also clear that at the same time the leaders maintained their control, they deliberately extended participation in these new extralegal governments. This participation both broadened support for the whig leadership and, no doubt, pushed it toward a more radical position.[36]

In addition to providing an extensive popular base for future resistance to Parliament, the committees of inspection performed a wide assortment of duties. Although Congress outlined the method of electing committees, it left many of the details of organization to the peculiar needs of each community and authorized the adoption of "such further Regulations as they may think proper, for carrying

---

Selectmen to Boston Comm. of Corres., Aug. 7, 1774, Boston Comm. of Corres. Papers, N.Y. Pub. Lib.

[32] Timothy Pickering Papers, Mass. Hist. Soc.

[33] When Martin asked the Assembly to discourage the illegal meeting of the Congress, it answered that it was the "undoubted right" of the American colonies to petition for a redress of grievances. The Assembly also thought that the provincial convention "deserve not to be called an illegal meeting, or to have the imputation of sedition cast upon them" (Saunders, ed., *N.C. Records*, IX, 1198).

[34] Compare the membership of the House of Burgesses with that of the Convention (Kennedy, ed., *Journals of Burgesses*, XIII, 67–68; Force, ed., *American Archives*, I, 449, 493, 494, 523, 528, etc.).

[35] Comparison of the available lists of the justices of the peace with the committees appointed in 1774/75 shows some remarkable similarities. Of 13 justices listed for Warwick County in Oct. 1773, 11 appear on the Comm. of Inspection elected in Nov. 1774. Of 19 justices listed for Westmoreland in Oct. 1770, 15 were on the committee in Jan. 1775. In thirty counties where it was possible to obtain lists of both the justices and the committees, I found that at least 270 of 528 served in both capacities. This figure takes no account of the fact that many of the justice lists were three or four years old and may have included the names of persons deceased, retired, or removed to another county.

[36] The organization of militia companies was also used to increase participation in the whig movement. Thomas Young wrote from Newport that "Military Companies are forming and a great ambition runs through all ranks to become skillful in the use of arms. For God's sake endeavor to stir up some such thing in New York! No means which have hitherto been tried have served more to convert young gentlemen, of Tory sentiments, than to get them embodied with the Whigs and begin to taste of their Spirit by being often in their company" (Young to John Lamb, Nov. 19, 1774, John Lamb Papers, N.-Y. Hist. Soc.).

into execution this Association." Consequently the new system proved remarkably adaptable; as long as a committee continued to enjoy local support, it could extend its activities into almost any aspect of community life. This flexibility was to some extent restrained by the pressure of surrounding communities. An excellent example occurred in Falmouth, Virginia, where in January 1775 the citizens decided that a committee elected by themselves would be more sympathetic to the mercantile interests of the community than the one already established by King George County. Many county residents saw this as an attempt by the merchants in Falmouth to evade the Association, and so the King George Committee solicited advice from Richard Henry Lee concerning the legality of Falmouth's action. Lee replied that "the insertion of the word Town was intended only for the very populous large Towns in the North and the few considerable Ones that are to be met with in the Southern Provinces." Since the county had already appointed a committee, it would be "purely subversive" that a "small Village like Falmouth should presume to have a Committee of their own private and partial election whose determinations in a variety of Cases may differ from those of the said Committee of the County."[37] The King George County Committee subsequently called the Falmouth committee to appear at a meeting and explain its behavior. Each of the "culprits" was sentenced "agreeable to the method of advertising laid down by the Congress," although the county committee did prevent some residents of a more "Fiery disposition" from throwing the offenders "out of Windows . . . into the Street."[38]

The committees' activities affected almost every conceivable aspect of colonial life. They set the price of salt, promoted the manufacture of malt liquor, inspected customhouses, questioned those suspected of being tories, and even regulated the moral standards of the inhabitants. The first and most important of their duties was of course the enforcement of nonimportation. This function proved most time-consuming during the two-month period of grace Congress had granted to merchants who might have sent orders before the Association was approved.[39]

When a ship arrived in port during the months of December and January the local committee would appoint a number of its members to investigate. If the consignee elected to sell his merchandise at auction, the subcommittee then made provisions for the sale, adver-

[37] Lee to King George Co. Comm. of Inspection, n.d., Lee Family Papers, UVa. Lib. (microfilm, Col. Wmsbg. Foundation).

[38] William Allason to Thomas Markin, Feb. 6, 1775, William Allason Letterbook, Allason Papers, Virginia State Library, Richmond (microfilm, Col. Wmsbg. Foundation).

[39] Ford, ed., *Journals Cont. Cong.*, I, 78–79.

tised it in the local papers, and supervised the auction. The importer rarely chose the other two options, to return or to store his goods, because of the risk of damage and uncertainty as to the Association's duration. Moreover, the committees generally favored sale because of the problems involved in supervising storage and the prevailing notion that goods already imported might as well be made available to the public. In some cases, perhaps most, importers were permitted to buy back their goods at little or no additional cost. The Norfolk, Virginia, committee attempted to persuade a local doctor to sell badly needed medicines with the argument that the local inhabitants had never bid against the consignee unless it appeared that he had deliberately attempted to violate the Association.[40] Philadelphia and Wilmington, North Carolina, also permitted importers to repurchase their goods.[41]

Before the first of February, little reason existed for anyone to oppose the nonimportation clause of the Association, and the committees had a relatively easy time enforcing it. Exactly how much merchandise came into the several ports to be sold at auction is uncertain, but some idea may be gained from the reports of those committees which kept a record of their sales. The committee in Wilmington, North Carolina, reported that during the first two months of enforcing the Association, total sales reached £9,650. New York City's committee did not estimate total value but reported the sale of goods from twenty-one different vessels and calculated the profit for the Boston poor at £347. Salem counted £109 profit for Boston, and Plymouth sent £31.[42]

After February 1, the insistence that goods be shipped out of the colony meant a greater loss for the importer and, in spite of a reduction in the number of vessels entering port, brought increased efforts to evade the Association. Reshipment proved so expensive that some consignees elected to have their goods thrown overboard rather than sent to another port.[43] Importers made few attempts to violate the boycott forcibly, but they sometimes tried to smuggle goods into a colony or to obtain special permission from the committee.

In Baltimore, Dr. John Stevenson asked permission to land one hundred tons of British salt, contending that the product was ballast and thus not prohibited by the Association. When the committee refused, Stevenson proceeded to consign portions of the salt to local vessels for sale in other parts of the colony. Summoned before the

[40] Dixon and Hunter's *Va. Gaz.* (Williamsburg), Feb. 25, 1775.

[41] Cargo Manifests of the Nonimportation Association, Hist. Soc. of Pa.; Saunders, ed., *N.C. Records,* IX, 1098.

[42] *S.C. Gaz.* (Charleston), April 3, 1775; *New York Gazette and Weekly Mercury,* May 1, 1775; *Essex Gazette,* April 4, 1775.

[43] *S.C. Gaz.* (Charleston), Feb. 27, 1775.

committee to explain his behavior, the doctor replied that he had believed the decision applied only to the city of Baltimore. He then offered to furnish the names of each captain to whom he had consigned salt, promised to donate the proceeds from any sales already made to Boston, and guaranteed that the remainder should not be landed in any part of America between Nova Scotia and Georgia. The committee voted to accept his apology and then made certain that their prohibition would be effective by sending messages to inland committees suggesting that they be on the lookout for smuggled salt.[44]

The most notorious attempt to evade the nonimportation agreement occurred in New York City when the *Beulah,* arriving shortly after the February deadline, was refused permission to unload. Some of the tory elements in New York had expected the *Beulah* to be an important test case; Benjamin Booth wrote that the vessel was "daily expected from London, when the matter will come to a fair trial."[45] Perhaps because of the importance of this early case, the New York committee appointed a small group to keep the vessel under observation so long as it remained in the harbor. Despite these precautions, the captain managed to transfer a portion of the shipment onto a boat from Elizabethtown, New Jersey, in order to evade the Association.[46] This infraction came to the attention of the committee in Elizabethtown, and cooperation between that group and the New York City committee resulted in the apprehension of those involved. Robert and John Murray, owners of a major portion of the cargo, confessed before the New York committee, and Elizabethtown censured Ichabod Barnet for his part in the affair.[47] Both the persistence and the intercommittee cooperation demonstrated in this instance are typical of efforts throughout the colonies.

In many parts of the colonies where the commercial aspects of the Association were of minor importance, committees were appointed for entirely different reasons. The use of tea, for example, proved a major problem in many areas, and despite its symbolic representation of British tyranny, long years of habit made it a difficult vice to control. In Hartford, Connecticut, an elderly couple, distraught over the recent death of their daughter, brewed a pot of tea at the suggestion of neighbors. The town committee summoned them to appear. The couple apologized for their breach of the Association,

[44] *Md. Gaz.* (Baltimore), March 30, 1775; Mar. 22, 1775, Harford Co. Comm. of Inspection Papers, Lib. Cong.
[45] Booth to James & Drinker, Feb. 10, 1775, James & Drinker Business Papers, Hist. Soc. Pa.
[46] Force, ed., *American Archives,* I, 1257.
[47] *New York Journal,* Mar. 23, 1775; Benjamin Booth to James & Drinker, Feb. 22, 1775, March 2, 1775, March 20, 1775, James & Drinker Business Papers, Hist. Soc. Pa.

and the committee let them off with a warning.[48] In some areas the use of tea probably continued, at least in secret. One signer of the Association was permitted to append a note excepting the use of tea for his wife, and one New York merchant reported that "tea is bought, sold and drank as usual, in defiance of Congress and Committees."[49] But in general there can be little question that tea was an emblem of toryism and was eschewed by most colonists. John Harrower, a recent immigrant from England, reported that he had not tasted tea during a six-month stay in Virginia and supposed the prohibition of that article to be effective throughout the colonies.[50] Rumors that tea was unhealthy or that it was often used for embalming the dead and then sold to unwary tories may have helped to effect the boycott.[51]

Another aspect of the Association that occupied both local and provincial committees was the injunction to promote a program of economic nationalism. This provision promised not only to distress the British and lead to repeal of the Coercive Acts but also to lessen permanently the economic dependence of the colonies on the mother country. To encourage the development of home manufacturing, many committees offered premium payments to the first person who produced certain articles needed in the locality. Nearly all of these premiums aimed at stimulating the production of clothing or cotton and woolen goods. Essex County, Virginia, promised £50 to the person who first produced five hundred pairs of stockings within the county.[52] In North Carolina the Chowan County committee resolved in late January to promote a subscription to provide payments for the manufacture within the county of "Wire Wool and Cotten Cards, Fulled Woolen Cloth, Bleached Linen and Steel." By March 4, £80 had been subscribed, and the committee set up specific terms for awarding the prizes. They admitted that the amounts offered were small but hoped that other counties would join in helping them provide larger sums.[53]

Committees in every colony took steps to encourage the production of essential articles, and the proposal was considered advantageous even by many who opposed other provisions of the Association.[54] In both Pennsylvania and Virginia the provincial conventions adopted

[48] *Connecticut Gazette* (New London), April 14, 1775.

[49] Kenyek Shattuck, *A History of the Town of Concord* (Boston, 1835), 92–93; Benjamin Booth to James & Drinker, March 2, 1775, James & Drinker Business Papers, Hist. Soc. Pa.

[50] Edward Miles Riley, ed., *The Journal of John Harrower* (Williamsburg, Va., 1963), pp. 56, 73.

[51] *Essex Gaz.*, March 7, 1775.

[52] Force, ed., *American Archives*, II, 14.

[53] Saunders, ed., *N.C. Records*, IX, 1134, 1142.

[54] Charles Yates to Samuel Martin, July 5, 1774, Yates Letterbook, UVa. Lib. (microfilm, Col. Wmsbg. Foundation).

elaborate resolutions encouraging the manufacture of a variety of articles, including woolens, cottons, flannel, blankets, rugs, hosiery, coarse cloths, all sorts of dyes, flax, hemp, salt, saltpeter, gunpowder, nails, wire, steel, paper, glass, copper products, and malt liquors.[55] The Massachusetts Provincial Congress adopted a similar list with the addition of tin plates, firearms, and buttons.[56]

Local committees gave special attention to particular articles. From King and Queen County in Virginia a group of gentlemen reported an attempt "to extract molasses" from pumpkins and proclaimed that the effort had "yielded liquor of a good quality, and in such quantities that two rendered three quarts fit for distilling." From this experiment they concluded that it would not be long before the entire colony might "be thoroughly supplied with rum without extra-imports of molasses."[57] Upon reading this report, Landon Carter, not to be outdone, wrote to the *Virginia Gazette* that he had long been familiar with a procedure for extracting beer from corn stalks.[58]

One of the most ambitious programs the colonists attempted was the organization of "the United Company of Philadelphia for promoting American Manufactures." This group, set up in February 1775, was to consist of two hundred persons, each of whom would purchase a share in the company for £10. Their intention was to promote a factory for the production of linen and woolen and cotton cloth. On March 16 they met to elect officers. Daniel Roberdeau, president of the company, described the benefits that might be expected from the venture. He noted particularly the savings for the province in reducing foreign importation, employing local residents, lessening colonial dependence on Great Britain, and reducing importation of European vices. A few days later the company managers rented a house, and by the end of April the company was, at least temporarily, in regular operation.[59]

Almost all of the committees recognized the importance of protecting sheep as a means of reducing colonial dependence on Great Britain. Some even added their own provisions to the recommendations of Congress. In Virginia and Pennsylvania the provincial conventions forbade the slaughter of all sheep less than four years old, and the butchers of Philadelphia, at the request of the city committee, agreed not to slaughter any sheep before the first of May.[60] The *South Carolina Gazette* reported that neither lamb nor mutton had been

[55] Force, ed., *American Archives*, I, 1171–72, II, 170–71.

[56] *Ibid.*, I, 1001–2.

[57] *Essex Gaz.*, Feb. 28, 1775.

[58] Purdie's *Va. Gaz.* (Williamsburg), Feb. 17, 1775, supplement.

[59] Force, ed., *American Archives*, I, 1256–57, II, 140–42; William Duane, ed., *Extracts from the Diary of Christopher Marshall* (Albany, 1877), pp. 14, 16.

[60] Force, ed., *American Archives*, I, 1171–72, II, 170–71.

offered for sale in the city since the Association became effective.[61] So uniform was the prohibition of killing or exporting sheep that the committee in Newport, Rhode Island, wrote with some agitation to inquire whether it were true that the committee in Salem, Massachusetts, had permitted the sale of sheep to South Carolina. Salem admitted the truth of the charge but could not see "why the salt water which intervenes between some of the associated colonies should cut off or lessen ... trade ... any more than the small rivers or other boundaries between the New England colonies, among whom the usual commerce, particularly in Sheep, is continued."[62]

Among the most difficult, and pervasive, of the duties taken on by the committees of inspection was the enforcement of Congress's recommendations regarding frugality and simply living. Horse races, dances, gambling, county fairs, and all sorts of "dissipating vices" were canceled in obedience to the Association. The Baltimore County committee, after "reflecting on the many mischiefs and disorders, usually attending the fairs held at Baltimore town, and willing in all things, strictly to observe the regulations of the continental congress, who ... have advised to discountenance and discourage every species of dissipation, especially horse racing, cock fighting, etc., have unanimously resolved, to recommend it to the good people of this county, and do hereby earnestly request, that they will not themselves nor will suffer any of their families to attend, or in any wise encourage the approaching fair." The committee thought the fairs would serve no purpose save "debauching the morals of their children and servants, affording an opportunity for perpetrating thefts, encouraging riots, drunkenness, gaming, and the vilest immoralities."[63]

In North Carolina the annual horse races were canceled, and the Saint Cecilia Society in South Carolina suspended all concert plans.[64] The committee in Wilmington, North Carolina, condemned all balls and dancing, warned tavern keepers against permitting such entertainment in their establishments, and even forbade local residents from holding dancing parties in their homes.[65]

In the New England colonies the committees were no doubt even more thorough in their suppression of frivolity. A resolution passed in Marblehead, Massachusetts, condemned all dancing and feasting, and Portsmouth, New Hampshire, warned those who persisted in "Cards & Billiards" that they must discontinue such practices in

---

[61] March 6, 1775. See also Force, ed., *American Archives*, I, 1051; *Pa. Gaz.* (Phila.), Jan. 11, 1775, and *Pennsylvania Journal and Weekly Advertiser* (Phila.), Jan. 4, 1775.

[62] Salem, Mass., Comm. of Corres. to the Newport, R.I., Comm. of Corres., Feb. 22, 1775, Pickering Papers, Mass. Hist. Soc.

[63] *Md. Gaz.* (Annapolis), April 15, 1775.

[64] Saunders, ed., *N.C. Records*, IX, 1091; *S.C. Gaz.* (Charleston), Nov. 21, 1774.

[65] Saunders, ed., *N.C. Records*, IX, 1091.

these times of "deep distress and danger."[66] Somersworth, New Hampshire, hoped to suppress all kinds of "gaming, tavern haunting & idleness, that by frugality, industry and good economy we may be able to administer relief to our friends who stand in the gap."[67] In that same colony, Epsum condemned all those who tempted "Women, Girls and Boys, with their unnecessary Fineries, which is a Moth to our Country."[68]

The colonists accepted this interference in their social activities with little complaint. Virginia youths quite regularly apologized to their local committees for participating in horse races. Occasionally confusion arose over what constituted dissipation and what was good clean fun. A letter to the *Virginia Gazette* inquired whether a dance "tending to an innocent and pleasing intercourse between the two sexes" could be considered "extravagant, or fall under the description of dissipation." The writer could see no harm in such amusement "calculated evidently upon a frugal plan" but admitted that he found it difficult to be certain of the "true standard whereby we are to judge and determine between gaming and amusement." He concluded his letter by suggesting that it might be best to "desist altogether from playing, lest a contrariety of opinions and dissentions amongst the people may be introduced."[69]

No aspect of the Association better illustrates colonial determination and sincerity than the article calling for simplicity in the conduct of funerals. The purpose of this provision, like all those eschewing finery, was to lessen the dependence of the colonists on England by permanently reducing the quantity of goods purchased from British manufacturers. To this end, Congress resolved against the long-standing custom of wearing costly mourning garments at funerals and against the exchange of such expensive gifts as scarves and gloves. Newspaper reports indicate that this prohibition gained wide acceptance, and that it soon became a matter of local pride to note that even the wealthy were buried with a minimum of extravagance. The *South Carolina Gazette* reported the death of a prominent local woman and remarked that "few had more friends than this most amiable and excellent Lady, yet the latter Clause of the 8th Article of the Continental Association was strictly adhered to at this Funeral."[70] De-

---

[66] *Essex Gaz.*, Jan. 10, 1775; Nathaniel Bouton, ed., *Documents and Records Relating to the Province of New Hampshire*, VIII (Nashua, N.H., 1873), 445.

[67] William D. Knapp, *Annual Report of the City of Somersworth* (Somersworth, N.H., 1894), 61.

[68] *New Hampshire Gazette* (Portsmouth), Jan. 20, 1775.

[69] Dixon and Hunter's *Va. Gaz.* (Williamsburg), Jan. 28, 1775.

[70] Dec. 19, 1774. See also *Massachusetts Spy* (Boston), Nov. 24, 1774; *Conn. Gaz.* (New London), Dec. 16, 1774; *Pa. Gaz.* (Phila.), Nov. 9, 1774; *N.H. Gaz.* (Portsmouth), Jan. 20, 1775; *N.Y. Gaz.*, Jan. 16, 1775.

spite the delicate nature of the offense some committees passed resolutions to enforce this provision. The Newburyport, Massachusetts,
committee recommended the boycott of all funerals not conforming
to the requirements for simplicity in mourning.[71]

Such a variety of activities made it necessary for the committees to
employ many methods of detecting violators. Larger committees often
divided themselves and assigned different groups to specific aspects
of enforcement. Some of these groups might be sent to neighboring
committees to exchange information or instructed to visit all persons
in town and ascertain their opinions about contemporary affairs. New
York City appointed a subcommittee to maintain a watch over the
vessels entering the harbor, and many committees circulated copies
of the Association and required all inhabitants to sign a pledge that
they would obey the agreement. Especially popular in Virginia and
Massachusetts, this practice found favor in various towns throughout
the colonies. Groton, Massachusetts, voted to enter the names of all
persons who refused to sign the document in the town records and on
April 12 listed four persons for that offense.[72] Acton, also in the Bay
Colony, decided that signers should include every person over sixteen.[73] Women were not normally required to sign, although some
who were property holders did so.

Some committees appointed certain persons to circulate the Association for signatures, and in other cases the entire committee appealed to local citizens. In Wilmington, North Carolina, the committee voted to "go in a body and wait on all the Householders in
Town, with the Association before mentioned, and request their signing it, or declare their reasons for refusing, that such Enemies to their
Country may be set forth to public view and treated with the contempt they merit." The committee found one doctor, seven merchants, a planter, and two tailors who refused to sign and later published the names of the eleven as recommended by the Association.[74]
The committee in Norfolk, Virginia, on the other hand, seems to have
assumed that persons who did not sign the Association did not have
to abide by its terms—although they were not, of course, permitted
to engage in importing British goods.[75]

[71] Benjamin Labaree, *Patriots and Partisans: The Merchants of Newburyport* (Cambridge,
Mass., 1962), pp. 36–37.

[72] Caleb Butler, *History of the Town of Groton, Massachusetts* (Boston, 1848), 124.

[73] Samuel Adams Drake, *History of Middlesex County, Massachusetts,* I (Boston, 1880),
199.

[74] Saunders, ed., *N.C. Records,* IX, 1150, 1152, 1166. On March 13 the committee reported that eight of the recalcitrant citizens had changed their minds and "subscribed
their names within the time limited."

[75] James Parker to Charles Steuart, Dec. 6, 1774, and Feb. 11, 1775, Steuart Papers,
Nat'l. Lib. of Scotland (microfilm, Col. Wmsbg. Foundation).

Many committees found it difficult to determine whether a certain parcel of goods had been imported before or after the Association went into effect. Windham, Connecticut, suggested that the seaport towns make a list of those who were considered enemies of the Association so that the districts in the interior might refuse to accept their goods.[76] In many localities merchants had to show a certificate from a committee at the point of entry stating that the goods had been brought in according to the rules of Congress. Virginia's Governor Dunmore, for example, found that some of the goods he had imported and sent to the western part of the colony were accompanied by such a certificate.[77] Traveling salesmen complicated this problem by selling merchandise from door to door. More than one committee passed resolutions regulating or even prohibiting these itinerant traders. New Market, New Hampshire, resolved that any "Inhabitant that shall harbour any Hawker, Pedler, or Petty Chapman, offering as such, to purchase or sell any Goods, Wares, or Merchandise shall be esteemed and treated as an Enemy of his Country."[78] The committee in Westmoreland County, Virginia, ordered vendors selling goods there to produce proof that they had imported their merchandise before February 1.[79]

Judging from the records of committee activities, the article asking merchants not to take advantage of the nonimportation to raise prices proved most difficult to enforce. To seek out violators the committees often called upon various merchants to open their books for inspection. In Caroline County, Virginia, three subcommittees were appointed to investigate the books of certain merchants to see if they were guilty of raising prices. Six of these at first refused to cooperate, but after being publicly condemned as enemies of their country, they submitted.[80] These gentlemen were not so clever as Robert Gilmore of Northumberland County, Virginia. Accused of selling pins at too high a price, Gilmore persuaded the committee to give him a clean bill of health when some of his friends swore that he had charged the same price for at least four years previous.[81]

Enforcement of the Association varied in any number of ways from colony to colony, and even from town to town. In some places unique "crimes" forced the committees to add new offenses to the list forwarded by Congress. Deerfield, Massachusetts, broke off all "com-

[76] Windham, Conn., to the Boston Comm. of Corres., Dec. 10, 1774, Boston Comm. of Corres. Papers, N.Y. Pub. Lib.

[77] William Allason to Andrew Sproule, May 28, 1775, Allason Letterbook, Allason Papers, Va. State Lib. (microfilm, Col. Wmsbg. Foundation).

[78] *N.H. Gaz.*, Jan. 20, 1775.

[79] Force, ed., *American Archives*, I, 1222.

[80] T. E. Campbell, *Colonial Caroline* (Richmond, 1954), pp. 236-38.

[81] Pinckney's *Va. Gaz.* (Williamsburg), Jan. 19, 1775.

mercial connection" with one John Williams because he appeared at
the town meeting and "read the several definitions of treason, and
their horrible punishments."[82] In other towns the committees
adopted special measures to insure that every citizen agreed with
the Association. Hingham, Massachusetts, sought to insure cooperation by persuading the two town ministers to appear at a meeting
and encourage all the inhabitants to obey the Continental Congress.[83] New Cambridge, Connecticut, was less subtle. That town
appointed a special committee to interview all persons suspected of
being "unsound in their political sentiments" and presumably to
ostracize those whom they found guilty.[84] Punishment seems also to
have varied not only from place to place but with individuals. Long-
time residents enjoyed greater immunity, and some committees
waited for weeks to publish the names of offenders because of their
reluctance to expose "fellow townsmen" to such castigation. Such
leniency did not of course apply to strangers. The committee in
Rehoboth, Massachusetts, allowed Caleb Wheaton, "who lately
came here from the Eastward," exactly twelve hours to "depart the
Town."[85]

The procedures adopted by the committees in investigating cases
of violation also varied. New Haven County in Connecticut adopted
an extraordinarily detailed set of regulations, which were then
adopted throughout the province. These rules provided that any person accused of a violation should be notified of the charge in a summons issued to him and signed by at least one member of the committee. This summons explained the charges brought against the accused
and asked him to appear before the committee and defend himself.
Each summons had to specify a time and place for the defendant to
appear and was to be served not less than six days prior to the appointed hearing. Members of the committee promised that the charge
would be thoroughly heard and the accused given ample opportunity
to present his case. To assure the fairest possible decision, no member involved in bringing the charge or in presenting evidence could
vote to condemn the accused except "upon the fullest, clearest and
most convincing Proof."[86]

The procedures endorsed by the New Haven committee, though

[82] *Boston Evening Post,* Mar. 20, 1775, transcript among the Peter Force Duplicates,
packet for Feb. 1775, Lib. Cong.

[83] Falmouth, Mass., appointed a committee to wait upon the "several Ministers of
this Town, and desire them to propose a Contribution . . . for the relief of the Town of
Boston" (Falmouth Resolves, July 21, 1774, Boston Comm. of Corres. Papers, N.Y.
Pub. Lib.).

[84] Carleton Beals, *The Making of Bristol, Connecticut* (Boston, 1954), p. 59.

[85] *Providence Gaz.,* Feb. 4, 1775.

[86] *Conn. Gaz.* (New London), Feb. 17, 1775.

more detailed than most, were probably not atypical. Because there was not a great deal of opposition to the Association, the committees usually did not find it necessary to proceed harshly. Many offenders were repeatedly summoned to appear before they were condemned, and in many instances persons were judged guilty and then forgiven on the basis of a simple apology. On the other hand, there is no doubt that several of the committees made themselves unpopular and that the sudden acquisition of almost unlimited power must have fed the egos of unnumbered tyrants. Charles Yates wrote from Virginia that dictatorial power was "lodged with Men whom I should think must themselves be surprised at the great authority they have stepd. into."[87]

Exactly how far the punishment of being condemned an "Enemy to the Liberties" of America extended also varied. Harwich, Massachusetts, although determined to boycott all those who did not obey Congress, agreed that it would be going too far to refuse to "grind" for enemies of the country.[88] Westmoreland County, Virginia, published the name of a local schoolteacher, David Wardrob, and insisted that all persons who had sent their children to him should "immediately take them away" because he was a "wicked enemy to America." The committee also instructed Cople Parish "no longer to furnish the said Wardrob with the use of the vestryhouse for his keeping school therein."[89]

The most detailed statement of punishment was that adopted by Sutton, Massachusetts. Having warned that any person who continued to associate with those found guilty of violating the resolves of Congress would himself be subject to exposure as an enemy of his country, the committee proceeded to explain exactly what was allowed. One might associate with an "enemy" provided that "it shall appear to the Committee that such person did no more than to help in case of absolute sickness or some casualty, in which a Building or the Life of some person or creature was in danger of immediately perishing, or spake nothing other to the offender than to demand, or pay a debt or Tax, or about the Things of the Eternal World, or to convince him or her of his or their error in transgressing as above, or if he only spake a word inadvertently, and desisted upon being reminded of the state of such Offender."[90]

This sort of punishment proved quite effective. Rarely did an offender hold out for long under pressure from the local committee and

---

[87] Yates to Samuel Martin, Feb. 20, 1775, Yates Letterbook, UVa. Lib. (microfilm, Col. Wmsbg. Foundation).

[88] Paine, *Harwich*.

[89] Pinckney's *Va. Gaz.* (Williamsburg), Feb. 9, 1775.

[90] William A. Benedick and Hiram A. Tracy, *History of the Town of Sutton, Massachusetts* (Worcester, 1878), p. 94.

community. A typical apology was that of Andrew Leckie, printed in the *Virginia Gazette*. Admitting that he had spoken evil of the delegates to the Continental Congress, Leckie found himself at a loss to explain "how such words should escape from a person of my sentiments." He added that "having made this open and candid confession of my folly, I hope to regain the favour and good opinion of the public; an assurance of which would be the greatest consolation I could have under the insupportable weight of public censure and public hatred."[91]

No aspect of the committee system is more intriguing than the role that it played in arousing, or suppressing, mob violence. Virginia's Governor Dunmore contended that the use of coercion was widespread. He wrote that the committees in Virginia had assumed total authority in most counties; they watched "the conduct of every inhabitant, without distinction, and . . . send for all such as come under their suspicion into their presence; to interrogate them respecting all matters which, at their pleasure, they think fit objects of their inquiry." To stigmatize "such as they find transgressing what they are now hardy enough to call the Laws of the Congress" was, according to Dunmore, "no other than inviting the vengeance of an outrageous and lawless mob to be exercised upon the unhappy victims."[92]

Dunmore's charge of mob violence was often repeated by opponents of the Association, and yet it appears that the committees more often acted to suppress lawlessness than to encourage it. The committee in Falmouth, Massachusetts, resolved to "exert their utmost endeavors to prevent all the inhabitants to this Town from engaging in any riots, tumults, and insurrections, or attacks on the private property of any person." Falmouth thought that such activities were "pernicious to the real interest . . . as well as injurious to the liberty of *America* in general."[93] The town meeting in Somersworth, New Hampshire, also viewed the Committee system as a support for order in society and instructed its own group to suppress "vice and criminality." Wilbraham, Massachusetts, resolved that "the many Mobs & Riotous Practices that have been amongst us have been so far from helping the Common Cause of Liberty, that they have retarded it."[94] Thomas Ellison, a New York merchant, urged his father and brother to sign the Association because the weakness of civil government made it necessary to support the committees "to keep order, and prevent running into confusion, till these troubles can be settled."[95]

[91] Pinckney's *Va. Gaz.* (Williamsburg), Nov. 14, 1774.

[92] Gov. Dunmore to the Earl of Dartmouth, Dec. 24, 1774, Force, ed., *American Archives*, I, 1061–62.

[93] *Ibid.*, II, 313.

[94] Wilbraham Town Resolutions, July 29, 1774, Boston Comm. of Corres. Papers, N.Y. Pub. Lib.

[95] Ellison to his father, Apr. 29, 1775, *Magazine of American History*, VIII (1882), 283.

In almost every case where violence occurred the committees opposed it. In Cumberland County, New Jersey, some members of the committee seized some tea landed at Greenwich and resolved to store it until the full committee could meet and discuss its final disposition. During the night a group of more zealous local inhabitants carried the tea away and destroyed it. The committee later held a meeting and condemned this procedure as an unnecessary act of violence.[96] An even better example of committee problems with unruly persons is found in the records of Newburyport, Massachusetts, where the group apprehended a store of East India tea and decided that it ought to be confiscated and stored. This decision aroused the ire of certain unidentified citizens who took possession of the tea and destroyed it. At the annual town meeting, the Newburyport committee appealed to the assembled freeholders for support, and the meeting voted its unanimous approval of the conduct of the committee, finding "the manner in which the Tea was taken out of their hands by no means Justifiable."[97] Such incidents occurred in almost all of the other colonies.

Nevertheless the committees did face a serious problem in their efforts to enforce the Association and at the same time maintain local order. They were, after all, engaged in an extralegal activity that could be pursued only in defiance of the regularly established government. There was no basis in law for the proceedings of the committees, and some quite openly admitted that when individuals refused to obey the resolutions of Congress, it might be necessary to adopt coercive methods. A county congress in Worcester, Massachusetts, condemned the use of violence "except so much as is necessary to carry the Resolves of the Continental and Provincial Congresses into Execution."[98]

As the regular local governments declined in power, the committees gradually extended their authority. In December 1774 the Provincial Convention in Maryland recommended that each county collect funds to buy military provisions; by the first of the year several of them had begun to do so.[99] In January 1775 the members of the committee in Fairfax County, Virginia, noted the example set by Maryland and also voted a tax for military supplies.[100] This extension of power made it increasingly necessary for the committees to insist that the inhabitants render them the same kind of obedience they had previously given the constitutionally established governments.

[96] *Pa. Gaz.* (Phila.), Jan. 4, 1775; Joseph Sickler, *Tea Burning Town* (New York, 1950).

[97] Labaree, *Patriots and Partisans*, 37.

[98] Force, ed., *American Archives*, I, 1194.

[99] *Pa. Gaz.* (Phila.), Dec. 21, 1774; Minutes, Jan. 2, 1775, Jan. 23, 1775, Feb. 23, 1775, Harford County, Md., Comm. of Inspection Papers, Lib. Cong.

[100] Force, ed., *American Archives*, I, 1145.

Since this was the only way to prevent anarchy, it was little wonder that so many committees handed out their stiffest penalties to those who made slurs on the dignity of their proceedings. The committees of inspection were in the process of becoming committees of safety, and the possibility that they would take on the full responsibilities of revolutionary government was rapidly growing. Effective government requires the threat, and often the use, of coercion.

CHAPTER IX

Great Britain Declares War

THE adoption of the Continental Association signaled the British government's failure to isolate and subdue Massachusetts. In deciding upon a new policy, the North ministry had to consider not only the crisis in Massachusetts but the stated resolution of the other colonies to join in opposing attempts to discipline that colony. Only two courses of action remained open. The British cabinet could abandon its effort to force colonial acceptance of parliamentary supremacy, or it could attempt to implement that policy through more aggressive measures. On that decision depended the future of the empire.

Many colonists had hoped that the endorsement of the Continental Association would persuade the North ministry to alter its policy or perhaps result in the appointment of a new cabinet. Others were not so optimistic. John Adams, writing in 1818, recalled that Virginia's delegation to the Congress had held widely divergent views on the question. Richard Henry Lee thought the colonists would "infallibly carry" all their points, Patrick Henry believed it would be necessary to fight in order to win redress, and George Washington "doubted between the two."[1]

Had the colonists been more familiar with conditions in Great Britain, fewer would have entertained hopes of compromise. Without exception the members of the cabinet were determined to stand firm in their policy toward the colonies, and George III heartily endorsed that conviction. Even before Congress formulated its program the king had clearly stated his opinion that the government could not compromise. He thought that "the dye is now cast, the Colonies must either submit or triumph." Although the king agreed that the cabinet ought not come to "severer measures," he also insisted that "we must not retreat; by coolness and an unremitted pursuit of the measures that have been adopted I trust they will come to submit."[2]

Several factors had contributed to strengthening the opinion that the aggressive policy initiated by the Coercive Acts must be continued. Among these were the repeated injunctions of the colonial

---

[1] J. Adams to William Wirt, Jan. 23, 1818, C. F. Adams, ed., *Works of J. Adams*, X, 278–79.
[2] George III to Lord North, Sept. 11, 1774, Fortescue, ed., *Corres. of George III*, III, 131.

governors. Gage in Massachusetts proposed that the government should immediately begin hiring Hanoverian and Hessian mercenaries for action in America since "these provinces must be first totally subdued before they will obey."[3] Thomas Hutchinson, who had only recently arrived in Great Britain from Massachusetts, endorsed the coercive policy adopted by the government in the spring of 1774 and reported to George III that the Boston Port Act constituted the only effective means of bringing the colonists to a "speedy submission."[4]

The proceedings of the Continental Congress increased these demands for determined action. Virginia's Governor Dunmore hoped that "these undutiful People" would be forced to endure the misery "of which they have themselves laid the foundation."[5] From North Carolina, Governor Martin expressed indignant "revoltings" at the proceedings in Philadelphia and predicted that the crisis had come. He thought that "Britain must assert and establish her just Rights and authority in the Colonies whatever they may be or give up forever all pretensions to dominion over them."[6]

Another factor reinforcing British determination to force the issue with the colonies was the widespread opinion that the Americans would not fight. Just as the colonists believed that the ministry would retreat in the face of a united refusal to obey the Coercive Acts, the cabinet was convinced that the Americans would back down once they realized that Britain intended to stand firm. Before his departure from England, General Gage had assured the king that if Britain was resolute the colonists would "undoubtedly prove very meek."[7] Henry Ellis, governor of Georgia from 1757 to 1760, expressed a typical point of view in writing that as far as the Bostonians were concerned, he had "no apprehensions from their power, nor yet from their courage."[8] Governor Hutchinson had reported the people of Boston "much dispirited" by the new British attitude of determination, and as late as April 1775 he predicted that they would not fight.[9]

Reports from the troops stationed in Boston increased the conviction that the colonists were bluffing. In September 1774 Gage wrote

[3] Thomas Gage to Thomas Hutchinson, Sept. 17, 1774, *Dartmouth MSS*, II, 226.

[4] George III to Lord North, July 1, 1774, Fortescue, ed., *Corres. of George III*, III, 116.

[5] Gov. Dunmore to the Earl of Dartmouth, Dec. 24, 1774, C.O. 5/1353/47–48, Public Record Office, London (Library of Congress Transcripts).

[6] Gov. Martin to the Earl of Dartmouth, Dec. 4, 1774, Saunders, ed., *N.C. Records*, IX, 1083–84.

[7] George III to Lord North, Feb. 4, 1775, Fortescue, ed., *Corres. of George III*, III, 59.

[8] Ellis to Henry Knox, June 27, 1774, Historical Manuscripts Commission, *Reports*, ser. 55, *Manuscripts in Various Collections*, VI (Dublin, 1909), 112.

[9] George III to Lord North, July 1, 1774, Fortescue, ed., *Corres. of George III*, III, 116; Peter O. Hutchinson, ed., *Diary and Letters of His Excellency Thomas Hutchinson* (Boston, 1884), p. 428.

that the army did not hold the provincials in "high Estimation."[10] Hugh Percy, a ranking officer in that army and later Duke of Northumberland, described the inhabitants as "sly, artful, hypocritical rascals," labeled them cowards, and admitted that he could not but "despise them compleately."[11] An army captain there, W. Glanville Evelyn, wrote his father that while "on paper" the Bostonians appeared the "bravest fellows in the world," there existed no greater set of "rascals and poltroons."[12] Another officer thought that if it came to blows, "any two Regiments here" would be able to defeat the "whole force of the *Massachusetts* Province."[13] A number of the troops, according to Evelyn, not only disliked the provincials but eagerly hoped for the chance to engage them in battle: "Never did any nation so much deserve to be made an example of to future ages, and never were any set of men more anxious (than we) to be employed on so laudable a work. We only fear they will avail themselves of the clemency and generosity of the English, and by some abject submission evade the chastisement due to unexampled villainy, and which we are so impatiently waiting to inflict."[14]

A third consideration contributing to the cabinet's continuing inflexibility was the conviction that American resistance had been augmented by factionalism in Great Britain. Criticisms of British policy by such men as Lord Chatham, Edmund Burke, and John Wilkes, the ministry believed, had given the Americans reason to expect support for their demands by a sizable group in the mother country. Once the ministers demonstrated the determination of Parliament to subdue the colonies, the disturbances would cease. As James Murray wrote from Boston, "it has not been without great Nursing & tenderness from both sides of the Atlantick, that this fiend, Rebellion, is now come to be such a Giant."[15] To correct the "erroneous" notions that had helped propel the Americans into resistance, Lord Dartmouth sent a circular letter to the colonial governors. According to Dartmouth, the government believed that the firmness of the king's speech and the resolutions of Parliament would "remove those false impressions which have been made upon the minds of his Majesty's subjects in *America*." Such determination on the part of

[10] Gage to the Earl of Dartmouth, Sept. 2, 1774, C. E. Carter, ed., *Gage Correspondence* (New Haven, 1931–33), I, 371.

[11] Hugh Earl Percy, *Letters from Boston and New York*, ed. Charles K. Bolton (Boston, 1902), p. 31.

[12] Capt. Evelyn to his father, July 6, 1774, G. D. Schull, ed., *Memoir and Letters of Captain W. Glanville Evelyn of the Fourth Regiment* (Oxford, 1879), p. 27.

[13] From an officer at Boston, Nov. 22, 1774, Force, ed., *American Archives*, I, 992.

[14] Capt. Evelyn to Mrs. Leveson Gower, Dec. 6, 1774, Schull, ed., *Memoir and Letters of Evelyn*, p. 43.

[15] Murray to Charles Steuart, May 15, 1775, Steuart Papers, Nat'l. Lib. of Scotland (microfilm, Col. Wmsbg. Foundation).

Great Britain would dispel "those expectations of support in their unwarrantable pretensions, which have been held forth by artful and designing men."[16]

All these factors encouraged the government to pursue the policy outlined by the legislation passed in the early months of 1774. America had to accept her position of subordination within the British Empire, and this could be achieved only through a determined enforcement of the Coercive Acts. This determination of the cabinet to force American acceptance of parliamentary supremacy dominated British colonial policy from 1774 until after the Battle of Saratoga in 1777. Undoubtedly the ministry would have preferred to achieve this end without bloodshed, but as subsequent events would illustrate, the government was prepared to implement its policy by force if that proved necessary.

News that an American Continental Congress would meet in early September 1774 forced the British government to confront the possibility of an extended struggle. If the other colonies rallied to the support of Massachusetts, it would be necessary to adopt even more forceful measures. In order to catch their opponents unprepared, the ministry suddenly and unexpectedly dissolved Parliament in late September and called new elections.[17] This move resulted in a strong pro-government majority and assured the cabinet that measures taken in response to the Congress could be carried through without the interruption of a general election. Lord North openly admitted in a conversation with Thomas Hutchinson that "Parliament was dissolved on this account—that we might, at the beginning of a Parliament take such measures as we could depend upon a Parliament to prosecute to effect."[18]

While the ministry prepared to meet any situation resulting from the decisions of the Continental Congress, a more immediate threat of disruption loomed in Massachusetts. Since the arrival of General Gage in May 1774 the British government in Massachusetts had almost ceased to function outside the well-guarded confines of Boston. This crisis in the Bay Colony was of utmost importance. From the British, as well as the American, viewpoint, Massachusetts would be the testing ground. Whatever measures the British adopted to meet the resolutions of Congress would be implemented in the Bay Colony.

On September 2 General Gage wrote to Dartmouth in terms so alarming as to suggest that open conflict between his troops and the

[16] The Earl of Dartmouth to the Governors of the Several Colonies, Dec. 10, 1774, Force, ed., *American Archives*, I, 1034–35.

[17] The proclamation of dissolution was issued on Sept. 30, 1774 (Force, ed., *American Archives*, I, 810–11).

[18] P. O. Hutchinson, ed., *Diary and Letters of T. Hutchinson*, p. 298.

inhabitants of Massachusetts could not be avoided much longer. The governor proclaimed that civil government was "near its End" and predicted that "we shall shortly be without either Law, or legislative power." He strongly recommended that the cabinet adopt aggressive measures.

I mean my Lord to recurr all I can by Degrees, to avoid any bloody Crisis as long as possible, unless forced into it by themselves, which may happen. His Majesty will in the mean Time Judge what is best to be done, but your Lordship will permit me to mention, that as it is Judged here, that it will be resolved to stem the Torrent, and not yield to it, that a very respectable Force shou'd take the Field. The Regiments are now composed of small Numbers, and Irregulars will be very necessary in this Country, many of which of one Sort or other I conceive may be raised here. Nothing that is said at present can palliate, Conciliating, Moderation, Reasoning is over, Nothing can be done but by forceable Means. Tho' the People are not held in high Estimation by the Troops, yet they are numerous, worked up to a Fury, and not a Boston Rabble but the Freeholders and Farmers of the Country. A Check any where wou'd be fatal, and the first Stroke will decide a great deal. We shou'd therefore be strong and proceed on a good Foundation before any thing decisive is tried, which it's to be presumed will prove successfull.[19]

Gage's efforts to convince the ministry that a large force was required to subdue the New England colonies were only partially successful. The belief persisted that the Americans were neither brave enough nor sufficiently disciplined to fight effectively. The warnings seemed to the ministers a reflection of some timidity on Gage's part. When Gage wrote Hutchinson in November suggesting that the Coercive Acts be suspended to gain time for the recruitment of a force adequate to implement them, George III ridiculed the idea as "the most absurd that can be suggested."[20] Lord North noted that he knew of no provision for suspending the acts of Parliament, and Lord Suffolk advocated Gage's immediate removal. William Knox reported that the suggestion had turned the entire cabinet against the Massachusetts governor.[21]

The ministry did agree with Gage that action must be taken to bring Massachusetts into line, and it debated several means of effecting that goal. Among the measures most often considered were proposals for arresting certain colonial leaders and bringing them to trial for treason. The assumption that a majority in America supported British policy had led to the conclusion that the seizure of a few malcontents would result in the collapse of resistance to British authority. If such leaders as Samuel Adams and John Hancock could be

19 Gage to the Earl of Dartmouth, Sept. 2, 1774, Carter, ed., *Gage Corres.*, I, 371–72.
20 George III to Lord North, Nov. 18, 1774, Fortescue, ed., *Corres. of George III*, III, 154.
21 *Dartmouth MSS,* I, 370; *MSS in Various Collections,* VI, 257.

eliminated, so the cabinet reasoned, the disturbances in America would end.

The government laid several plans for seizing American leaders during the spring and summer of 1774 but abandoned each of them for one reason or another. John Pownall told Hutchinson that he had personally opposed the Massachusetts Government Act and had proposed instead that the Massachusetts authorities be instructed to "send over Adams, Molineux and other principal Incendiaries; and if found guilty, put them to death." Pownall added that "the Lords of the Privy Council actually had their pens in their hands, in order to sign the Warrant" but that "Lord Mansfield diverted it by urging the other measures."[22]

Throughout 1774 the cabinet made several attempts to obtain evidence of treason on the part of various American leaders. It repeatedly consulted Solicitor General Wedderburn and Attorney General Thurlow as to whether a particular act, or series of acts, could legally be construed as treason. In June, Lord Dartmouth asked Gage to obtain the originals of certain letters written by Benjamin Franklin and Arthur Lee, both of whom were then in England, which "might be the grounds of a proper Proceeding thereupon."[23]

Shortly after the news of the Boston Tea Party arrived in England, Thurlow and Wedderburn reported that the destruction of the cargo and the events leading up to it constituted "high treason," but they expressed doubts that sufficient evidence could be collected to assure a conviction.[24] Adoption of the Continental Association again raised the question, and Lord North was instructed to consult the attorney and solicitor-general concerning affairs in Massachusetts. If persons in that colony were found to have participated in open rebellion, then the legal experts were to draft a proclamation demanding that they either surrender or be proclaimed traitors.[25] On December 13 Thurlow and Wedderburn submitted the opinion that rebellion had broken out in Massachusetts, but they warned that all the province except Boston seemed united in refusing the king's government. As for the proclamation, they asked for "Your Lordships directions, concerning the terms which it is meant to hold out."[26]

As October passed it became evident that the Continental Congress would adopt measures in support of Massachusetts Bay. The Suffolk Resolves and the warning to merchants that nonimportation might be adopted arrived in Great Britain before the Association it-

[22] P. O. Hutchinson, ed., *Diary and Letters of T. Hutchinson,* p. 183; for a detailed account, see Donoughue, *Brit. Politics and the Amer. Revolution,* pp. 36–72.

[23] Earl of Dartmouth to Gage, June 3, 1774, Carter, ed., *Gage Corres.,* II, 167.

[24] C.O. 5/160 (Lib. Cong. Transcripts).

[25] Minutes of cabinet meeting held Dec. 1, 1774, *Dartmouth MSS,* I, 371.

[26] C.O. 5/159 (Lib. Cong. Transcripts).

self and strengthened the cabinet's determination to prepare for the worst.[27] As early as September 21 Lord North told Hutchinson that if the colonists adopted a commercial embargo, the cabinet was prepared to interdict American trade with the rest of the world.[28] Lord Dartmouth, commenting on the adoption of the Suffolk Resolves, gave it as his opinion that the government could not retreat.[29]

In early December news of the Continental Association arrived in London. On the fourteenth Dartmouth told Hutchinson that he considered everyone who signed the document guilty of treason and that the "most vigorous measures" would be pursued immediately to punish those involved. Yet despite the cabinet's determination to adopt stringent measures, it paused to observe the Christmas holidays. Dartmouth explained that the affair must be deliberated upon and expressed doubt that anything could be pushed through Parliament before its holiday adjournment. Knox told Hutchinson that a final decision must wait until after the vacation, but he indicated that a major alteration of policy was in the offing when he added that a stop would be put to measures that "were intended and to a ship under orders."[30]

Hutchinson, who advocated immediate and determined action, disapproved of the delay. He noted a "strange silence" on American affairs which he attributed to "amazement." Even after Christmas the former governor of Massachusetts found that "Lord North is gone to Banbury, Ld. Rochford to his seat, and there is the appearance of all the tranquility which might be expected if America was perfectly quiet."[31]

One explanation of this "strange silence" is found in the ministry's desire to mask its intentions. Representatives of the several colonies were at first led to believe that the resolutions of Congress would be given serious consideration. Less than two weeks after he had verbally condemned those who signed the Association as traitors, Lord Dartmouth reported that the king had received the petition of the Congress "very graciously."[32] Rumors prevailed in London that the decisions made in Philadelphia had forced the government to make concessions in order to conciliate American opinion.

Among those who accepted this viewpoint was Arthur Lee. He thought the ministry "disposed to give some relief" and advised his fellow countrymen to insist upon a "total compliance." Lee even

[27] P. O. Hutchinson, ed., *Diary and Letters of T. Hutchinson*, p. 273.

[28] *Ibid.*, p. 245.

[29] *Ibid.*, pp. 324–25.

[30] *Ibid.*, p. 325.

[31] *Ibid.*, p. 336.

[32] William Bollan, Benjamin Franklin, and Arthur Lee to the Speaker of the Delaware Assembly, Dec. 24, 1774, Force, ed., *American Archives*, II, 127.

suggested that the North ministry might be forced out of office and expressed his belief that the Rockinghams could be expected to join in supporting colonial demands. This opposition, "supported by the popular voice and petitions of the merchants," he labeled "irristible."[33]

Actually, the merchants had made no serious effort to pressure the ministry into complying with American demands, and in any case the popular voice could not be expected to have a strong effect on the British government. Although a number of merchants petitioned Parliament, their efforts were aimed more at pleasing the colonists than at changing government policy. One of the few points on which Hutchinson and William Lee agreed was that the merchants acted to protect their reputations with customers in America rather than for any other purpose.[34] Lee urged his brother Richard Henry "to pay no attention to the proceedings of the merchants. I am one of a Committee for drawing their petition, and can assure you it is only a blind to recover their lost reputation in America."[35]

There was no doubt that Parliament would support the ministry. A vast majority of the members elected in the autumn of 1774 either agreed with the effort to discipline America or were sufficiently indebted to the existing government to support its policies. The dissolution of Parliament had been remarkably effective in providing the North ministry with a compliant majority. The cabinet was able to pursue its colonial policy for many years without undue concern for the opposition in Parliament.

No man in England was more determined to use that favorable majority than George III. Convinced that only resolute action could save the empire, the king repeatedly advocated the adoption of forceful measures toward America. When Lord North and Pownall suggested sending a commission to the colonies to negotiate a settlement, the king replied that he was "not so fond" of the idea. He further emphasized his belief that such a move looked "like the Mother Country being more affraid of the continuance of the dispute than the Colonies." He insisted that he did not want to drive America "to despair but to Submission"; however, he was sure that "nothing but feeling the inconvenience of their situation" would bring the colonists to submit.[36] In an undated memorandum written in December or

33 Lee to Ralph Izard, Dec. 27, 1774, Deas, ed., *Izard Corres.*, pp. 35–37.

34 Hutchinson to his brother, Apr. 1775, P. O. Hutchinson, ed., *Diary and Letters of T. Hutchinson*, p. 432; see also Worthington C. Ford, ed., *Letters of William Lee*, I (Brooklyn, 1891), 124n.

35 Wm. Lee to R. H. Lee, Jan. 9, 1775, Ford, ed., *Letters of Wm. Lee*, I, 111n.

36 George III to Lord North, Dec. 15, 1774, Fortescue, ed., *Corres. of George III*, III, 156.

January, the king expressed a sense of relief that the colonies had made it easy for Britain to adopt severe measures.

Had the Americans in prosecuting their ill grounded claims put on an appearance of mildness it might have been very difficult to chalk out the right path to be pursued; but they have boldly thrown off the mask and avowed that nothing less than a total independence of the British Legislature will satisfy them; this indeed decides the proper plan to be followed which is to stop the trade of all those Colonies who obey the mandate of the Congress for non importation, non exportation, and non Consumption, to assist them no further with presents to the Indians and give every kind of assistance to those that conduct themselves otherways, which will make them quarell among themselves . . . and experience will then show them that the interference of the Mother Country is essentially necessary.[37]

This memorandum illustrated the government's refusal to consider compromise as part of its plan to settle the dispute with America. In all probability, two alleged attempts to conciliate the colonists were, as Benjamin Franklin said, simply a "deceptive motion" to make it appear as if the government "intended pacific measures."[38] Franklin was directly involved in one of these attempts, when Dr. John Fothergill, acting under the direction of Lord Dartmouth, opened negotiations with the Philadelphian concerning the possibilities of compromise. The other so-called concession was that adopted by Parliament in February on the urging of Lord North, consisting of a resolution proposing the suspension of Parliament's taxing power provided that the colonists voluntarily supplied funds for their own government and for emergencies.

Neither of these proposals suggested any real concession to colonial demands or even constituted a plausible basis on which to consider a reconciliation. Fothergill admitted this in explaining his failure to Lord Dartmouth. He pointed out that he had been given no authority to raise hopes that the Port Bill, the Massachusetts Government Act, or the Quebec Act would be repealed and that nothing less would satisfy the Americans. He informed Dartmouth that just as "a concession to pay a tax was the *sine qua non* on this side, so a rescinding of those Acts, or rather repealing them, is the term of reconciliation on the other."[39] Franklin agreed fully. He noted in March 1775 that "while the Parliament claim'd and exercis'd a Power of altering our Constitutions at pleasure, there could be no Agreement; for we were render'd unsafe in every Privilege."[40]

[37] *Ibid.*, III, 47–48.
[38] Franklin to James Bowdoin, Feb. 25, 1775, Smyth, ed., *Writings of Franklin,* VI, 309.
[39] Fothergill to the Earl of Dartmouth, Feb. 6, 1775, *Dartmouth MSS,* II, 266; David Barclay to James Pemberton, Mar. 18, 1775, Pemberton Family Papers, Hist. Soc. Pa.
[40] Smyth, ed., *Writings of Franklin,* VI, 373.

With regard to the proposed suspension of the taxing power, the king himself stated that the measure gave up no rights and only defined "the line to be held in America."[41] But the bill was violently attacked in Parliament by members who believed that even this meaningless gesture surrendered too much. Both the attempt to negotiate with Franklin and the North Conciliatory Resolution did more to delineate the divisions between Britain and the colonies than to offer a solution.

It might be noted finally that both of these efforts were advanced after the cabinet had decided to use the army in Massachusetts. This decision to initiate war with the colonies was formalized during the first weeks of 1775, if not before. On January 13 a meeting of the cabinet in Lord Rochford's office agreed that Gage's army in Massachusetts should be reinforced by regiments from Ireland. At the same meeting the cabinet discussed proposals for restricting colonial trade and considered the advisability of sending commissioners to "negotiate for union with the colonies for the mutual interest of both parties." This last suggestion was not acceptable to the king. The other two were adopted along with a decision to seize the outstanding leaders in the Massachusetts Provincial Congress.[42]

Whether this meeting formulated the particular means by which force should be used in America is not known. George Bancroft concluded that this conference "drifted the ministry into war," but there is no concrete evidence that the details of American policy were resolved. Hutchinson noted on January 20 that after spending half an hour in Lord Dartmouth's office he had learned that matters were only partly determined.[43] On January 25, Dartmouth "intimated" that a decision had been reached, and five days later he informed Hutchinson that the cabinet had decided to reinforce the troops in Massachusetts and to adopt a plan for restricting American trade.[44] By January 27 all details had almost certainly been ironed out since on that day a secret dispatch was sent to Gage ordering him to march his troops into the countryside and subdue the rebellion in Massachusetts Bay.[45]

The dispatch of January 27 explicitly instructed the general to make use of his army to apprehend the outstanding "rebel" leaders in the New England colony. Dartmouth gave a detailed summary of the decisions reached by the cabinet in response to the meeting of

---

[41] George III to Lord North, Feb. 19, 1775, Fortescue, ed., *Corres. of George III,* III, 177.

[42] *Dartmouth MSS,* II, 258.

[43] P. O. Hutchinson, ed., *Diary and Letters of T. Hutchinson,* pp. 357–58.

[44] *Ibid.,* p. 365.

[45] The extensive quotations which follow are taken from the secret letter written to Gen. Gage by the Earl of Dartmouth, Jan. 27, 1775, Carter, ed., *Gage Corres.,* II, 179–83.

the Continental Congress and the continuing crisis in New England. He began by reviewing the ministry's efforts to provide Gage with the troops and matériel he had requested in order to act with vigor in exercising his authority. The time had now come.

The King's Dignity & the Honour and Safety of the Empire, require, that in such a Situation, Force should be repelled by Force; and it has been His Majesty's Care not only to send you from hence such Reinforcement of the Army under your Command as general Considerations of public Safety would admit, but also to authorize you to collect together every Corps that could be spared from necessary Duty in every other part of America.

Dartmouth then detailed the provisions that were under way to provide Gage with additional forces. He noted that "your object has hitherto been to act upon the Defensive, and to avoid the hazard of weakening your Force by sending out Detachments of your Troops" and agreed that such precautions had no doubt been necessary in the past. But now Gage was to adopt forceful measures.

It is hoped however that this large Reinforcement to your Army will enable you to take a more active & determined part, & that you will have Strength enough, not only to keep Possession of Boston, but to give Protection to Salem, and the Friends of Government at that Place, & that you may without Hazard of Insult return thither if you think fit, & exercise Your Functions there, conformable to His Majesty's Instructions.

In case Gage was still not sufficiently impressed with the government's determination to enforce its decisions, Dartmouth emphasized that the cabinet wanted him to use the army.

I have already said, in more Letters than one, that the Authority of this Kingdom must be supported, & the Execution of its Laws inforced, and you will have seen in His Maty's Speech to both Houses of Parliament, & in the Addresses which they have presented to His Majesty, the firm Resolution of His Majesty and Parliament to act upon those Principles; and as there is a strong Appearance that the Body of the People in at least three of the New England Governments are determined to cast off their Dependence upon the Government of this Kingdom, the only Consideration that remains is, in what manner the Force under your Command may be exerted to defend the Constitution & to restore the Vigour of Government.

Dartmouth then proceeded to answer Gage's contention that his army was inadequate for the task at hand. In doing so he implied that the disturbances in Massachusetts might not have been so serious had the general been less timid.

I have stated that the violences committed by those who have taken up Arms in Massachusetts Bay, have appeared to me as the acts of a rude Rabble without plan, without concert and without conduct, and therefore I think that a smaller Force now, if put to the Test, would be able to encounter them with greater probability of Success than might be expected from a greater

Army, if the people should be suffered to form themselves upon a more regular plan, to acquire confidence from discipline, and to prepare those resources without which every thing must be put to the issue of a single Action.

Having prepared the way by underscoring the government's determination to settle the question with the colonies by armed force, Dartmouth proceeded to outline the plan endorsed by the cabinet. This decision, as noted earlier, had long been under consideration and represented a careful study by the North ministry of both its application and probable results.

In this view therefore of the situation of The King's Affairs, it is the Opinion of The King's Servants in which His Majesty concurs, that the first & essential step to be taken towards re-establishing Government, would be to arrest and imprison the principal actors & abettors in the Provincial Congress (whose Proceedings appear in every light to be Acts of Treason & Rebellion if regardless of your Proclamation & in defiance of it, they should presume again to assemble for such rebellious purposes [the meeting of the Provincial Congress]; and if the steps taken upon this occasion be accompanied with due precaution, and every means be devised to keep the Measure Secret until the moment of Execution, it can hardly fail of Success, and will perhaps be accomplished without bloodshed; but however that may be I must again repeat that any efforts of the People, unprepared to encounter with a regular force, cannot be very formidable; and though such a proceeding should be, according to your own idea of it, a Signal for Hostilities yet, for the reasons I have already given, it will surely be better that the Conflict should be brought on upon such ground, than in a riper state of Rebellion.

Dartmouth need not have been so repetitive in insisting that Gage use his army to subdue the province. Although the general had earlier feared that seizing the provincial leaders might lead to war, by the beginning of 1775 he had concluded that such a course would present the best possibility of success. In a letter dated January 18 he advocated sending a "respectable Force" into the field, seizing the "most obnoxious" provincial leaders, and proclaiming pardon for the others.[46] On February 10 Gage reiterated this decision, reached at the same time as the cabinet adopted its similar plan. The general noted that he had previously acted with discretion but that "your next Dispatches will probably require a different Conduct, and I shall wait for them Impatiently as I conclude they will require me to make Many preparations to act Offensively." The time had come to attack, "for to keep quiet in the Town of Boston only, will not terminate Affairs; the Troops must March into the Country."[47]

Thus by January 1775 the cabinet had decided on war and its gen-

[46]Gage to the Earl of Dartmouth, Jan. 18, 1775, *ibid.,* I, 390.
[47]Gage to Lord Barrington, Feb. 10, 1775, *ibid.,* II, 669.

eral awaited the order with impatience. Both agreed that the best plan would be to seize the leaders of the Massachusetts Provincial Congress then sitting at Concord and try them for treason. The secret orders endorsed in late January did not reach Gage until the second week in April. Hutchinson reported that the dispatches had been sent aboard the *Falcon* with a duplicate on the *Nautilus* but that as of March 12 adverse winds had prevented either vessel from leaving England.[48] According to Gage, the *Nautilus* arrived in Boston on April 14 and the *Falcon* two days later.[49]

The British government was fully aware that the orders to Gage constituted an ultimatum which might lead to war. In the dispatch Dartmouth stated that the effect of the attack would be to test the colony's "Resolution to resist." Although the cabinet expressed hope that bloodshed might be avoided, it explicitly direct Gage to carry out his orders regardless of the consequences. Hutchinson also realized that the orders might signal the beginning of the war. In a letter written on April 10, he expressed his belief that the colonists would not oppose the king's troops and then stated that "before this reaches you it will be determined."[50]

When Gage later reported on his efforts to carry out the cabinet's directions, he did not mention an attempt to apprehend the leaders of the Congress. He explained that the march to Concord was an attempt to capture stores of arms and ammunition reportedly hidden there.[51] Whether the failure to arrest the Massachusetts leaders stemmed from his doubts that the attempt would succeed or simply from the troops' inability to achieve their objective is unclear. The arrest of such men as Samuel Adams and John Hancock would have given the Massachusetts governor considerable satisfaction and earned for him the gratitude of the British government. There is some evidence that the troops attempted to find Hancock and Adams while in Concord. A number of letters written in the spring of 1775, including one reputedly from an officer involved in the march, charged that the troops had searched the house in which the two leaders had been staying.[52] That Gage never mentioned this aspect of the march is hardly conclusive, since the attempt, if it was made, proved unsuccessful. Certainly the general had favored such an attempt earlier

[48]P. O. Hutchinson, ed., *Diary and Letters of T. Hutchinson*, pp. 416–17.

[49]Gage to the Earl of Dartmouth, Apr. 22, 1775, Carter, ed., *Gage Corres.*, I, 396.

[50]Hutchinson to his son in Boston, Apr. 10, 1775, P. O. Hutchinson, ed., *Diary and Letters of T. Hutchinson*, p. 428.

[51]Gage to the Earl of Dartmouth, Apr. 22, 1775, Carter, ed., *Gage Corres.*, I, 396.

[52]Force, ed., *American Archives*, II, 386; *Md. Gaz.* (Annapolis), May 4, 1775; *N.Y. Gaz.*, May 1, 1775; Margaret W. Willard, ed., *Letters on the American Revolution*, (Boston, 1925), pp. 83, 87–88; William V. Wells, *The Life and Public Services of Samuel Adams*, II (Boston, 1865), 270.

in the year, and his instructions indicated that the government preferred arresting these leaders to any other course of action.

On the other hand, by April conditions in Massachusetts had changed, and the alteration may have convinced Gage that his chances of arresting men as popular as Hancock and Adams were few. The important factor, for both Gage and the ministry, was to intimidate the colonists by demonstrating the power of the British army, and an unsuccessful attempt to seize the leading patriots would accomplish nothing. The ammunition stored at Concord presented a less risky objective. Moreover, though the secret instructions to Gage specifically directed him to apprehend the Massachusetts leaders, they left the final decision in his hands. Dartmouth had assured Gage that "this is a matter which must be left to your own Discretion to be executed or not as you shall, upon weighing all Circumstances, and the advantages and disadvantages on one side, and the other, think most advisable."[53]

The importance of the march to Concord, of course, lies not so much in the specific objectives of the troops as in the fact that it initiated war with the colonies. Throughout the colonies the engagement drastically altered public opinion and persuaded men that armed conflict could no longer be avoided. The North ministry would soon have its answer—America would resist by armed force rather than accept the dictates of Parliament. When the news of Lexington and Concord first reached England, Pownall remarked that if the account proved true, "some of the provincials . . . proved bolder than was to be expected."[54] In these few words he summarized one of the major miscalculations of British colonial policy. That error played as great a part as any other factor in bringing on the American Revolution.

[53]The Earl of Dartmouth to Gage, Jan. 27, 1775, Carter, ed., *Gage Corres.*, I, 181.
[54]John Pownall to William Knox, June 2, 1775, *MSS in Various Collections*, VI, 118.

CHAPTER X

The Last Event

A LMOST BEFORE the delegates arrived home after attending the First Continental Congress hopes for a peaceful solution to the crisis began to fade. In December word arrived that the ministry had forbidden the export of gunpowder to America and had taken steps to halt even the shipments of that article already in preparation.[1] Two months later American newspapers printed excerpts from the king's speech to Parliament promising "to withstand every attempt to weaken or impair the supreme authority of this Legislature."[2] Among the delegates who first began to eye a military solution was Samuel Chase. As early as December he concluded that war with the mother country was inevitable, and by February he had begun to lobby with some of the more conservative delegates. Writing to James Duane in February, Chase argued that "to resolve to resist without making the necessary Preparations for Resistance, appears to Me to be weak, & a Deception to ourselves & our Friends."[3]

More bad news followed. In March the colonists learned that Britain was sending additional troops to enlarge its army at Boston, and in early April word came that Parliament had declared the province of Massachusetts Bay to be in rebellion.[4] One of the British officers in Boston reported that by April 1 events in England had "convinced the Rebels (for we may now legally call them so) that there is no hopes for them but by submitting to Parliament."[5]

The crisis was most acute in New England. The gradual increase in the number of troops stationed at Boston and the repeated indications that General Gage intended to send his forces into the countryside soon convinced Massachusetts and her neighboring colonies that armed confrontation was imminent. On February 2 a meeting of thirteen town committees from around Boston took the king's speech under consideration and voted that no inhabitant should furnish any provisions to the British which might prepare them for "taking the

[1]Thomas Cushing to Josiah Quincy, Jr., Dec. 30, 1774, Force, ed., *American Archives*, I, 1080.
[2]Purdie's *Va. Gaz.* (Williamsburg), Feb. 3, 1775, supplement.
[3]Chase to Duane, Feb. 5, 1775, Duane Papers, N.-Y. Hist. Soc.
[4]*Pa. Gaz.* (Phila.), Apr. 12, 1775.
[5]Hugh Earl Percy to Rev. Thomas Percy, Apr. 8, 1775, Bolton, ed., *Letters of Percy*, p. 48.

In the Common Cause

Field early in the Spring.'''6 Five days later the Boston Committee
of Correspondence, in a slip of the pen, used the phrase "till the
grand crisis shall arrive" and then crossed that out and replaced it
with "should the important crisis arrive."[7]

The colonies realized that whatever policy Great Britain adopted,
it would be implemented in Massachusetts. It was not so much the
nonimportation agreement that threatened the peace of the empire
as the continued frustration of efforts to enforce the Coercive Acts,
especially the Massachusetts Government Act. Unlike the revenue
measures over which previous controversies had flared, the Government Act could not be ignored. The Boston Port Act had been, tac-
tically, a good law because its enforcement did not necessitate initiat-
ing hostilities. The Government Act presented a different problem;
the ministry had staked its prestige on implementing an act requiring
a certain amount of cooperation from the inhabitants. When that
cooperation was not forthcoming, government in the Bay Colony
came to a standstill. The British were left either to admit that they
could not rule or to do so by armed force. The former was unthink-
able because it would entail an admission of total failure on the part
of the government, and the latter could not be achieved without
arousing the entire continent to opposition.

Meanwhile, Massachusetts walked a narrow line. The First Continental Congress had promised to support Boston in case General
Gage attempted to use force against the colony, and so it was important for the New England leaders to avoid measures that might
appear aggressive to the other colonies. They understood that they
could expect support from the other provinces only in case of British
attack, but they also feared the consequences of not preparing to
defend themselves.

In December some of the more radical elements in the Massachusetts Provincial Congress decided that the colony could delay no
longer. They proposed that the delegates abrogate the charter, elect
a governor, and begin to raise and equip a provincial army.[8] This
suggestion raised immediate opposition from more moderate leaders.
The latter insisted that Massachusetts must not appear to be provok-
ing the British into an attack. According to one account, Sam Adams
suggested taking over the government and raising an army and
stated that America would support such measures. To this assertion
Thomas Cushing responded, "That is a Lie Mr. Adams & you know
it & you know that I know it is a Lie."[9] Since Cushing had also been

[6]Box 1 (Gen. Corres.), Boston Comm. of Corres. Papers, N.Y. Pub. Lib.

[7]Boston Comm. of Corres. to the Marblehead Comm. of Corres., Feb. 7, 1775, *ibid.*

[8]Thomas Cushing to Samuel Purviance, Feb. 13, 1775, Brock Collection, Henry E.
Huntington Library, San Marino, Calif.

[9]Stephen Collins to Robert Treat Paine, Jan. 14, 1775, Stephen Collins Letterbook,
Lib. of Cong.

a member of the First Continental Congress, his statements probably carried considerable weight. Still there were those who thought that Massachusetts should adopt a more aggressive stance. Shortly after the Provincial Congress adjourned, John Adams wrote that he sometimes wished the First Continental Congress had accepted "the Motion made by Mr. Ross and Seconded by Mr. Galloway, that this Province Should be left to her own Discretion with Respect to Government and Justice, as well as Defence." Had they done so, Adams thought, some "Sublime Conceptions" recently debated in the Provincial Congress would have "been carried rapidly into Execution."[10]

Nevertheless, the majority in the Massachusetts Congress was right; the appearance of moderation was essential to the viability of the American union. In fact, the rumor that Massachusetts had considered electing a governor and raising an army had alarmed colonial moderates. Philadelphia's Stephen Collins wrote immediately for reassurance, warning Robert Treat Paine that there were "real Friends to Liberty . . . who are really fearfull of som Steps being taken in New England, that will tend to a Division of the Colonies."[11] Collins reported that the Philadelphia tories had used the rumors from New England to buttress their charge that "Independency & Republican Government is the object in view."[12] From Maryland, Samuel Purviance wrote expressing his pleasure that a project which he had beheld with "horror" had been laid aside and that Massachusetts intended to guard against a rupture of the "public Tranquility."[13]

Massachusetts did not authorize the establishment of a provincial army until ten days before Gage sent his troops to Concord, but it did make some defensive preparations. In October the Provincial Congress appointed Harrison Gray to receive the taxes of the colony, authorized the expenditure of funds for the purchase of arms and bayonets, and established a Committee of Safety empowered to "alarm, muster, and cause to be assembled" any number of local militia it might consider necessary in case of an emergency.[14] After word arrived that the king had promised to support the authority of Parliament, the Provincial Congress instructed one Colonel Robertson to deliver four brass fieldpieces and two brass mortars to the Committee of Safety and, the following week, authorized the committee to assume possession of all implements of war belonging to the province. In late January the Committee of Safety met with another congressional subgroup, the Committee of Supplies, and arranged for the deposit of cannon, mortars, balls, and shells in the two towns of Worcester and Concord. On February 21 a similar meet-

10J. Adams to Edward Biddle, Dec. 12, 1774, Adams Papers Microfilm, reel 344.
11Collins to Paine, Jan. 14, 1775, Stephen Collins Letterbook, Lib. Cong.
12Collins to William Tudor, Jan. 14, 1775, *ibid.*
13Purviance to Thomas Cushing, Mar. 4, 1775, S. Adams Papers, N.Y. Pub. Lib.
14Force, ed., *American Archives,* I, 843.

ing instructed the Committee of Supplies to purchase military stores
sufficient to provision an army of 15,000 men. When in early March
additional reinforcements arrived for Gage, the Committee of Safety
appointed night watchmen at the three towns of Charlestown, Cambridge, and Roxbury and arranged for couriers to carry news of any
advancing troops to the ammunition depots at Worcester and Concord.[15]

These defensive measures were not adopted without opposition,
and again the main objection came from those who feared that
Massachusetts would separate herself from the general union. One
member of the Provincial Congress who spoke out against authorizing the Committee of Safety to summon the militia contended that
"nothing but an absolute necessity of preserving ourselves from
immediate & sudden destruction will justify us with the other
Colonies in commencing Hostilities." He warned that the militia,
once mustered, might find it difficult to resist making an attack. Such
an engagement "must be suspended, *if possible,* untill the Continent
by their Representatives shall in the most explicit manner say when
and precisely upon what occasion or Event the Scene shall open."[16]

However, Massachusetts was not alone in preparing for the possibility of a military engagement; the other New England governments also saw the growing threat of attack and began to prepare for
defending themselves. In early November the Connecticut Assembly
resolved that the towns in that province should provide themselves
with double the amounts of powder, balls, and flints required by
previous militia laws.[17] The New Hampshire Provincial Convention
met on January 25, and although recommending that the inhabitants
try to preserve "peace and harmony," it also thought that local
officers should "strictly comply with the laws of this Province for
regulating the Militia."[18] In Rhode Island preparations for defense
were enormously boosted by the December arrival of Lord Dartmouth's directive forbidding the importation of gunpowder. Samuel
Ward wrote Richard Henry Lee that "our General Assembly immediately ordered Copies ... to be sent to Mr. Cushing to be com-
municated to the [Massachusetts] Provincial Congress." Ward went
on to list the defense measures adopted by the Rhode Island Assembly.

They then ordered the Cannon at Fort George (which was not tenable) to
be sent to Providence, where they will be safe and ready for service; 200 lbs.
of Powder, a proportionate quantity of Lead and Flints, and several pieces

[15]*Ibid.,* I, 1329, 1337, 1367, 1370.
[16] Thomas Cushing? to Joseph Hawley, Feb. 27, 1775, Joseph Hawley Papers, N.Y.
Pub. Lib.
[17]Force, ed., *American Archives,* I, 858.
[18]*Ibid.,* I, 1180–82.

of brass Cannon for the Artillery Companies, were ordered to be purchased. A Major General (an officer never before chosen in the Colony) was appointed, several independent companies of light Infantry, Fusileers, Hunters, &c., were formed; the Militia was ordered to be disciplined and the Commanding Officers empowered to march the troops to the assistance of any sister Colony.... The idea of taking up arms against Great Britain is shocking, but if we must become slaves or fly to arms, I shall not hesitate one moment which to choose.[19]

Outside New England, Maryland again took the lead. Just as it had earlier voted to adopt trade restrictions while the other colonies hesitated, it now became one of the first provinces to take steps toward preparing the militia for battle. Samuel Chase played an important part in this decision. By December, Chase had decided that war with Britain was inevitable and that the colonies courted disaster by ignoring that fact. On December 12 the Maryland leader wrote John Adams a letter which in outright militancy surpassed anything that had yet come from New England. Chase believed that Britain would not retreat and would soon launch an invasion of the colonies. He therefore concluded that since Canada would be the key to a military confrontation with the mother country, "we must at all Events procure and keep Possession of that province." He proposed that an army of 30,000 men should be maintained in Boston and one of 20,000 in New York. Chase also suggested that the colonists begin immediately to outfit ships for waging war on the British merchant marine, and he favored immediate destruction of the army stationed at Boston. "In short I would adopt every Scheme to reduce G[reat] B[ritain] to our Terms."[20]

Even as Chase wrote, the Maryland Provincial Convention put the finishing touches to a series of proposals reflecting his militant outlook. The meeting resolved that "a well regulated militia, composed of the gentlemen, freeholders, and other freemen, is the natural strength and only stable security of a free government" and proposed that all males between the ages of sixteen and fifty form themselves into companies and "use their utmost endeavours to make themselves masters of the military exercise." The Convention instructed each county in Maryland to raise a specified sum of money for the purchase of arms and asked the local committees to see that each militiaman was provided "with a good firelock, and bayonet fitted thereon, half a pound of powder, two pounds of Lead, and a ... powder-horn, and bag for ball, and be in readiness to act on any emergency." The Maryland delegates further proclaimed that if the British attempted to use force to implement the Coercive Acts or to collect a tax in any

[19]Ward to Lee, Dec. 14, 1774, *Southern Literary Messenger,* XXVIII (Jan.–June 1859), 188–89.
[20]Chase to J. Adams, misdated Jan. 12, 1775, Adams Papers Microfilm, reel 344.

part of America, "this province will support such colony to the ut-most of their power." Finally, the congress expressed its hope that the other colonies would "enter into such or like resolutions for mutual defense and protection."[21]

The resolutions from Maryland had a pronounced effect in other parts of the continent and helped to prepare the way for further armament. From Massachusetts, Joseph Warren wrote that he ad-mired the votes of Maryland and thought that "they Breath a Spirit of Liberty & Union which does Honour to them and Indeed the whole Continent."[22] On December 21 the county committee in New Castle, Delaware, met and adopted resolutions for training the militia in terms exactly like those earlier approved in Annapolis.[23] In Fairfax County, Virginia, a meeting chaired by George Washington con-curred "with the Provincial Committee of the Province of *Maryland*" that a militia was necessary and resolved to establish four county companies of sixty-eight men each. When the Virginia Convention met in March, it appointed a committee to prepare plans for "arm-ing and disciplining" a number of men. The committee's report, as endorsed by the congress, called for the recruitment of both infantry and horse troops and instructed the county committees to collect money for provisioning the men so enlisted.[24]

New York and Pennsylvania, although less enthusiastic about the proceedings in Maryland, were nonetheless affected by them. James Duane of New York wrote Chase that "the step you have taken which will be called an Assumption of the Militia into your own hands is certainly of a very serious nature, and here it produces great anxiety." Duane noted that the resolutions adopted in Annapolis constituted the "first public act out of the pale of New England which indicates a preparation for war" and admitted that Maryland's "calm delibera-tion" had had a much greater effect in New York than the conduct of those "more immediately engaged."[25] In Pennsylvania the whigs be-gan preparations for a second Provincial Convention amid specula-tion that such a gathering might follow the lead of Maryland and provide for arming and training the militia. This action was strongly opposed by the more conservative elements in the colony, and Thomas Warton, Sr., reported that "some of Us have told them that We will meet the Committee & oppose openly such a measure."[26] The congress which met in late January did not propose taking up arms, but it adopted a strongly worded resolution promising to resist British aggression. The delegates vowed that if Great Britain, "in-

[21]*Pa. Gaz.* (Phila.), Dec. 21, 1774.
[22]Warren to J. Adams, Jan. 15, 1775, Adams Papers Microfilm, reel 344.
[23]*Pa. Gaz.* (Phila.), Dec. 28, 1774.
[24]Force, ed., *American Archives*, I, 1145, II, 168–70.
[25]Duane to Chase, Dec. 29, 1774, Duane Papers, N.-Y. Hist. Soc.
[26]T. Wharton to Joseph Wharton, Jan. 18, 1775, Wharton Letterbook, Hist. Soc. Pa.

stead of redressing our grievances, should determine by force to effect a submission to the late arbitrary acts of the British Parliament, ... we hold it our indispensable duty to resist such force, and at every hazard to defend the rights and liberties of America."[27]

By the time General Gage sent his troops to Concord, the actual outbreak of conflict was almost anticlimactic. Those closest to the scene had long realized that unless Britain suddenly announced a capitulation and began to withdraw her troops, she must advance. Chase had predicted that "delay must ruin the Minister" and that "some decisive Mode must be adopted, & instantly executed, or he must fail."[28] In early February, Gage had observed that "to keep quiet in the Town of Boston only, will not terminate Affairs; the Troops must March into the Country."[29] The Boston Committee of Correspondence had for many weeks been cautioning other towns in the province to maintain calm and avoid precipitating military conflict, on the assumption that Gage would do so himself. The precarious situation of the ministry—both militarily and psychologically— was a godsend for radical Bostonians: it permitted them to adopt an ostensively defensive posture in the knowledge that the British could not maintain a passive attitude. Gage's attack forced the war on America.

A number of historians have explained the rapidity with which Americans moved to armed rebellion in ideological terms. Bernard Bailyn among others, has offered valuable suggestions about the fierce hostility with which Americans reacted to British policy. From frontier towns to urban seaports, from the county courts to the floor of the First Continental Congress, the traditions of English radicalism and the residue of the Puritan ethic combined to intensify colonial determination to resist.[30] These intellectual biases were undeniably important, perhaps essential to the American Revolution, but they cannot be considered determinative. The Battle of Lexington occurred in 1775 because the British government had decided to enforce an unenforceable policy. The Coercive Acts were oppressive not just in theory but in fact, and they forced Americans to choose between abject submission to arbitrary authority on the one hand and armed resistance on the other.

To argue that civil war came to the British Empire in 1775 because Parliament attempted to assert its right to tax the colonies and to enforce the Coercive Acts is not to contend that war would not have come ten years later for different reasons. The First Continental Congress carefully avoided demanding repeal of acts that touched on

[27]*Pa. Gaz.* (Phila.) Feb. 1, 1775.
[28]Chase to Duane, Feb. 5, 1775, Duane Papers, N.-Y. Hist. Soc.
[29]Thomas Gage to Lord Barrington, Feb. 10, 1775, Carter, ed., *Gage Corres.*, II, 669.
[30]See especially Bailyn, *The Ideological Origins of the American Revolution* (Cambridge, Mass., 1967).

Parliament's right to regulate trade or to control American manufacturing, but it also reserved the right to complain of such legislation at some future time. Parliament's regulation of imperial commerce and colonial manufacturing, though oppressive, was not yet so
objectionable as to force the colonists into a united opposition. But
the five statutes passed in the spring of 1774 were indeed coercive.
They represented so sweeping an attempt to turn back the imperial
clock that they assured American resistance and provided it with the
broadest possible basis from which to gather popular support.

The Coercive Acts, much more than the Stamp Act or the Townshend duties, rang the changes on American fears and grievances.
They appeared to threaten the Protestant religion, the availability
of land in the west, the integrity of the colonial assemblies, the right
of taxation, the traditional procedures of jury trial, the civil control
of the military, and the sanctity of colonial charters. There was almost no complaint voiced by the Americans in the past century
which Great Britain did not manage to revive by one or more of the
provisions of the Coercive Acts. Not since the Dominion of New
England had the mother country attempted anything comparable,
and 1774 was not 1685. The legislation was so out of tune with the
situation in America that many colonists could not believe Parliament
actually intended to see it implemented.

Nor is it surprising that the colonists rushed to the support of
Massachusetts Bay. In the first place, most Americans, whig and
tory, agreed that the legislation directed against the New England
colony was intended as a warning to the other provinces as well, and
they had increasing reason to believe in the accuracy of that evaluation. Great Britain had obviously decided to tighten the reins of
empire, and that was, after all, the basis of American discontent.
Moreover, a large number of colonists believed that the mother country would not initiate hostilities; that the real danger of armed conflict lay in the possibility that Massachusetts would become im-
patient and take action on its own. As the Continental Congress saw
it, one of the best means of avoiding this possibility was to promise
the Bay Colony support in case of attack while threatening to leave
her stranded if she began any hostilities. That strategy may have
cooled tempers in Massachusetts, but it also committed the other
colonists to respond in case of an attack such as that which took
place at Concord. Finally, many Americans believed that the best
prospect for peace was to demonstrate a willingness to fight. A remarkable number of colonial leaders were thus led to make public
commitments to the resistance because of private belief that the
mother country would back down in the face of a united opposition.[31]

---

[31] James Duane to Samuel Chase, Dec. 29, 1774, Duane Papers, N.-Y. Hist. Soc.

By asserting the power of Parliament in such an extreme form, the Coercive Acts forced the colonists to become political radicals. There was almost universal condemnation of British policy among the colonists, and those who thought differently seldom said so. Many who were inclined to support the government's position discovered that it was difficult to formulate an acceptable defense. Thomas Wharton, Sr., was a man of conservative outlook who was later imprisoned as a tory. He had thought at first that the Port Act might be implemented without too much difficulty, provided Parliament refrained from passing rumored legislation affecting the constitution of the Bay Colony.[32] When the British legislature passed not only the Government Act but three other objectionable laws for good measure, the Philadelphian despaired. By the time news of the Quebec Act arrived, he concluded that the colonists "from One End of this Continent to the other" considered it "the greatest departure from the English Constitution of any ever yet Attempted." The tone of Wharton's correspondence shows that he shared that opinion, even though he continued to argue that the colonists should adopt moderate methods of opposing such legislation.[33]

The unanimity with which the colonists moved to oppose the Coercive Acts was enhanced by the widespread belief that Parliament had only passed the legislation because of its misconception that Boston would be left to suffer alone. Just as the British cabinet subscribed to the theory that America would back down once it was convinced that Parliament meant business, so the colonists assumed that the government would retreat when it realized the colonies were determined to resist. The Americans repeatedly argued that measures illustrating colonial determination were bound to make the British back down. Acton, Massachusetts, resolved that a nonimportation of British goods was "the only Method of Preserving our Land from Slavery without Drenching it in Blood," and Sherburne, in the same colony, proposed that each town adopt specific resolutions so that the British would give up their idea "that the People in general are disposed to Submission—and that their Representatives voting and Resolving contrary to such Supposed disposition . . . was owing to an undue influence of some aspiring factious Demagogues upon them."[34] A similar attempt to demonstrate American resolve came out of a committee meeting in Wilmington, North Carolina. The county delegates voted to ban all horse racing, gaming, and other entertain-

[32]T. Wharton to Samuel Wharton, May 17, 1774, Wharton Letterbook, Hist. Soc. Pa.

[33]Wharton to Thomas Walpole, Aug. 20, 1774, *ibid.*

[34]Selectmen of Acton, Mass., to the Boston Comm. of Corres., Aug. 10, 1774, and Sherburne, Mass., Comm. of Corres. to the Boston Comm. of Corres., and Boston Comm. of Corres. Papers, N.Y. Pub. Lib.

ments, because "nothing will so effectually tend to convince the British Parliament that we are in earnest in our opposition to their measures, as a voluntary relinquishment of our favorite amusements."[35]

Americans, with few exceptions, did not understand that they could not affect British policy by measures short of armed resistance. The belabored letters of Virginia planters instructing their factors and merchants in Britain to bring pressure to bear on the ministry reflected their inaccurate assessment of the political situation in England. The colonists could not see that their proposals for imperial reorganization were, in British eyes, tantamount to a call for independence. As long as an individual retained some hope that the government would meet colonial demands peacefully, he naturally supported moderation. It could easily be argued that radicalization in prerevolutionary America depended more upon a realistic evaluation of the political situation in England than on any other single factor.

John Adams in the early summer of 1774 favored restructuring the empire along lines not unlike those advocated by far more conservative spirits. He foresaw an annual American Congress which might become a seminary of "American Statesmen, a School of Politicians, perhaps at no great Distance of Time, equal to a british Parliament, in wiser as well as better ages."[36] This suggestion varied only slightly from that of Wharton, who supported a plan similar to that proposed by Joseph Galloway at the First Continental Congress.[37] Both Wharton and Adams realized that Britain might oppose such a suggestion, but both thought that it would eventually be accepted without disrupting the empire. Wharton wrote a friend in England that "some with You may for a time Obstruct it, Yet I do give it as my Sentiments, that nothing I know of, can take place, which will so long continue You & Us as One people."[38] Adams thought, similarly, that "the whole Policy and Force of the Ministry will be bent against it.... But I dont see how it is possible for them to prevent it or hinder its Effects."[39]

Few realized that the bright panacea projected by men like Adams and Wharton might well necessitate severing the connection between Great Britain and the colonies. One of these, Joseph Hawley, wrote anxiously to Adams to convince him of his error and persuade him

[35]Saunders, ed., *N.C. Records,* IX, 1091.

[36]J. Adams to Joseph Hawley, June 27, 1774, Hawley Papers, N.Y. Pub. Lib.

[37]Wharton to Thomas Walpole, July 5, 1774, and T. Wharton to Samuel Wharton, Oct. 9, 1774, Wharton Letterbook, Hist. Soc. Pa.

[38]Wharton to Walpole, May 31, 1774, *ibid.*

[39]J. Adams to Joseph Hawley, June 27, 1774, Hawley Papers, N.Y. Pub. Lib.

that the colonies should prepare for war. He seconded Adams's suggestion that "the institution of annual Congresses ... will brighten the chain, and would make excellent statesmen and politicians," but he thought it inevitable that "such an institution would breed extremities and ruptures." He pointed out that a structural reorganization such as that entailed in the establishment of an annual congress would shake the foundations of the empire. It was unrealistic to believe that Britain would accept such an institution, and Hawley wanted Adams to prepare for a more activist role. He predicted that an American Congress, "if formed, must be discontinued, or we must defend it with *ruptures*."[40] John Adams's conversion to radicalism seems to have come sometime in the late summer of 1774, and there is every reason to believe that it accompanied his conversion to the views of Joseph Hawley.

In pointing out the connection between conditions in England and preparations in America, Hawley had put his finger on an important point about the movement toward war and, in the end, toward independence. The disagreements that most often divided the colonists in 1774–75 concerned the state of politics in the mother country. The conservatives were those who expected Great Britain to respond favorably to a petition for redress; the moderates hoped to succeed by adopting an embargo of trade; and the radicals anticipated the necessity for taking up arms. This categorization often had nothing to do with the ideas an individual entertained about the proper status of the colonies within the empire or about the extent of parliamentary authority. Chase of Maryland, for example, stood with the moderates in Congress when he argued that Parliament should have the right to regulate trade. Yet Chase must be considered a radical because he soon decided that "the present unhappy Dispute with Great Britain would not wait the Event of a commercial Opposition." The Marylander argued that the mother country "must either give up the Right of Taxing America, or enforce obedience by the Sword," and concluded that the Americans must prepare for civil war as the "most effectual Means to prevent one."[41]

Conversely, many who took a radical position in arguing that Parliament ought to have no control over imperial trade must be categorized as moderate or even conservative because they were reluctant to adopt aggressive measures in pursuit of that objective. The Pennsylvania Convention asked for repeal of the Hat Act of 1732 and the Iron Act of 1750 and proposed that no future regulations of the "commerce of the Colonies" be adopted without "mutual consent." Yet

[40]Hawley to J. Adams, C. F. Adams, ed., *Writings of J. Adams*, IX, 342–45.
[41]Chase to James Duane, Feb. 5, 1775, Duane Papers, N.-Y. Hist. Soc.

the delegates to that convention expressed their hope that the Continental Congress would petition for a redress of grievances before adopting restrictions on British trade. In retrospect, it is remarkable that such a group of men could have believed that Britain would grant the colonies virtual autonomy, even from the Acts of Trade and Manufacturing, upon receipt of a "humble petition."[42] Similarly, Galloway's proposal for restructuring the empire represented a much more radical turn of mind than did the suggestions of a man like Samuel Chase. It was because Galloway expected Britain to respond to a colonial petition that he finally condemned the whigs and deserted the cause. Politically, the First Continental Congress would have been wise to have endorsed Galloway's Plan of Union. Because Parliament would have rejected the American proposals anyway, the result would have been an even more overwhelming colonial consensus.

Since the colonists had no reason to suspect the extent of the British commitment to enforce the Coercive Acts, they calmly and deliberately bound themselves to oppose that enforcement in the expectation of defeating it. The most probable means of securing repeal seemed to be nonimportation. The adoption of trade restrictions, far from being an impetuous reaction to the Coercive Acts, was based on precedents established at the time of the Stamp Act in 1765 and the Townshend duties in 1767. In neither case had the boycott of British trade led to war with the mother country, and the colonists had no reason to suppose that conditions had changed. Springfield, Massachusetts, endorsed nonimportation because the town considered such proposals to be "prudent, Peaceable, Constitutional Measures, for the redress of our Grievances."[43] The county congress in Berkshire, Massachusetts, defended trade restrictions as "neither Unwarrantable; hostile, traiterous nor contrary to our Allegiance due to the King, but tends to promote the Peace, good Order and Safety of the Community."[44]

In fact, since the colonists had achieved a unanimity in 1774 which they had only aimed at in the earlier crises, there seemed to be every reason to suppose that their victory would be swifter and more complete. When the First Continental Congress announced its unanimous support for nonimportation, many of those who had originally opposed such methods decided that it would be best to go along. Thomas Johnson, Jr., wrote from Annapolis that "though I do not imagine the Resolutions of the Congress are agreeable to every In-

[42]Force, ed., *American Archives,* I, 555–62.

[43]Resolutions of Springfield, Mass., July 12, 1774, Boston Comm. of Corres. Papers, N.Y. Pub. Lib.

[44]Berkshire Co. Congress Resolutions, July 6, 1774, *ibid.*

dividual of our Province yet I believe all are so well convinced of the
Necessity of Unanimity that we shall have no Trouble at all to execute the Association or by Degrees to go to any Length that may be
necessary to defend the Rights of America."[45]

Upon the unanimous endorsement of the Association by Congress,
and with the prevailing belief that unanimity would bring victory,
the colonists flocked to assert their support. By the time the Americans clashed with the British troops at Lexington, they had established hundreds of committees instructed to enforce the trade boycott. Thousands of colonists, by accepting membership on these
committees, identified themselves with the leadership of a movement
which the British would soon label rebellion and move to subdue by
armed force. Moreover, every colony except Georgia and New York
approved the Association either in its Assembly or in a specially
elected congress. Eleven of the thirteen colonies thus placed their
political prestige on the table; they had officially objected to the
Coercive Acts and committed themselves to procuring repeal. When
that repeal was not forthcoming, the Americans were forced to confront the stark fact of political impotence. Not even the sacrifices
of nonimportation and the force of unanimity had affected British
policy.

The significance of this widespread commitment to opposing the
Coercive Acts can hardly be overstated. Whatever the previous
ideological outlook of the individual involved, the decision to support
the Continental Association helped to propel him into armed rebellion. Many who joined in support of the Congress had no expectation that this support would force them to take up arms; some committee members participated in organizing the American resistance
for the express purpose of exercising a moderating influence. But
these men expected that Britain would give some attention to American grievances and propose at least token measures of conciliation.
They had only the vaguest idea that the mother country might initiate hostilities, and when confronted by that prospect, they found it
difficult to retreat. Professing a willingness to stop drinking tea, they
found themselves holding a rifle. Intending only to participate in an
intercolonial demonstration of solidarity, they found that troops had
begun to attack the front lines. James Duane is an excellent example.

Duane attended the Continental Congress, fought consistently to
modify measures he considered extreme, and decided, with some
reservations, that the Association offered a sufficient possibility of
success to merit his active support. The New Yorker was aware that
hostilities were possible, but he thought the danger of Boston's ini-
tiating them much greater than the possibility that Britain would

[45]Johnson to James Duane, Dec. 16, 1774, Duane Papers, N.-Y. Hist. Soc.

attack. Duane was convinced that if Massachusetts could be restrained, the mother country would propose some sort of compromise and the crisis would cool. In December he wrote Chase of his disappointment that Maryland had decided to discipline and arm her militia, because he feared that this step would "inflame the ardor of our Friends in Boston and precipitate an attack on the King's Troops." Duane explained that he especially worried about the excesses of Boston because he knew that the British would not dare shed American blood unless given a good reason. It was therefore essential for the colonists to maintain calm and await news that the British government had fallen. "Let us but act with wisdom and temper, avoid the Imputation of commencing hostilities—and persevere with virtue and fortitude in our Association and all will yet be well."[46]

Had Duane understood the determination of Great Britain to implement the Coercive Acts, he might have realized that all would not be well. He, like many moderate leaders, soon found himself in an impossible situation. He clung desperately to the hope that conflict between the troops and the Bostonians could be delayed until some kind of accommodation was worked out that would permit both sides to withdraw and tempers to cool. But that hope depended on a conciliatory statement from Parliament, and it was extinguished as news from Great Britain went from bad to worse. Other moderate and conservative leaders reported a similar finding of despair. Wharton thought in January that a moderate "Spirit is now Rising & will gain the Ascendance, provided what We hear from you [in England] shall Carry the face of Justice with it."[47] Three months later the Philadelphian thought it only a matter of time until the Bostonians and the army came to blows.[48] In February, James Pemberton of Philadelphia condemned the resolutions of Congress but predicted that "we have a faint hope" that things would improve. Shortly after the engagement at Lexington he wrote a friend in England that "if your Rulers have any public Virtue or feelings of humanity remaining they must be convinced of their mistaken policy in attempting to enforce their rigorous measures." Pemberton had worked to keep the Quakers disassociated from the whig movement, but he now reported that "our hands are weak & influence small and we are become here a People disunited in sentiment and Conduct."[49]

From the passage of the Coercive Acts to the skirmish at Lexington, the British ministry forced the Americans to unite in opposition to its policy. Those colonists who sought to prevent war were frustrated

[46]Duane to Chase, Dec. 29, 1774, *ibid.*

[47]Wharton to Thomas Walpole, Jan. 18, 1775, Wharton Letterbook, Hist. Soc. Pa.

[48]T. Wharton to Joseph Wharton, Apr. 6, 1775, *ibid.*

[49]Pemberton to Dr. John Fothergill, Feb. 15, 1775, and Pemberton to David Barclay, May 10, 1775, Pemberton Family Papers, Hist. Soc. Pa.

by the intransigence of the mother country. They tried to smooth troubled waters following news of the Boston Port Act, only to be confronted with the Government Act, the Justice Act, and the Quebec Act. They insisted on petitioning the king, only to find that he received their effort with contempt. They cautioned Boston not to adopt offensive measures and comforted each other with reports that the "substantial" citizens would step forward once the ministry offered to negotiate, only to discover, as Pemberton admitted, that the British troops were the aggressors.

It would take another year, and another round of escalations calculated to demonstrate yet another level of determination, before men such as James Duane and John Dickinson would realize that their concept of American government was not possible within the existing framework of the British Empire. Men like Washington, Jefferson, the Adamses, and the Lees were now aware of that fact. Others would waver in between. And yet George III had been quite correct when, in the summer of 1774, he predicted that "the dye is now cast, the Colonies must either submit or triumph."

Critical Essay on Sources

The following essay is not intended as a comprehensive bibliography of materials used in this work, but rather as an indication of the more important collections on which the study was based. I have especially attempted to note sources that are less commonly known and used.

I. Primary Sources

Manuscripts

A major source, especially for the material on Virginia and Maryland, is to be found in the microfilm collections of the Research Library at Colonial Williamsburg. Among the most important of these are the papers of mercantile firms microfilmed in Great Britain, notably the Charles Steuart Papers from the National Library of Scotland and the James Russell Papers from Coutts and Company in London. These collections include hundreds of letters written from Virginia and Maryland in 1774–1775 as well as a few extraordinary accounts of life in Boston by tories Nathaniel Coffin and James Murray. The Samuel Purviance Papers of the Maryland Historical Society were also available in Williamsburg and provided excellent, though incomplete, information on the political situation in Maryland.

An equally rich source for the colonial period is the Historical Society of Pennsylvania, where a number of often used collections provide the historian with a wealth of material. Among the most important of these are the Shippen Family Papers, the Pemberton Family Papers, the James & Drinker Business Papers, and the Thomas Wharton Letterbook. A good source for events in Pennsylvania during this period is the R. R. Logan Collection, which contains extensive materials on John Dickinson.

The Library of Congress in Washington, D.C., also contains several collections of value to historians of the early Revolutionary period. Included among the most helpful collections for this study were the Stephen Collins Papers, the Thomas Wharton Letterbook, and the transcripts from the Public Records Office in London.

The Boston Committee of Correspondence Papers at the New York Public Library are invaluable for an insight not only into events in Boston but into communications between the Massachusetts capital and other colonies. Also useful among the collections of the New York Public Library were the Samuel Adams Papers and the Joseph Hawley Papers.

For reconstructing events in New York the library at the New-York Historical Society is essential. The Alexander McDougall Papers and the James Duane Papers are cited extensively in this text.

Occasional letters at the Connecticut Historical Society in Hartford, especially among the William Samuel Johnson Papers, were helpful, as were the Webb Papers at Yale University's Sterling Library.

Printed materials

Three collections of source material provided the bulk of information on the Congress itself and events in the several colonies related to it: Peter Force, ed., *American Archives* . . . , 4th ser. (Washington, D.C., 1837–46); Worthington C. Ford, ed., *Journals of the Continental Congress, 1774–1789*, I (Washington, D.C., 1904); and Edmund C. Burnett, ed., *Letters of the Members of the Continental Congress,* I (Washington, D.C., 1921). The Force volume is packed with documents, reports, letters, and newspaper clippings and provides excellent introductory reading for a study of the period. The *Journals* are now available in the microfilmed Papers of the Continental Congress. Burnett's edition of the *Letters* is a monumental effort and, along with the *Journals,* is indispensable to any study of the Congress. An extraordinarily helpful, if limited, account of Congress is Christopher Collier, ed., "Silas Deane Reports on the Continental Congress," Connecticut Historical Society *Bulletin,* XXIX (1964).

Collections of the various colonies are also rewarding. Perhaps the best of these is J. P. Kennedy, ed., *Journals of the House of Burgesses,* XIII (Richmond, 1905), which contains not only the legislative journals but many communications from the various colonial committees of correspondence. Also useful are J. R. Bartlett, ed., *Records of the Colony of Rhode Island and Providence Plantations in New England* (Providence, 1856–65); W. A. Whitehead et al., eds., *New Jersey Archives,* 1st ser., X (Newark, 1886); William L. Saunders, ed., *Colonial and State Records of North Carolina* (Raleigh, 1890); Elizabeth Merritt, ed., *Archives of Maryland,* LXIV (Baltimore, 1947); Nathaniel Bouton, ed., *Documents and Records Relating to the Province of New Hampshire,* VIII (Nashua, N.H., 1873); and E. B. O'Callaghan and Berthold Fernow, eds., *Documents Relative to the Colonial History of the State of New York* (Albany, 1853–87).

Collections of personal and official correspondence are readily available for most of the major figures in this period. Many such might be cited, but among the most descriptive writings are John C.

Fitzpatrick, ed., *The Writings of George Washington*, III (Washington, D.C., 1931); Charles Francis Adams, ed., *Works of John Adams* (Boston, 1850-56); James C. Ballagh, ed., *The Letters of Richard Henry Lee* (New York, 1911-14); and Harry A. Cushing, ed., *The Writings of Samuel Adams* (New York, 1904-8). On the other side of the political fence are Peter O. Hutchinson, ed., *Diary and Letters of His Excellency Thomas Hutchinson* (Boston, 1884); C. E. Carter, ed., *Gage Correspondence* (New Haven, 1931-33); and Hon. Sir John Fortescue, ed., *The Correspondence of King George the Third from 1760 to December, 1783*, III (London, 1928).

John Drayton's *Memoirs of the American Revolution*, I (Charleston, S.C., 1821) is often unreliable but can provide insights into the period if approached carefully. Also useful for events surrounding the Congress as well as reports on happenings within is William B. Reed, *Life and Correspondence of Joseph Reed* (Philadelphia, 1847). An especially interesting aspect of this volume are the letters from Reed to Lord Dartmouth before, during, and after the meeting of Congress.

Three sources by Joseph Galloway provide some tantalizing hints about the events of Congress but must be approached with considerable care. *The Examination of Joseph Galloway before the House of Commons* (London, 1780) recounts the questions asked of and answers given by Galloway on the Revolution and includes a number of direct references to the First Continental Congress. Also interesting are Joseph Galloway, *A Candid Examination of the Mutual Claims of Great Britain, and the Colonies* (London, 1780), and Joseph Galloway, *Historical and Political Reflections on the Rise and Progress of the American Rebellion* (London, 1780).

A fascinating journal of the period is Jack P. Greene, ed., *The Diary of Colonel Landon Carter of Sabine Hall, 1752-78*, II (Charlottesville, Va., 1965). A less volatile but in some ways more informative account of Virginia during the period is Edward M. Riley, ed., *The Journal of John Harrower* (Williamsburg, Va., 1963).

Colonial newspapers have been widely utilized in this study, especially for the sections dealing with the election of Committees of Inspection and enforcement of the Continental Association. Many newspapers not only reported the elections and activities of such committees but listed the names of those chosen to be members as well. Most of these papers are now available on microfilm, although I found the library at the American Antiquarian Society essential in compiling such local statistics.

II. Secondary Accounts

A readable and reliable account of the First Continental Congress is Lynn Montross, *The Reluctant Rebels* (New York, 1950). Edmund C.

Burnett's *The Continental Congress* (New York, 1941) devotes but a few pages to the first meeting in Philadelphia although it is a clear and succinct statement. The best account of this period is still Arthur M. Schlesinger, Sr., *The Colonial Merchants and the American Revolution* (New York, 1917). Although the author allows his emphasis on the merchant class in the colonies to slant his view of the First Continental Congress, the work remains a superior history.

Edmund S. and Helen M. Morgan, *The Stamp Act Crisis: Prologue to Revolution* (Chapel Hill, N.C., 1953) presents an excellent account of an earlier colonial congress, and the influence of that work on the present account is obvious. Two other works which provided background for this study are Benjamin Woods Labaree, *The Boston Tea Party* (New York, 1964), and John Shy, *Toward Lexington* (Princeton, N.J., 1965). On the political background in England see Bernard Donoughue, *British Politics and the American Revolution: The Path to War, 1773–1775* (New York, 1964), a work which parallels this volume from the other side of the Atlantic.

A number of local accounts have provided background for this study. Two older but still useful works are H. J. Eckenrode, *The Revolution in Virginia* (Boston, 1916), and Charles H. Lincoln, *The Revolutionary Movement in Pennsylvania, 1760–1776* (Philadelphia, 1901). Roger Champagne has contributed significantly to our understanding of New York in this period, most notably in "New York and the Intolerable Acts," *New-York Historical Society Quarterly*, XLV (1961), 195–207, and "New York's Radicals and the Coming of Independence," *Journal of American History*, LI (1964), 21–40. Most helpful on Massachusetts in this period is Richard D. Brown, *Revolutionary Politics in Massachusetts: The Boston Committee of Correspondence and the Towns, 1772–1774* (Cambridge, Mass., 1970). See also Benjamin W. Labaree, *Patriots and Partisans: The Merchants of Newburyport* (Cambridge, Mass., 1962). Among the other reliable and generally readable background accounts used for this study are David L. Jacobson, *John Dickinson and the Revolution in Pennsylvania, 1764–1776* (Berkeley and Los Angeles, 1965); Charles A. Barker, *The Background of the Revolution in Maryland* (New Haven, 1940); Oscar Zeichner, *Connecticut's Years of Controversy* (Chapel Hill, N.C., 1949); and David S. Lovejoy, *Rhode Island Politics and the American Revolution, 1760–76* (Providence, 1958).

Included among the thesis works which have provided thoughtful considerations of the period are Bernard Bailyn's *Ideological Origins of the American Revolution* (Cambridge, Mass., 1967); Pauline Maier, *From Resistance to Revolution: Colonial Radicals and the Development of American Opposition to Britain, 1765–1776* (New York, 1972); Gordon Wood, "Rhetoric and Reality in the American Revolution," *William and Mary Quarterly*, 3d ser., XXIII (1966), 3–32; and Jack M. Sosin,

"The Massachusetts Acts of 1774: Coercive or Preventive?" *Huntington Library Quarterly*, XXVI (1963), 235–52.

Finally, this essay would not be complete without a note on the information provided by town and county histories. An excellent collection for local materials is the American Antiquarian Society in Worcester, Mass. It was from such volumes that many of the figures on committee membership were compiled, supplemented by the very ready assistance of town clerks and local historical societies in New England.

Index